I Think There's a Terrorist in My Soup

Also by David Brenner

Soft Pretzels with Mustard
Nobody Ever Sees You Eat Tuna Fish
Revenge Is the Best Exercise
If God Wanted Us to Travel . . .

I Think There's a Terrorist in My Soup

How to Survive Personal and World Problems with Laughter—
Seriously

David Brenner

**Andrews McMeel
Publishing**

Kansas City

Library of Congress Cataloging-in-Publication Data
Brenner, David, 1945–
    I think there's a terrorist in my soup : how to survive personal and world problems with laughter—seriously / David Brenner.
        p. cm.
    ISBN 0-7407-3822-4
        1. Brenner, David, 1945– 2. Comedians—United States—Biography.
3. Conduct of life—Humor. I. Title.

PN2287.B685A3 2003
818'.5402—dc21

2003052154

03 04 05 06 07 MLT 10 9 8 7 6 5 4 3 2 1

To my three sons, Cole Jay, Slade Lucas Moby, and Wyatt Destry Slater, who have learned the importance of laughter and how to make people laugh from their father, David Norris, who learned it from his father, Louis Yahuda, who was so funny he must have learned it straight from God.

Contents

Contents

Introductory Words by Bill Maher

When I was in high school, it was always a big day when David Brenner was on the *Tonight Show* or *Merv Griffin*. I was a kid dreaming about being a comedian, and here was this hip, young guy actually doing it on television. It was inspiring, because I figured if he could do it, anyone could.

I'm joking of course.

I tell this story for another reason: to show I'm younger than David Brenner. Not that he shows it, and that's because he stays, and thinks, funny. This book reads like a nonstop onslaught of his best, most sidesplitting stand-up routines, except all the material is new, and funnier than ever. I should know because, did I mention that David Brenner was around when I was still in *high school*?

Back then, I thought he was the hippest guy around, and the years since, and getting to know him, have only confirmed that. I can make this call because I *know* I'm hip; I was fired by ABC.

Enjoy this book from a master of American humor.

Comedian and political provocateur Bill Maher recently earned a Tony nomination for his Broadway debut, *Victory Begins at Home*. He is best known for the critically acclaimed television shows *Politically Incorrect* and *Real Time with Bill Maher* and is the author of several books, including the bestseller *When You Ride Alone, You Ride with Bin Laden: What the Government Should Be Telling Us to Help Fight the War on Terrorism*.

Introductory Words by Chris Matthews

David Brenner is one of the great comedians of our time. I mean that *of our time* part literally. Like what happens when I get to the airport. "Love your show, now take off your shoes!" Unlike me, David doesn't get mad; he gets *funny*. He finds the insanity at work. Some nut lights a fuse to his shoes and we spend billions of people hours taking off and putting on our footwear at airport security checks.

I have to admit my bias. David Brenner is from Philly. That means, among other qualities, he is one of those few Americans who speak without a regional accent. (Now *I'm* the one that's kidding.) He also loves F. Scott Fitzgerald, another giant prejudice leaning in his favor. In fact, I came across a line in *I Think There's a Terrorist in My Soup* that carries an unmistakable trace of the great Jazz Age author. It comes from David's uncle who prides himself in a sexual rap sheet as long as his randy nephew. "I understand. I was in the army." I will never, ever forget Brenner's wondrous reaction to that line. What a wild heart this man has!!

Chris Matthews is host of *Hardball* on MSNBC and *The Chris Matthews Show* on NBC. He was once chosen "Washington's Funniest Celebrity."

Acknowledgments

Every book written has always had a long list of people to thank 'without whom this book could have never been written." I don't have that long a list, so I am going to make up a lot of names and how they helped me. You can have fun trying to separate the sincere from the bullshit, just like in life itself.

I thank Andrews McMeel Publishing for believing in this project or I'd be trying to sell this book door-to-door across the country, and for the help provided by their editor, Jennifer Fox; a superspecial thanks to my hands-on literary agent, Randi Glass Murray, who brilliantly nursed me practically daily through the entire process and edited the entire book (except this part); Randi's husband, Gordon, who heard me on a San Francisco radio station talking about the germ of the idea for this book and called his wife, who, in turn, called Amy Rennert, the owner of The Amy Rennert Agency, who fifteen minutes later called me on her cell phone from the Hawaiian beach where she was vacationing and consummated the deal; Beth Goldsmith for providing me with the perfect writing studio in Aspen, Colorado, always my favorite creative environment; my Aspen friends, Chuck and Barbara Besanty and Joey and Marcy DiSalvo, for their encouragement; Sony for inventing the VAIO laptop computer, which is a sensation; my attorneys, Bob Dickerson and Denise Gentile, who kept the dogs of divorce from biting off my head, which would have made it difficult to create; my executive assistant, Shannon DeBoer, for her efficiency in handling all the annoying details of my comedy career; my live performance agent, Rich Super, who lives up to his last name in every respect and who never wavered from believing in me; Jeff Abraham, who is the best press agent in the country and proves it every day; Bill Zysblat, who has guided me through all the horrors of my financial upheavals, along with my show business lawyer, Larry Shire, both of whom kept me from blowing my brains out; Kenneth Cole, a special friend, whose kindnesses are too numerous and personal to mention; my street corner friends, including The Bird, The Dancer, and Moose, who have been laughing at my jokes for as long as I've been telling them; my two best childhood friends, Dee Dee and Beb, who are no longer here physically but are forever in my mind and heart (I can still hear your laughter); my dear friend George Schultz, who is also no longer with us, but without whom I might not have been as successful a stand-up comedian as I have been; Johnny Carson for that first TV appearance and then some; my fellow comedians, Richard Lewis and Steve Landesberg, for all the belly laughs, especially when I needed them; my New York City Amsterdam Billiard Club partner and friend, Greg Hunt, for all the deep and funny conversations and for losing to me in nine ball; last and definitely least, Nick Ramoundos, who did absolutely nothing to help me with the writing of this book but who has never seen his name in print and loves the bullshit limelight; *USA Today* for supplying me with jokes about all the things in life that, on the surface, are anything but funny; all the world leaders, good guys and bad, and all the governments, good and evil, and all the other assholes who make life so difficult and miserable for the everyday man and woman that a book like this becomes an important necessity; the NYPD, NYFD, and EMS for their bravery, inspiration, and tears and in memory of the brothers and sisters they and we lost; my sister, Bib, who has always stood by my side throughout my life and has always believed in me; my sons, Cole, Slade, and Wyatt, who unknowingly give me the very reasons for trying to make life better not only for them but for all children; my mother, father, and my big brother, Moby, who are no longer here but continue to inspire me to do something special now and forever; and, finally, all the people who came to see me work live onstage or watched me on TV during my Laughter to the People Tour, which began three days after September 11, 2001, and continues today, for teaching me that during these difficult and sometimes seemingly impossible times laughter and humor are essentials pushing me to keep creating, to keep looking for the funny side of everything that is hurtful and frightening, which, in turn, drove me to write this book and has given to me a new and special purpose in my life.

To each and every one of you, I thank you for giving me this opportunity to do something so worthwhile and important, something of which I can be proud for my entire life.

And to each of you who is not mentioned, there's a damn good reason why you're not.

"Comedy must be daring.
It must skirt the edge of bad taste.
If it doesn't, it's not challenging
or exciting—or funny."

Mel Brooks
Comedian, Actor, Writer
2001, at age seventy-seven

Introduction

At 6:00 P.M. on September 11, 2001, I interrupted my daylong vigil of being glued to the TV news and sending e-mail messages to my New York friends and acquaintances in desperate attempts to find out if they were okay. I showered, put on a suit and tie, drove to the Las Vegas showroom where I had been working since the previous November, stepped onto the stage, and performed ninety minutes of comedy.

My opening line to the audience of two hundred plus was, "I know why I'm here. I have a contract I have to honor. I have no idea why you're here. But it has been said that laughter is the best medicine, and we Americans have never needed that medicine more than we do tonight. So, let me be your doctor."

It was the second most difficult show I had ever done. The most difficult was a concert I performed the night my mother died in 1986.

When I walked off the stage that night, I left my cushy job in Las Vegas and three days later began my Laughter to the People Tour, which has taken me to forty-eight states, so far. In the more than thirty years that I have been a comedian, I have never had such appreciative audiences. People rushed the stage to shake my hand and to thank me for making them laugh *again,* something a lot of Americans had forgotten how to do.

My tour was supposed to end in January 2002, after five performances at the theater in Madison Square Garden. But a young NYC fireman on a self-imposed leave of absence, after losing eight "brothers" in the World Trade Center, told me that this was the first time, since that black day in September, that he laughed at anything that was going on in the world and said that I had given him a whole new perspective on life. He said he was going to go back to work the next day.

I was so moved, and I was so impacted by the realization that laughter could be so powerful, so important, so life altering. I called my agent that night and told him to extend the tour, which is still going strong now in 2003.

Laughter has always helped me get through tough times—growing up in the mean streets of Philadelphia and dealing with the challenges in my adult life—but I never realized as I do since September 11 how vital and necessary laughter is for all of us.

It was this epiphany, born from touring around the country, that led me to write this book, *I Think There's a Terrorist in My Soup*, in which I show and teach you how to search for and find what's funny in some of the most perplexing, anxiety-provoking personal and world problems that we all face, from the unavoidable, like aging, to the uncontrollable, like war, to the universal, like money.

For each subject, I explore where the humor is, sometimes incorporating material that has been created for, well tested, and honed with my audiences all over the country. I'm not too embarrassed to reveal my own insecurities, anxieties, worries, and fears. I, too, am only human, but I'm a funny one.

I *cannot* teach you how to be funny, just as I can't teach you how to be tall. Both are in the genes. You're born to be funny and tall. Nothing you can do about it. But I *can* teach you how to *search for and find* the funny side of and the laughter in everything that stresses you, from the problems and worries in your personal life to the problems and worries that are heaped on top of you by world events and circumstances.

My father told me that there is something funny in everything. He said that all you have to do is look for it. He taught me how and I learned well, and I can teach well.

I believe with all my heart, soul, and funny bone that laughter truly is the best medicine. So, my dear patients and students, turn the page and let's get started. It's time to laugh.

I Think There's a Terrorist in My Soup

Sex

This is an important subject to discuss, very important. It has been said that money makes the world go around. Maybe in today's world, but sex was here a long time before money and the world was going around pretty damn good then. But for something that has been with us since the beginning of time, or after a couple days when Adam got bored and asked God for something to play with other than gorillas and centipedes, Man still hasn't gotten a good grip on the sex handle. It might very well be life's greatest pleasure, but, paradoxically, it may very well also be the greatest cause of worry and problems, which would explain why sex is also the main subject for jokes and the first subject in this book.

I'm not privy to psychiatric sessions. I'd love to be a fly on the couch, just to listen to the range of sexual problems discussed. I don't mean this in a perverted or a light way. Bedroom problems are real and can be devastating to a relationship or an individual. I would never belittle anyone who suffers from such problems, and I certainly don't have any answers for those who do. However, what I can do is shine a humorous light on the subject that I would hope might make some of you with a sex problem lighten up a bit, see your problem in a new way, find something humorous about it, and, finally, ease the worry and pain of it. But don't cancel your next psychiatric appointment. Laughter relieves; it doesn't cure.

Sex is a lot of different things to a lot of different people, but its one universal is that it can be seen as funny by everyone. If, after reading what I am about to write, you still don't find the subject of sex funny in any way, toss out this book and go buy a copy of *Mein Kampf.* You'll split your sides laughing.

I'm sure that when you were a kid, a lot of your peers acted as though they knew everything there was to know about sex (which of course they didn't), and if you didn't fake knowing as much as they claimed to know, you would be tagged a loser and be ostracized. Tough punishments for merely not knowing about a wang, a woody, and a womb, which could be easily mistaken for a midwestern law firm.

"Good morning. Wang, Woody, and Womb. How may I direct your call?"

My first encounter with this childhood phenomenon of not knowing about something sexual happened in third grade. A wadded-up note landed on my desk. Keeping an eye on my teacher, I opened it. Scrawled in bold letters across the middle of the sheet of paper were the words: "If you had it last night, smile."

All I had the night before was a cup of hot chocolate, and I had no idea why anyone would think that was something to smile about, but most of the other kids were staring at me, so I smiled. I passed; I made the grade; I was accepted in the Had It Club. To this day, whenever I have hot chocolate, I get a little aroused. I think I'll have one now.

Sex education was not taught in school when I was a child. Our extracurricular sexual education began in fourth grade, the day we discovered *National Geographic*. This was our only "dirty magazine." Almost every issue was filled with gorgeous color shots of naked women in some African country. Any kid who could get his hands on a copy was a neighborhood hero. He would lead us panting boys down an alley where he would open the magazine to the page showing bare-breasted native women. It wasn't until I was fourteen years old that I found out when a woman gets naked, she isn't holding a spear.

The only thing that has changed, in this department of discovery, from my generation to the present one, is format. It took me quite a while to figure out why my thirteen-year-old son, Cole, was spending so much time in the bathroom with his laptop and had the tap water running full blast.

Without getting into details, my entrée into the active world of sex was at age eight. Yes, eight! There was a fourteen-year-old living across the street who . . . how should I put this . . . who liked lollipops, all-day suckers, and things like that. Before her, I never knew I had a "thing like that." The truth is that I had no idea what the hell she was doing to me in the backseat of my friend's father's car, but it felt good, and who was I to be unneighborly? But, as usual, we moved, and The Licker of Spruce Street was lost forever. But hope isn't the only thing that springs eternal.

Like all kids who grow up in city streets, the bulk of my sex education came from the "older guys." Parents never talked about sex to children. The bullshit stork was alive and well in Philadelphia, as was the widespread fear of going blind from excessive masturbation. By the time we had sex education classes in high school, we had done everything there was to do, outside of the Tijuana Spinning Basket, which was just a rumor until Juan and his sister Rosa moved into the neighborhood from Mexico.

My "older guy" lived across the street from me. When I was ten, he was fourteen. When I turned fifteen, he turned nineteen. It kept going that way. His name was Tommy. One day, when I was twelve and he must've been around sixteen, he asked me if I had ever whacked off.

There is no way one can conceptualize the meaning of an expression like "whacked off." Whatever it was, it sounded like something painful, so I said I hadn't. He gave me explicit instructions on how to do it, which not only sounded like it might be painful, but also weird. He said that I was too young to "shoot jit," but I would get a "good feeling." He was right on both counts. This new art form, which didn't cost a dime, became a daily ritual, except on days of funerals or male cousin sleepovers. I remember thinking that girls might not be necessary in life except as the object of imagery. One of my dumbest concepts, which I happily negated a couple summers hence.

This is an example of life's little ironies. In the summer of my fourteenth year, Tommy left the city to work in an auto repair shop upstate somewhere. Every summer a beautiful young woman came up north from Georgia to visit her grandparents, who lived next door to Tommy. This sixteen-year-old Southern Belle became Tommy's summer romance, which included that perennial favorite, summer sex. Tommy was now out of town and I, a horny fourteen-year-old who had recently "jitted," was in town.

One particularly hot Friday evening after work, I was taking my front stoop two at a time. My mother was doing the weekly food shopping and my father was hanging out in a neighborhood bar with his pals. Need I tell you that both these activities were standardized because it was payday? I was also in a Friday night good mood.

The Southern Light, dressed all in white, including an off-the-shoulder blouse that framed her large breasts, and wearing a very short pair of short-shorts, waved to me from her grandparents' porch. I smiled and waved back. She signaled me not to go in my house. I nodded. She walked across the street seductively and up my stoop, and stopped with only inches to spare between her and me. I embarrassingly spanned those inches with my excitement. She looked down and laughed.

"Let's go in your house and make that bad boy go away."

Moments later, I was on top of her on the living room sofa. Like two insane cats, we pulled off each other's clothing. I couldn't believe that, at last, I was about to be able to answer that wadded-up note honestly. "Yes, I had it last night! Hail to all the gods and their offsprings!"

Now, I hate making excuses, but you have to keep in mind that this was my first time and I was in my parents' house, on their sofa in their living room, in bright summer light with my mother liable to walk in any second and . . . oh, what the hell . . . the whole thing was over in less than a minute, counting foreplay. I had burps that lasted longer. Now tell me that sex isn't funny.

This is such an embarrassing story to admit, but I don't mind telling it, because it has a happy male-ego-feeding ending. I spent the rest of the summer perfecting my act with the Georgia Peach. It was all any boy would want it to be. Matter of fact, I could use a summer like that one right now. I'll settle for a weekend. Hell, I'll even risk a Friday evening.

At the end of the summer, Tommy came back. My Southern Belle never did. I'll never forget Tommy, and I sure as hell will never forget all the midnight rides in Georgia. You never forget your first, and, thank God, you never know which one is your last.

How important is sex? Well, it must be pretty damn important for us to spend so much time thinking about it, how to get it, and get it again and again. The most recent Kinsey Institute study reported that 16 percent of women between the ages of twenty and fifty think about sex every day, while another study I read reported that the average male has a sexual thought every three minutes. This helps explain why men are so damn horny and helps reconfirm that I am not the average man. If I didn't have to eat and go onstage, I have no idea what else I would think about, and I'm far from alone.

I saw another survey in which they asked men what was the first thing that attracted them to a woman physically, what turns them on. Seventy-eight percent of men said "their eyes." Eyes? If that's true, how come we don't have a chain of restaurants called Pupils?

Forget that survey. My personal survey through the years is that 99.6 percent of men are attracted to one of three female anatomical areas: legs, ass, and/or breasts, and women know this is true, too. Why else would they go to such trouble to enhance the "mighty three"? Have you seen all this hype over a cream that makes a woman's breasts bigger? It doesn't work. It makes a man's hands smaller. Women aren't the only ones who buy products to enhance what nature hasn't given them, in order to attract the opposite sex. More and more men are getting cosmetic surgery and not just for their eyes.

I should imagine, and thank goodness I can only imagine, that it must be awful to be a man who is not richly endowed, who nature shortchanged. It is a shortcoming that might be among the worst of all shortcomings. Psychiatrists' couches must have had many a man lying on them with such tales of woe. Yet, as with just about everything in life, there is humor in it. I am not just talking about the cruel jokes one must endure if you are the subject of such mirth, but of the idiocy of those who try to take advantage of such sad souls.

For example: Have you seen the ads for The Bulge? You buy

this . . . this thing, and you put it down the front of your pants. You look in the mirror at yourself and you are looking damn good. You've got a natural-looking bulge going for you. Your self-confidence also bulges, so you go out and hit a singles place, like Pupils. You order a drink and just walk around, just you and your bulge. The Bulge's makers claim it will attract women "like metal shavings to a magnet." Personally, I would hate women flying across a room and smashing into my crotch, but to each his own or what looks like it is his own.

Okay, let's say The Bulge works as advertised. Let's say a good-looking woman with long legs and huge gazooms digs your bulge and invites you back to her place. She leads you into her bedroom. By this time, you've made a mental note to call your shrink and cancel all the appointments for the next year. She wets her lips and takes off her Wonderbra; you take off your Bulge. Now, she looks like you and you look like her.

There's an ad that appears in a men's magazine I always read. Its headline is "What Do Women Secretly Say Behind Their Lover's Back?" I never bothered to read it, because I was happily married with no sexual problems, but once I was on my way to getting divorced and going back into the marketplace, I thought I'd better check it out. Maybe women were whispering new stuff.

It turns out that the ad has nothing whatsoever to do with behind-the-back secrets, but everything to do with in-the-front secrets. It is an ad for a product to "enhance" a man's treasure. Not needy, but curious, I read on. It is a pill that is made from "nature's own ingredients" like "the root of the Buffo Tree" and other shit like that. Anyway, you are instructed to take two pills a day, which will "increase the length and thickness by [wait 'til you hear the descriptive word] a *whopping* 26 percent"!

It continues, claiming that they have had a "96 percent success rate in growing one . . . two . . . or three." This is how it ends. It doesn't say what. It could be pubic hairs.

"You look different, Joe. Working out?"

"No."

"New suit, Joe?"

"No."

"Hi, Joe. Are you working out?"

"Nope."

"You look like a different man, Joe. In love?"

"No, I've grown three new pubic hairs. Want to see?"

"Love to, Joe, but I've to pick up my new Bulge."

The pill takes three to four months to start working, but they claim that once it does (ladies, you've got to read this; it was definitely written by a man who has no understanding of women whatsoever), "Once it starts to work, when your wife, lover, or girlfriend sees it for the first time . . ." In other words, for four months, the guy's going "Turn out the light. I'm coming to bed. The big surprise didn't arrive yet. I'm still Mr. Peanut Man. Turn out the goddamn light!" Anyway, when she sees it for the first time (ready?), "watch her *gasp!*" Come on, is there one woman in the world who, upon seeing the new expansion, would clutch her throat and go "Arghhhhhhh!"?

But the authors of the ad really understand the male ego and hit a perfect bull's-eye with their sales pitch. They ask, "Men, would you settle to live in an average home . . . drive an average car . . . or make an average income? . . . Then why settle for the average dick?" Well, they didn't write "dick ; they wrote penis, but penis is so nondescript and asexual. It sounds more like a disease.

"Bob, I've got penis. I have no idea where I got it and it's spreading. Look, I've got penis all over my back."

Never in my life have I ever heard a man say the word "penis." "I've got a problem with my penis. I'm going to see the penis doctor." Never. Guys say "My dick's killing me. I'm going to the dick doctor, Dr. Penis. He's around the corner."

Then there is a disqualifier, a warning, so they don't get sued. "Do not let it grow more than nine inches! You'll be too large for most women." This shows a complete misunderstanding of the male ego. If this pill really worked, there isn't a man in the world who would stop using it.

"You call that a dick, Dick?" *(Unwrapping his from around his waist and twirling it above his head lasso style)*

"Go ahead; try to make a run for it."

(Tossing it) "Okay, dick, go get Dick!"

(Reeling him in) "Yahoo! Ride 'im, dick!"

"Where's the fire? On the roof? I'll get it!"

"Your cat is up a tree, lady? Here, climb up this."

For those men who might have need of such a product, let me give you something to think about that hopefully will make you feel better and more adequate. It is not the size of the fuse but the dynamite behind it. Now go have some fun, and not by yourself.

Sex can be not only a weapon but a tool. In a survey, 63 percent of men and women questioned said the best way to settle an argument is to have sex. I would just warn you men to keep this in mind, before you start screaming at a careless truck driver on a dark stretch of highway.

It has also been proven, according to a major study, that 50 percent of married couples said "vacation sex" is the best sex. Before you order those plane tickets, in the same study, 50 percent also said they believed in separate vacations.

So, yes, sex is very important. I have always believed that the pull of one pubic hair is greater than that of all the Roman Legions. If you doubt this, look at the risks the most powerful kings took for Queen Nookie. Of course, history books tone it down for schoolchildren. For example, it was not Helen's *face* that launched those thousand ships and the real words spoken were, "My kingdom for a Whore."

I think I have made my point about the importance of sex. Now, let's move on to the differences between men and women, when it comes to sex. Men will never tell you how much money they make but will give you every detail of their sex lives.

"So, Bill, how's the new job? What are they paying you?"

"Well . . . I mean . . . they . . . I bring home a nice dollar. Did I ever tell you that before Margaret and I get into bed, I dip my dick in margarine, and she shoves a knotted leather shoelace up my ass and then . . ."

"Eh, good luck in the new job, Bill. See you in church Sunday."

The other thing men do that is so cruel to their fellowman is brag about their sexual prowess. This can give other men insecurity or major psychological hang-ups. I think every man knows or has run into a man who says something on the order of, "I don't know what happened to me last night, but after the fifth time I had problems getting it up."

Five times? Five fuckin' times? Hearing someone claim this prowess can send most men into a psychological tailspin. Well, let me be presumptuous and speak for all men. I have always considered myself a great sexual partner, but let's be honest: After the first time, it's like trying to drive a nail in a wall with a fish, and I'm not talking about a frozen one, either.

The next time you run into a "Five-Timer," remember that men are bullshitters and this guy probably couldn't whack off twice in twenty-four hours. So don't get uptight if after you reach your climax, even your fingers stay soft until the next night. You're normal, my friend. Even if you are so-called older, keep in mind that you may not be as good as you were once, but once, you're as good as you ever were, and if you're not, there is Viagra.

Thank goodness for Viagra. It sure must be depressing to have all the equipment, maybe even be hung like a dinosaur, and all it does is look at your shoes and pee. Did you hear that they developed a Viagra mouth spray, but took it off the market, after one man's tongue shot right through the roof of his mouth?

It can't be easy for anyone who has a condition that lessens the joys of sex. Science is working to find the cure for each and every one of them. Of course, most scientists are men. Here are my takes on some of the advances in science and medicine that have made the news, legitimate stories, horrible stories, but there is still the funny side, as there is with everything.

Imagine having your penis or testicles cut off, accidentally or otherwise:

A man in Russia had his penis cut off in a factory machine accident.

Doctors replaced his penis with one of his fingers. When I read this, I thought, "Oh, my God, can you imagine if this guy were your uncle?"

"Come on, kids, pull my finger."

A woman in Italy had a fight with her husband, and, like America's Mrs. John Bobbitt, she cut off his penis. But, unlike Mrs. Bobbitt, instead of driving off in a car and throwing it out the window, the Italian version tied it to a hot air balloon. Can you picture this guy running all over Rome trying to leap up and catch it? He's got to be the only man in history to try to *get it down.*

Imagine being a woman trapped inside a man's body or vice versa:

A man saved money for most of his life for a sex change operation, went all the way to Manila to have it done, and by mistake, they took out his appendix. Everyone felt so sorry for him, but I thought, "What about the guy who went in for the appendectomy?"

Imagine being a man who cannot procreate:

Scientists have confirmed that they have developed artificial sperm. How lazy can we get? They ought to bottle it and call it, "I Can't Believe It's Not Bill."

Imagine not being able to decide when to become pregnant or not being able to limit the size of your family:

One of the latest developments is a birth control pill that greatly cuts down the risk factors. It is a pill that lasts for one hour. I think most women are more interested in finding a man who can last one hour. What someone should do for women is invent a pill that makes a man want to cuddle after having sex.

Of course, one of the greatest scientific contributions to man and mankind, woman and womankind, is the condom. I always wondered how the first one was invented. I mean, did some guy before climbing into bed and on his wife say, "I won't have to pull out. I wrapped some rubber around my dick"?

Did you know that in order to help decrease the population explosion of kangaroos a scientist in Australia has suggested a new kind of contraceptive? Obviously, it can't be condoms, because their arms are too short. They could never roll one on. You can prove I'm right. Lift your shoulders, and then press your upper arms tightly against your sides and try to slip one on. Then, explain to the woman waiting for you in the bed what the hell you're doing. Whatever you say, even the truth, how much do you want to bet she won't believe you?

Condoms have changed radically over the years. When I was a kid growing up, there were maybe four brands, and they were hidden on a little rack behind the druggist's counter. You had to be very secretive when buying one, and God forbid if there was a woman shopping in the drugstore at the time. You would have to use a code.

"Hi, doc, is everything under *control*? You don't want to give *birth* to any new ideas, especially with your wife. She might think you are just covering up and that would *rub her* the wrong way."

Nowadays, not only are the condoms on display in plain sight, but there are aisles of them, like Campbell's soup. You can tell that some of them appeal strictly to the male ego, just from the names they're given. One of my favorites is Magnum. It comes in three sizes: Large, Extra Large, and Traveling with a Circus.

Then there is a condom that is a gel. You keep rubbing it on and it turns into a condom. If you keep rubbing it on, you won't need a woman.

There are camouflage condoms. Now, I don't know about other men, but when I'm hunting in the woods and I see a beautiful woman, I don't want to give away my position.

There's even a klutz-proof condom. It seems that there are some men in this country who can't figure out how to put one on. These are the guys you really want to use condoms.

Imagine persons who suffer from psychological sexual problems:

A man in Long Branch, New Jersey, was having sex with his vacuum cleaner. Yes, it's true! Anyway, it pulled off about half an inch of his yakahula (my father's word for dick). I don't get it. With my vacuum, I can't pick up a paper clip. I wanted to call this guy in the hospital.

"Hey, man, I'm sorry what happened. So, what was it? A Eureka?"

Imagine an accident interfering with your otherwise healthy sex life:

A woman sued a fast-food chain for millions of dollars. She ordered a sandwich. With it came a hot pickle. When she put the pickle in her mouth, it burned her lower lip and her chin. She is suing on the grounds that, because of her burnt chin and lower lip, she and her husband cannot have sex. Come on, the woman couldn't even keep a pickle in her mouth.

You can see from these stories that people have all kinds of different sexual problems. Sometimes the sex act itself can be very upsetting, but it is also fun and funny. I truly believe that the more you make fun of it and have fun doing it, the better it seems and, maybe, even gets. So, as a personal note, I say to all the wonderful women with whom I have had sex, thank you for the laughs, and I hope you feel the same way. I think I just put my foot in it. Well, better my foot.

Childbirth

You want to talk about fingernail biting, cold sweats, hot flashes, lying awake all night, worrying your ass off, being terrified, shaking in your boots, quivering under your blankets and praying that God is not off on a holiday, then let's talk about childbirth, which is Mother Nature's way of increasing the population of the human race while driving it almost stark raving mad. I don't believe there is anything more frightening or worrisome than giving birth to a child. In second place is being a man who is with a woman who is giving birth.

The only aspect of pregnancy and the resulting birth of a child that isn't scary as hell is conception (with a few exceptions). How could childbirth not be? How weird is it to walk around knowing that something is growing inside of you or growing inside the person with whom you are walking? As a starter, there are hundreds of thousands of questions.

Among those for women:

"Did you reserve a table next to the bathroom?"

"Why do I hate the man I love?"

"Can anyone help me to my feet?"

"Oh, my God, where are my feet?"

"Do you have this in dark black, size 64?"

"Am I allowed by law to kick the baby back?"

"Where are my goddamn drugs!?"

"Is the son of a bitch out yet?"

Among those for men:

"How many times in one hour can a human being urinate?"

"All I said was 'Hi, my love,' so why the hell is she crying hysterically?"

"Where the hell can I get sesame-sprinkled broccoli and angry chicken at four-thirty in the morning?"

"Is she going to keep growing until she explodes?"

"Will she look this way forever?"

"Does she think she looks good in a dark black camping tent?"

"Where are her feet?"

"What's that smell?"

"Will my penis hurt the baby?"

"Why are nine months taking four years?"

"Where are my goddamn drugs!?"

"What the hell is that slimy, bloody thing?"

I have lived through three pregnancies, each of which was enough to get me admitted to an insane asylum. I faced and endured the myriad of terrors and survived. How? By finding the funny side, of course. Let me now guide you through my living horrors, but along the Avenue of Laughter, so you can someday make the trip there yourself.

First off, I must confess that, in spite of having three sons, I know little to nothing about the medical aspects of pregnancy and childbirth, but I am an expert when it comes to its horrors. I also know that God knew what He was doing, when He gave childbirth to women and not to men. Women can take discomfort, worries, and pain so much better than men. There is no comparison. When we men get a little cinder in our eye, we are screaming bloody murder about the pain and how we won't be able to work for at least a month or two. Meanwhile, women have something live inside of them that is kicking the shit out of them like a jackhammer, until he forces his way out of an opening smaller than his fist. Richard Pryor described childbirth best when he said, "Men, if you want to know what it feels like, grab your top lip and pull it over your face and head." So, my hat is off to the "weaker" sex; I praise you women to high heaven, and someday, I shall build a monument to you, if not in the middle of Central Park, then everlastingly in my mind and heart.

For decades, women have asked for, pleaded for, and, eventually, demanded that we men get more involved in the birth of our children, other than conception and driving them to a hospital nine months later. When my first son, Cole, was born, not only wasn't I in the birthing room, I wasn't even in the same city or state. He was sliding home in New York City, and I was walking onto a stage in Cincinnati.

When my second son, Slade, was born, I was a little more involved and a little braver. I wasn't in the middle of the battlefield, but more like behind the lines, in the lobby of the hospital with my first son, Cole, then fourteen years old, holding my hand and mopping my brow.

The horror, yes, horror, began a couple minutes after 5:00 A.M. on May 18, 1995, in the West Village of New York City. My nine-month-pregnant girlfriend, like almost every woman who is alive or ever lived, was totally brave and self-sufficient. She shook me gently, until I opened my eyes and focused on her smiling face.

"David, everything is fine. I'm going to the hospital. I'll call you later."

I, being the man, the provider, the hunter, the slayer of dragons, sprang up to a seated position and took masculine command. In a quivering, barely audible voice, I squeaked, "Look, I'm not doing anything, just having the usual nightmare about the giant, blue rabbit eating my testicles, so I'll go with you."

She, and I imagine most women, had prepared for this very moment. She had her color-coordinated go-to-the-hospital-outfit selected and hanging in the closet and a packed sundry bag under the bed. I think she placed it there the night of conception; after, hopefully, not during. As she calmly slipped into her clothes, checking herself in a full-length mirror, I staggered into the closet and grabbed the first things of cloth that touched my trembling fingers.

Fifteen minutes later, we left our loft, she, in her gorgeous, earth tone outfit with matching boots and bag, and me in an inside out and backward sweatshirt, crumpled jeans, two different color socks, and two left-footed sneakers. She was calm and smiling happily, in spite of the contractions, and I was a total nervous wreck, wincing at every contraction, including hers.

We walked to Sixth Avenue to get a cab. Luck was with us. As soon as we got to the corner, a cab was coming. I hailed it and helped her shimmy, shake, turn, twist, and lunge into the backseat. Additional good luck—the driver was wearing a new turban. He spoke the only English words he knew, "JFK or LaGuardia?" I told him that I thought it best to go to the hospital by car, rather than try to catch an inner-city flight to it this early in the morning. The American humor flew over his head like a meteor, so I just told him the cross streets of the hospital and hoped for the best.

He took off like a rocket and was cruising into a Mach 2 speed. Whenever I am in a cab in Manhattan, I always feel like I should be leaning out of the window, shooting at the car behind us.

When we got to the hospital, we ran into a lobby elevator. Well, I ran; she waddled. I pressed the twelve button. That's where the birthing rooms were, on the twelfth floor. Of course. The emergency room was on the roof. At least we were in the hospital, which was reassuring. I turned to my girlfriend, who was leaning against the wall in the corner of the elevator. She was obviously in a lot of pain. It was my manly job to make her feel better.

"Everything is going to be okay. We're in the hospital."

"I didn't think we were in the Museum of Natural History," she smiled.

Even under these circumstances, I was being reminded that I was the nervous-shitting-in-his-pants-cowardly male and she was the calm-cool-collected-brave female. I have to admit, now, years later, that her remark was also funny.

The doors opened at the twelfth floor, and I helped her out. The contractions were coming much closer together. Some nurses led her to the birthing room; I was led over to the reception desk to fill in all the forms containing the usual stupid questions, like "What is your mother's maiden name?" "Can your grandmother go to her left on a ground ball?" And my favorite: "Who to notify, in case of an emergency." I can't believe people write in the name of a relative who knows nothing about medical procedures. I don't want my Uncle Joe showing up at the hospital in his baseball cap and beer-stained T-shirt.

"Yo, David, wow, are you bleeding. Want a soda or something?"

In answer to the question on the admittance form, I always write in the name of the Surgeon General of the United States.

The list of questions was endless. I said to the nurse on duty, "Look, I'll tell you everything about my grandmother, including her affair with a one-legged man with three nostrils, but, please, let me fill out this form later. I just want to comfort my girlfriend, until her mother arrives."

"She's in Birthing Room Four-A, as in apple."

That's exactly as she said it, "A, as in apple," as if I, a grown man with a college degree, would not be able to find the room without the fruit reference. So damned insulting. Anyway, I walked down to Four-A, as in apple, and entered quietly. Immediately upon going in, I was a witness to an example of New York City when she is at her finest. Becalming, dark blue lighting blanketed the room and comforting classical music was being piped in in quadraphonic sound.

I made my way slowly across the darkened room to a low stool next to the bed, and gently took the left hand of my blond, green-eyed lady. I was shocked. Her hand was so fat. Now, as I admitted, I know very little about pregnancy and childbirth, but I didn't think that when the water bag breaks, all the water rushes into the left hand. Then I heard a female voice speak Spanish. I dropped the weighted hand and felt that I had to say something to this woman, whoever she was, but the only Spanish I could remember from high school was "Su burro es grande." I don't think, at this particular time in her life, this woman was happy to hear that her donkey is big.

Obviously, I was in the wrong room. I rushed back to Reception. The nurse had made a mistake. She gave me the wrong fruit. I was supposed to go to Four-B as in banana. As I started down the hall, I could hear women cursing loudly and screaming at their husbands things like, "Get me some Demerol, you bastard! You did this to me, you lowlife piece of shit!" The hall suddenly filled with frightened men, running toward the nurses' station. I got caught up in the drama and found myself charging with them, screaming for Demerol, without even knowing what the hell it was, but I didn't want the mother-to-be of my child to be the only woman without it. Two pills in hand, I charged into the room, and threw the pills at her, "Here's your Demerol!" She had no idea what I was yelling about.

She held my hand and settled me down, until her mother showed up. I kissed her good-bye, wished her luck, and got the hell out of the area as quickly as possible. I went down to the lobby and called my fourteen-year-old son, Cole. It was now only about 7:00 A.M., so he was still sleeping. This was confirmed when he didn't pick up the phone until the thirty-fourth ring.

"Hel-lo," he gurgled.

"Cole, this is Dad. Wake up, kid."

Now, Cole didn't know we had left the loft, so he thought I was a raging lunatic, sitting in my bedroom, calling him in his bedroom.

"Cole, I'm at the hospital. You're going to have a brother or sister today. You have to be here when it happens. You can skip school. You're never going to use the Louisiana Purchase, anyway. Take a cab on Sixth. Look for a new turban. I'll wait outside and pay him. Cole? Cole? Shit. Wake up, Cole!"

"I'm only messing with you, Dad. I'm up. Be there in twenty-five. One question, Dad. How come you're not in Cincinnati?"

The boy got the Brenner funny gene. Cole kept me company, much needed company, until that wonderful moment when the doctor came into the waiting room and told me I had a healthy baby boy who had a healthy mom. There's nothing to match the feelings that run through your mind like streams of colorful ribbons, gathering together in a pool of joy.

I saw my newborn son, Slade Lucas Moby Brenner, at age ten minutes. On Day Two, I picked up mother and baby in a stretch limousine to celebrate the occasion. As we were heading down Fifth Avenue, the strangest thing happened. I was sitting with my arm up on the back window shelf of the car. Forty-eight-hour-old Slade reached up and gripped my index finger tightly and held on to it all the way home. It was the starting moment of a special bond between us that exists to this very day, and will forever.

The first night at home, we put the baby in whatever it is that you put babies in, and placed it at the foot of our bed. Now, you have to keep in mind that I had never seen a newborn baby, let alone slept in the same room with one.

My girlfriend fell asleep within seconds, as she always did. I'm pretty fast to go under myself. Just as I was heading into dreamland, I heard a weird sound, "Grr google rah grip."

I thought, "What the hell was that?" It came again. "Gripple groll clah bip."

"Oh, my God!" I woke up my girlfriend. "Something's wrong with the baby. Listen." . . . "Grop grop ahgh hoof."

"David, the baby is just clearing the liquid out of his lungs. It's natural. Go to sleep."

With that said, she passed out, leaving me wide-awake with worry. I was not convinced that she was right. Besides, those were the exact last words my grandmother spoke.

"Where'd you hide your money and jewels, Grandma?"

"They're in . . . in the . . . Grop grop ahgh hoof . . . arghhhhhhhh . . ."

We never did find the stuff. Anyway, I took no chances with my baby boy's life. I went downstairs and got a flashlight. Throughout the night, every time I heard those weird gurgling sounds, I jumped out of bed, shined the light on the ceiling for reflective light so I wouldn't wake the baby, and checked to see if he was still breathing. For the next three weeks, I got up an average of thirty to forty times a night. I was sleep deprived and hallucinating. "Watch out for that flying moose!"

Then one night I climbed into bed and lay there waiting for the first gurgle. "Come on, Slade, let's have a 'Groppel, bish, hah, whoggle.'" Not a sound came. I sprung up and listened. No gurgle. Nothing! In a panic, I shook my girlfriend awake.

"Get up! There's something terribly wrong with the baby. Listen."

After listening for a moment, she said, "I don't hear anything."

"Exactly! Where's the 'google google gob bleb' stuff?"

"David, all this means is that the baby has finally cleared his lungs and is breathing like any other human being. Good night."

She turned her back to me and was gone. I sat there, still panic-stricken. So what I did for the next four or five weeks was set the alarm to get me up every twenty minutes. I would quietly shuffle over to the baby and—oh, he's going to be so neurotic when he grows up—I would blow in his face to see him move and know he was still with us. Can you imagine Slade, when he's about twenty-five years old, ready to leave the house with friends?

"Wait! I can't go out; it's windy!" Poor kid.

Now, I'm going to walk you through a birthing room and the actual birth of a baby, which could be titled simply "Men in the Birthing Room," or, more honestly, "How to Be Scared Shitless When Absolutely Nothing Is Happening to *You*." How would a frightened rabbit like me know anything about the birthing room experience? Well, I don't want to brag, but I will. Unlike the births of my sons Cole and Slade, when my third son was born on May 28, 1998, I want all of you, especially the ladies reading this book, to know that I was right there, on the front line, in the birthing room foxhole with all the bullets flying everywhere, holding my girlfriend's hand, just like women have been asking us men to do for decades. I can hear your applause, ladies, and your thoughts of how wonderful it is to read about a man who stood up to be counted. Now I want to tell the men reading this something. It was the worst fuckin' experience of my life! Why you women want us to witness this is beyond me. I would never say to my girlfriend, "Come in the operating room with me while I have my double hernia operation. Honey, watch the slice this scalpel makes."

Now for the details of my first, and, believe me, my last, experience of seeing a child born. I was the only man in the birthing room. All the doctors, nurses, other medical professionals, and, of course, my girlfriend, were women. I felt as though my machismo was on trial and felt pressured not to be too much of a wuss.

Now, I have been through some harrowing experiences in life, such as growing up in the mean streets, serving in the army, near-disastrous flights, and performing in front of millions of people live and on TV. Never once was I nervous. By always keeping it together in the neighborhood, one of my nicknames was The Prince of Darkness, fearing no one and nothing, and, because I was always perfectly calm and relaxed before going onstage, I got the early tag of Ice Blood. But that day in the antiseptic environment of a birthing room, far from the slums and stages, I felt my knees knocking together, literally. I couldn't believe it. Meanwhile, all the pros, including my girlfriend, were as calm as a group of women preparing a picnic lunch.

As everyone moved about quietly and calmly, doing whatever they had to do, I looked down at my girlfriend and saw a little head between her legs. I thought, "Either that is a midget hiding from the police, or . . ." I called out to the birthing staff, calmly, believe it or not, "Excuse me. I hate to bother you. Maybe it's me, but isn't this a head?"

The main doctor sauntered over, smiling at me. She casually glanced down to where my shaking finger was trying to point, and, as though announcing that it was time to serve the chicken salad, she said, "Ladies, it's time to go to work." They all smiled and walked over, one degree faster than slow motion.

As soon as they manned their posts, they made the transition into a remarkably efficient team. They told my girlfriend to push and take deep breaths, which she did. Push turned to pull, and all of a sudden something that looked like a broken shoulder slid out, followed by something that resembled a smashed, featherless chicken wing, then either a hip or the bone of an ass, all of these objects were covered with some kind of protective slime. The total "thing" looked like an out-of-space alien. I expected Sigourney Weaver to follow it out, firing an automatic weapon.

The women cooed. I almost vomited. Next, a lasso came whipping out. The doctor handed me a scissors and yelled, "Cut the cord!" (She told me later, when I was lying down with a cold compress on my forehead, that the reason she yelled was because she knew that was the only way to jar me into doing such a dastardly deed.) Then she said, "Remember, it's real tough, so cut hard. Real tough!" So I thought raw calamari and went for it. Now, no one bothered to tell me that there was blood inside the cord, which squirted all over me.

I thought, "Oh, my God, I just ruined my son," and made a mental note to cancel the Mohel (the name of the person in the Jewish faith who circumcises).

A nurse wrapped the pink worm in a blanket and shoved him at me so I had to take him. As she pushed him into my arms, she smiled and said, "Isn't he cute?" I don't know how many of you have ever seen a newborn baby, and I don't mean to upset anyone, but they are ugly! They look and move like little, drunken, rubber Rush Limbaughs. I thought, "Oh, my God, what did I do wrong? What evil did I do for which I am paying?" I thought, "Did I accidentally kill God's dog?" Or maybe it was simply the result of wearing pairs of too tight jockey shorts.

When you get your sense of humor turned up to maximum, keep the needle on Ultra High for one of the strangest and most annoying phenomena attached to the early days of new parenthood.

You know how people who own a certain brand of automobile wave to drivers in the same model car? Even more stupid to me than that is a bond that new parents feel they must have and exhibit with other new parents. It's like a secret society, TNBC: The Newborn Baby Club.

Almost every time I was taking one of my newborn sons for some fresh air in his carriage and got within forty feet of another new parent wheeling a carriage, I knew it was only a matter of seconds before I was bombarded with the same stupid questions. If you like being a member of TNBC, fine. If you hate it, as I did, here is how I answered. The other parents didn't always find it funny, but I did, and that's exactly who I'm trying to make happy, isn't it?

1. "Is it a boy or a girl?"
    "We're not sure. Scientists are still trying to make that determination."
2. "How old?"
    "I'm forty-two. How old are you?"
    "I meant your baby."
    "He hasn't told us, yet. I'm guessing under a year."

3. "Is this your first?"

"No, we had another carriage, but the wheels got stuck."

"I mean your baby."

"Yes, this is his first carriage."

"I mean, is this your first baby?"

"No, we had three others but we sold them. Hey, that's a cute baby you got there. Any interest in . . . Where are you going? Let's talk business!"

4. "What's his name?"

"Randolfooieahgrepson, after the constellation." *Or*

"Yitsumanger Boogeemahala, after the Indian fruit."

5. "My baby has my eyes and my husband's mouth."

"Mine has my gums and my girlfriend's colon. Would you like to see?"

6. "Is your baby a sound sleeper?"

"Not until we started diluting Quaaludes in his formula."

7. "How long was your girlfriend in labor?"

"An hour and four minutes short of nine days."

8. "Was it an easy birth?"

"No, the Caesarean failed, so they had to pull him out of her ass."

9. "Does your baby cry a lot?"

"No, but he shits his brains out every half hour."

I got rid of everybody this way, and had some great belly laughs thinking about what I had said, and telling friends. As a matter of fact, this bantering was so much fun, I suggest that even if you are not a new parent or not a parent at all, buy a carriage and a baby doll, walk around the neighborhood, and have some fun with TNBC members.

Although I am far from being an expert concerning pregnancy and/or childbirth, I feel that having had three sons and dealing with the women who physically had them qualifies me to give some advice, if you will, to both men and women who are dealing with this natural, although seemingly unnatural, phenomenon of life. First, the men.

Men, there are some key expressions you should memorize, practice saying, and use, when dealing with your pregnant lady:

1. "Honey, it's normal."

Example: "Honey, it's normal in the middle of the night, when there's a torrential storm, to want take-out pigs' feet soaked in red wine and mustard. I'll be back in no time."

2. "Yes, sweetheart."

Example: "Yes, sweetheart, only when you stand sideways and point at it can you tell you're pregnant."

3. "Me, too."

Example: "I understand that you feel like a broken blimp. Me, too."

4. "You're one hundred percent right."

Example: "You're one hundred percent right. My mother should have never asked if she could help you with dinner."

5. "It's the lighting."

Example: "No way do your breasts look like an air hose pumped them up. It's the lighting."

6. "Forget about it." (New Yorkers: "Fuhgehtahbowtit.")

Example: "So what, if you screamed I was an 'insensitive asshole' in the restaurant in front of my boss three times tonight. Forget about it."

7. "Why would I mind?"

Example: "Why would I mind if your mommy sleeps with you this week instead of me?"

8. "More than ever."

Example: "Yes, more than ever, I'd rather just cuddle than have sex."

9. "I'm sorry."

Example: "I'm sorry I laughed when you couldn't pull your jeans up further than your knees."

10. "I was an idiot."

Example: "I was an idiot to compare your discomfort and pain with the time I broke my kneecap, collarbone, and ankles in that motorcycle accident."

Now, ladies, I am not going to tell you what to say, because when you go into one of your mood swings, you're going to say whatever the hell you want anyway, so what's the use? What I am going to do is advise you what you should try to keep in mind about the father of your future child:

1. He's an idiot.
2. He's stupid, but let him think he is smart.
3. He means well.
4. Ignore when he sneaks a peek or stares at you in shock.
5. His mother lied.
6. Let him overeat and overdrink.
7. There is no other woman. Honest!
8. He's a little boy in a man's body.
9. You're still gorgeous, but hold off on the thong underwear until after.
10. Yes, God should have given pregnancy to men, but She didn't.

I survived the ordeal, and today, the ugly alien Wyatt is gorgeous, a little movie star. All three of my sons are handsome and precious wonders, and, maybe, this is what one has to keep in mind when the worrying and fears begin. Also, the children you have or are going to have someday, are going to make you laugh, just by being children, so why not start the laughter ball rolling, before you even meet them?

There are a lot of funny aspects to the entire process of childbirth and childhood, starting with the night of conception, through those wondrous early years, right up to the moment they grow into adults and leave you to start their own families and leave you wondering how you're ever going to replace what they have given you. But the sad truth is that nothing can replace that or them, so enjoy it all while you can. I have never heard a greater sound than that of a child's laugh, and I have no fonder memories than those given to me so generously by my three sons.

Children

I have always said that children are like hemorrhoids, in the sense that, even when they are perfect, they are a pain in the ass. Well, I actually first thought that before I had my own and was just observing other people's kids. Now that I have three sons, I don't think this is true anymore—I know it is! Absolutely! One hundred percent! . . . And I'm willing to wager that most of you parents, mothers and fathers, if you are open-minded enough to shine a bright light into your truth tunnel, will agree.

The oldest of my three sons, Cole, is twenty-one years old and is a university student back east. He's taking video game design and drugs. Come on, I'm only kidding. Why the hell would he want to design games?

My other sons, Slade and Wyatt, are eight and five. I can read your minds. "He has three sons ages twenty-one, eight, and five. Ha-ha." Well, you can stop chuckling. I had other children in between, but they were disgusting, so I gave them away.

I love my three boys. They are all any father would ever want from sons. I'm glad I have them in my life, but let me be frank. Fatherhood is not all it is promoted to be. Let me be more frank—nothing about it is like it's promoted to be. Lion tamers in the circus have it easier. Fatherhood is a three-hundred-ring circus with every wild beast doing exactly as he or she wants, with the ringmaster daydreaming of an easier life, like becoming a Special Forces Operative behind enemy lines during a nuclear attack.

Somehow, I think by watching my parents and the parents of my friends and the hundreds of parents in my neighborhood, I caught onto the tail of parental truth early in life. In spite of this rare knowledge, throughout my life, beginning when I was a young son, whenever I mentioned that I didn't want children, everyone, and I mean everyone, would say, "Just wait until you have one and you come home from work exhausted, with the weight of the world on your shoulders, and your son or daughter greets you at the door and says, 'Hi, Daddy.' It'll make your life all worthwhile." This didn't seem to correlate with the evidence, but since everyone, even the most beleaguered parent, said this, although it still didn't exactly have the ring of truth, there was a muted chime about it.

Okay, today I have three children, and sometimes I do walk into the house exhausted, feeling as though I do have the weight of the world on me, and one or all of those cute little buggers says, "Hi, Daddy," and it's . . . well . . . it's "nice" but no life-saver. I'll tell you the one thing that makes it all worthwhile. When I step out of the shower and one of my two youngest sons screams, "Wow, Daddy, you have such a huge penis," that's when I want another kid every week. If my twenty-one-year-old said it, I'd want another every second. If a woman said it, I'm sure I would have one every millisecond.

I know you've heard another cliché, that having a child or children changes your life. The kind of change like waking up one morning on your back and being transformed into a slowly moving target in a world of flying arrows. From the biggest things to the smallest, nothing in your life will ever be the same again. I suggest that as soon as you find out a child will be entering your life, take videos of everything you have and each other, because you will never see anything again as it is at that very moment.

From my personal experiences, I can tell you that in public, where you used to hum, whistle, or sing out loud a song that was on the top of the charts, you will hear yourself subconsciously warbling, "Rubber ducky, you're the one . . ."

At important business lunch meetings, when asked by the waitress, if you are finished with your meal, you'll hear yourself saying, "All gone."

When asked to describe a business associate, you'll say, "He's sooo big," and you'll bid adieu to newly met executives or persons with whom you are negotiating an important deal with a singsong "Bye-bye. Daddy's going bye-bye."

You'll become a conversational idiot with your newborn, as well as with other adults. When it is obvious that baby has spoiled his diaper, you will find yourself repeating, in that same stupid singsong voice, "What did you do? What did you do?" It's as if you are waiting for little baby to reply, "I shit in my pants. What the hell do you think is stinking up the house like this?"

You'll even go so far as to ask someone who has been on earth less than six months and who has no verbal skills whatsoever, "Why are you crying?" Usually, most parents will confuse their baby even more by asking him, in a manner that might make him think it isn't about him you are inquiring, "Why is baby crying?" Now the thought process in the little mind is thinking De Niro–esquely, "Are you talking to me?"

Yes, once you have a child, you lose the identity you had all your life. Personally speaking, I am a mere shell of the man I used to be. If you were to pick me up and press me against your ear, you would hear the ocean.

I remember an incident that so clearly emphasized this for me. I had attended a black-tie charity benefit in Aspen, Colorado. As my wife and I waited for a valet to bring our car, I slipped my hand into my tuxedo pocket and my fingers discovered a note. Immediately, I flashed back to my bachelorhood days, when women would put notes in my pockets, like "I'm the blond who asked you to help her fix her zipper. Angelica. 555-1342" or "I still want to have a drink with you. Anytime, night or night. The redhead, Lisa. 555-9870."

I didn't want to violate the trust between my wife and me, and I was no longer interested in . . . well, let's change that to I was no longer *seeking* that game which I had played so well, so long ago, oh, so very long ago. I had placed that life on a shelf with stickball and spin the bottle. However, like the majority of men, I am a victim of the fantasies of the male ego. What better way to feed the dead, or, at best, senile ego than to travel back in one's dust-laden mind for the briefest of moments and relive those days that are no more, when women sought me and went to creative extremes to be with me?

I turned my back on my wife and slowly slipped the note out of my jacket pocket, cautiously unfolded it, and, in the slyest of manners, read the enticing, sensually dripping words of a secret admirer. There it was in very neat block printing. "Buy Huggies and A and D ointment."

It was a note I had written to myself, so I would not forget that my youngest son needed these essentials, which I could pick up at the supermarket on the drive home.

With my fantasy exploited, my ego deflated, and my reality embedded in place, I turned to my wife.

"Were there any women here tonight named Huggies or A and D?"

"David, what are you talking about?"

"My past, honey."

She didn't understand and might have questioned me, but the valet brought our car, and we got in. As I was pulling out, I saw a very sexy brunette flashing me a big smile, but I had Huggies and A and D ointment on my mind and pressed down on the gas pedal.

Dribble and vomit will become your best friends. After a few months of paying high cleaning bills, you'll find yourself buying clothing that is prestained. A full night's sleep will be something that you'll remember vaguely from a long ago past life. Nights on the town will be remembered as fondly as childhood summers and just as distant. Dreams of boats, vacation homes, travel, ski trips, relaxing on beaches, and dozens of other plans you had for your future will be waitlisted. What you did and who you really are is part of your history, not your future. Well, not for at least eighteen years, anyway.

So what are the benefits of having children? you ask. Every parent would list different ones. Here are but a few of mine.

One of my favorites, probably because I am a comedian, is to make my sons laugh. This could be dangerous. For example, one day my son Wyatt was sitting in his room. As I walked in, I smashed my head on the door. He screamed with laughter. It was worth the momentary pain. But I had forgotten how kids are, until too late, when I heard him call out, "Again, Daddy." The "again" syndrome. I continued smashing my head, and he continued laughing hysterically. I stopped prior to forgetting the day of the week and my name.

Actually, my efforts to make my sons laugh go beyond my being a comedian. My father, who, in my opinion, was the funniest human being I ever met, including all the professional comedians I have known in my career, lived to make his children, family, and friends laugh. He got me every time. As he used to say, I was his "best audience."

My first true belly laugh, where I literally doubled up in convulsions and realized that I was living with a very special human being, happened when I was six years old and living in South Philly, a very tough Sicilian neighborhood. Think *Sopranos,* only real.

One afternoon, when my mother was shopping and I was home with my father, the front doorbell rang. My father went to answer it, and, as always, I went with him, because I loved being with him so much, even if it was only a walk across the living room rug to the front door.

I stood behind him. He opened the door. Standing on the stoop were two men in suits and ties, so I knew they weren't from the neighborhood. The only time I saw anyone dressed like that was at a wake. They reached into the inside pocket of their suit jackets and pulled out wallets, flashing big gold shields. FBI!

Now, my father always had a lot of "legitimate jobs," but his true occupation was a bookie, a numbers writer, so he fit in with lots of others in the neighborhood. This occupation would have been the best source of his income, except he was also a compulsive gambler. My dad would bet on anything. I can remember hearing one of the bets he tried to make. "Fifty bucks says the next person to walk through that door is a beautiful blond with long legs."

I remember tugging at his jacket and, as he leaned over, whispering, "Unless it's a Viking, you're going to lose the bet. We're in the men's room."

My father stood up, and, without losing a beat, said, "What odds you give me?"

Anyway, I knew what my father did, so with the two FBI agents standing there, I was certain that this would be the last time I would see him for a couple of years. My father focused his steel gray eyes on the FBI men, smiled that crooked smile of his, and asked quietly in his ever-raspy voice, "What can I do for you gentlemen?"

"Mr. Brenner?"

"I answer to that name, except on Tuesdays or when I owe someone money."

They didn't get it. "Mr. Brenner, we're here to ask you about the Tartucci brothers."

"I'm sorry, but I don't know any Tartucci brothers."

"Mr. Brenner, how long have you been living here?"

"Almost three years."

"Mr. Brenner, the Tartucci brothers live three doors down from you," the FBI agent said, pointing to his right.

Without losing a beat, my father pointed in the opposite direction of the FBI agent and said, "When we leave the house, we always go this way."

I went reeling back into the house, hysterical with laughter and knowing that I was the son of the strangest, most wonderful, funniest dad in the whole world. All these years later, I feel the same and will forever. What I didn't realize at the time was that I was learning how to be the kind of father my children would love.

We all know that children say the funniest things. What makes children special is how they innately use humor and laughter to help ease themselves through their life's problems. They don't have to read a book like this. Well, not until they become adults, when along with innocence and blatant honesty, they lose that inherent ability to see the funny side.

We constantly tell our children to stop being silly, when we could use some of that silliness in our lives. We can learn from our children. I have been and will always try to be open-minded enough to keep learning. Here are some examples of how my sons used humor to handle life's little upsets and reminded me to keep doing the same.

Dad is upset: Sometimes, when I am upset with my five-year-old, Wyatt, or for no apparent reason whatsoever, he will run in the room, pull down his pants, bend over, and slap his ass like a drum just to make me laugh, and I always do. What else I find interesting is that he will do the same thing when he is upset and wants to make himself feel better. You have no idea how many times I have wanted to do that at a business meeting.

Getting caught: Like every little boy, my son Slade adopted the disgusting habit of picking his nose and eating it. There is no genteel way of saying it. Every time I caught him doing it, I would tell him what a disgusting habit it was and that it was unhealthy and all the other logical arguments that aren't worth a bag of beans or boogers. I even tried humor. "Slade, are you digging for gold?" "When you get enough gold for a ring, stop." "Are you trying to tickle your brain?" Funny, but useless. Nothing worked.

One day, Slade didn't hear me coming down the hall. As I approached his bedroom, his back was toward me, but I could tell that he was engrossed in a major pick.

I startled him. "What are you doing, Slade?"

He spun around, and, without losing a beat, answered, "I am not picking a booger out of my nose, Dad. I am putting one in."

What are you going to say? "Well, as long as it's yours, I guess it's okay"? I just laughed. He then laughed. We both knew it was a made-up excuse, that it wasn't true, but neither one of us cared, because it was funny and the laughter defused the situation.

Dealing with reality: When my son Cole was about six years old, he was playing on a lawn. The biggest yellow jacket I had ever seen—it looked like a small bird, wearing a yellow-and-black-striped sweater—landed on Cole's head, crawled down his forehead, and stung him above one of his eyebrows. Cole looked at me accusingly and said, with some venom of his own, "Well, so much for the story about standing still!"

Getting out of trouble: Cole was attending one of those posh Upper East Side private elementary schools. I hated it and so did Cole, but there was nothing either one of us could do about it, at that time. Because of other circumstances out of his or my control, Cole was lax when it came to school.

One day, when no one else could be reached, the school principal called me and asked me to stop in to see her and Cole's teacher. I walked to the school and sat in the principal's office with her and Cole's teacher. I felt like I was the kid who was in trouble, which was understandably left over from all the times I was.

"Mr. Brenner," the principal barked, "in addition to being habitually late coming to school, Cole has a dismal record of handing in homework."

I had too much to say, so I didn't say anything.

Cole's teacher completed the double-teaming. "When I asked Cole this morning why he did not have his homework, do you know what he said?"

I thought that this is so typical of an uptight teacher to ask me a question for which I would have no way of knowing the answer. I resisted saying any of the words that were rolling around in my mouth like "uptight," "twats," "who gives a flying shit," etc. Instead I smiled as charmingly as I could and said, "No, I don't. Pray tell me."

"Your son Cole [as if I needed to be reminded of his name], looked right in my eyes, leaned closer to me, and whispered, 'Do you believe in flash floods?' What do you think of that?" she spit out.

"I think you should give my son an A for coming up with something so creative and so damn funny, instead of some bullshit excuse anyone could make up."

I was told by the principal that I obviously didn't understand the problem and that they would never contact me again. It really didn't matter, because Cole would soon live with me and would have no need for flash flood excuses.

Dealing with injury: It's way too long a story, so all I'm going to tell you is that one night while I was in New York for a few days to do

TV, I was rushed into surgery to relieve a recurring sac of blood in my right elbow which, left untreated or treated incorrectly, could result in the loss of my arm. There was no medical record of such an injury. The doctor told me it was a phenomenon and they were going to call it "Brenner's Elbow." Honestly.

I came through the operation with flying colors. With my arm in a cast, I flew home to Aspen, Colorado. My main concern was how much this would upset my then nine-year-old, Cole. I thought of different ways to tell him and decided on the truth. I always do that, search for ways of saying something and end up just telling the truth. I sat Cole down and showed him my cast, reassuring him that I would be fine. Then I told him about it being named after me. He took it all remarkably well; too well.

"I don't believe it," he said, slapping his hand to his forehead. "Other kids have fathers who have bridges or streets named after them. My father has a disease named after him!"

He walked away to join his friends who were waiting for him outside on bikes. I ran to the door, flung it open with my good arm, and called after him, "It's not a disease. It's an injury."

He yelled back, "Maybe to you, but not to the rest of the world," and pedaled off to have fun. I decided to do the same. Not pedal a bike; have fun. After all, it wasn't like I had some kind of disease. Again, Cole taught me one of life's lessons: Don't sweat the big stuff, once it has become small stuff, and, big or small, you can kick it in its ass with a joke.

Living with old people: As frightening as it might be for grown-ups to accept the inevitability that, if you are lucky, mind you, you will grow old, it is something that is scary to some children, too, when they realize that Grandma, Grandpa, Mom and Dad, and other grown-ups they love are getting old. This occurs when children realize the relationship of age to numbers. Slade recently told his friends that I was around eighty or ninety. I didn't tell you they understood the aging process completely, only that they were aware of it.

My oldest son, Cole, somehow had a realistic concept of age and aging from the time he was around five. We were walking down Third

Avenue in Manhattan on the way to a movie when we passed an elderly woman waiting in a bus stop. She was holding a big bunch of dried flowers. Cole looked at her and the flowers, then turned to me and said, "Wow, Dad, she's been waiting for a bus a long time."

Cole's best line about aging came when he was seven years old. He had a passion for GI Joe figures, so, of course, since I never owned one store-bought toy in my entire childhood, he had every GI Joe figure and every piece of battle equipment. We would play on the floor in my New York townhouse for hours at a time, hiding the enemy soldiers all over the living room, on and under chairs and sofas, pressed against the stairs, around the base of tables, in and around every nook and cranny, even though neither one of us knew what was a nook or a cranny. Then in a series of major battles we would rout the enemy forces with tanks, artillery, and, of course, charging foot soldiers.

One particular Saturday morning, after one of my very enjoyable sleepless bachelor nights on the town, Cole and I were playing war. It went on for hours. I was crawling around the floor so much I had rug burns. My body and I couldn't take it any longer. I realized that somehow, when I wasn't looking and least expected it, I had grown older. I also realized that this GI Joe war shit was accelerating the process. I stood up, stretching my aching, aging back.

"Cole, do you know why I spend hours of my adult life crawling around the floors of this house playing GI Joe with you?"

"Yes, Daddy, for two reasons."

"Really? What are they?"

"One, you're my daddy, and, two, you love me."

A great answer that hit the bull's-eye of my heart. However, it did nothing to ease the aches in the rest of my body.

"Well, both of them are true," I replied, waving my left arm to get feeling back into it, "but the main reason is because I know that someday, when I'm very, very old, sitting with slobber running down my chin, making a ka-ka in my pants, *you* will spend time with *me*."

Without losing a beat, Cole threw his arms into the air and exclaimed loudly, "Well, that's the end of GI Joe!"

So much for my fantasy of growing old, surrounded by my loving and devoted children! Yes, I still believe children are a pain in the ass and they flip-flop your life, but when it comes to problems in life, you can fret, brew, think, and obsess about them, or you can reach back to that time long or very long ago, when you were a child and had that natural ability to see everything through a veil of humor and recapture it once again, or twice again, or for always. Life deals each of us devastatingly difficult and crushing, cruel and oftentimes unfair, blows. You have a choice. You can get knocked on your ass or you can either roll with the punches or laugh at them. I prefer laughing, because you can crash when you roll; you can't crash when you laugh. Watch your children, really watch them, closely, and they'll teach you this and a lot of other wonders we all lose with every tick of life's clock.

Thank you Cole, Slade, and Wyatt for teaching Daddy so much and for helping me to remember another funny little Brenner boy, named David.

Marriage

If you are married and you are happy, then the following does not apply to you, but you can read it just for laughs. I am writing this for those who are married and not smiling in the morning, or for that matter, 24/7, and for those who are in the process of getting a divorce or are divorced. This is also for any of you who might be contemplating marriage anytime within the next eighty years. If you are in the latter category, I suggest you follow this advice: Read the following before you look, leap, and maybe go splat. Statistically, you are a couple of salmon swimming upstream, so some of you will make it—some.

Over 50 percent of all marriages in this country end in divorce. Now, you can add to this number at least another 25 percent who would divorce but don't, for various personal reasons—children, money, religion, the man doesn't feel like disco-dancing again, whatever. Add this to the total and you now have over 75 percent, or three out of every four marriages, that are unhappy failures. And yet, in spite of these horrific odds, people keep lining up to get married. I don't get it. If you pause to think about it, it doesn't make sense. Look at it this way: If three out of every four times you left your house, someone ran up and dumped a bucket of shit on your head, you wouldn't go out anymore. The odds are against you.

But the odds are way worse of pulling yourself out of a big city slum and I did it. However, I was not as lucky in my attempts to achieve success in the world of the little gold band—thrice. For some reason, when speaking of failure, the word "thrice" sounds so much softer than "three." But semantics aside, I've been to married hell and back three times. The first two times, each lasting a relatively short time, were in my early twenties. The third one was decades later, when

I was mature, had known and lived with the woman for over twelve years, had had two children with her, and was happier and more in love than I had ever been. Regardless, it, too, lasted only a little over a year.

This was when I concluded that marriage could ruin a shit sandwich, which isn't easy.

"There's something wrong with this sandwich."

"What do you mean? Doesn't it taste like shit?"

"No, worse."

"What could be worse than a shit sandwich?"

"This is. What'd you do to it?"

"Nothing. I just added a little pinch of marriage."

"Why?"

"I thought it would make it better."

"Better? You just screwed up a shit sandwich!"

"Sorry. How about a bowl of divorce?"

I don't know why marriage fails more than it succeeds, over 50 percent in the USA, and yet, according to a survey in *USA Today:* "Marriages tend to improve well-being. 40% of married people say they're very happy compared with 22% of the never married and 18% of the previously married." You realize that they're claiming that 82 percent of those who were unhappily married and got out of it are not happy. In other words, the previously married are saying they were happier when they were unhappily married. Even more shocking is that about two-thirds of those who were unhappily married at the outset and stuck it out were happy five years later. The conclusion is that a lot of problems resolve over time and married people tend to get happier.

So where the hell are all these unhappily married people coming from? I don't know about you, but I know hundreds of married couples, friends, and acquaintances (very few of whom are in show business), and I can count the number who are happily married on three fingers, and I'm not too sure about the middle-finger one. So, from my personal experiences and observations and soul-to-soul conversations, this study is one huge crock of shit.

You have to decide if this survey has any validity according to your personal experiences, but I must advise you don't, for God's sake, discuss it with your spouse. If you do, speak in a foreign tongue.

I think one of the most basic problems with marriage, and let's be honest about this, is that men and women are diametrically opposed, total opposites from the smallest aspects of life up to the largest. In my opinion, pairing us off is one of God's best jokes or biggest mistakes along with broccoli, the giraffe, and that monkey with the bulging red ass. It is a ridiculous assumption that a man and a woman can get along, even during a short ride in an elevator, let alone for a lifetime trip. I'll give you a good example of one of the small, but, nevertheless, relevant, differences from my last marriage, and I do mean my *last*! Or may God strike my dick dead.

We were living in Las Vegas. One morning, as I was coming down the stairs from the second floor, I passed by a large, circular window. Every house in Las Vegas has at least one large picture window, so you can look out your large window at people looking out of their large windows. A beautiful view is not to live next door to a large, ugly family. At certain times in the morning, the reflection of the desert sun transformed the window into a mirror.

As I descended the stairs, I saw a perfect mirrored reflection of my soon-to-be ex-wife, standing at the kitchen counter mixing something in a bowl. She was wearing her once-a-month-sour-lemon face. Scientists say you can tell when a woman has PMS by her fingernails. Yeah, when they're embedded in her husband's neck. Anyway, I did what is a man's nature to do. I avoided the confrontation. Men hate verbal confrontation. Women love it. No, women thrive on it, and they are far better at it than their male counterparts. During an argument, a woman has the ability to rev back into history and remember the smallest details, totally forgettable minutia.

"The last time we had this argument was six years ago in that Italian restaurant on Bleecker Street. You kept staring at the blond waitress with the huge knockers."

If pushed, she can remember exactly what you had hanging off the fork when you were goggling gazooms. Being a typical male, I can't even remember the restaurant.

Fearing the storm I see gathering on the horizon of my kitchen, I tiptoe down the stairs and slip into the dining room, and, acting very normal, I hide behind a curtain. This, too, will pass. But I hear her footsteps in the hall. "Uh oh." I head for my office. She's also heading there. I run up the stairs and duck into our younger son's bedroom. I hear her heavy, angry feet ascending six steps at a time. I charge out of the first bedroom and leap into the older boy's bedroom. She's on the landing. I could try to make it into the master bath, but how long can you run from someone, especially when you both live in the same house? So eventually, she catches up with me. (I never thought she'd look in the dirty-clothes hamper.) We then have a conversation that to me exemplifies the difference between men and women.

She says, "David, we have to talk."

I say, "Sure, how about a week from Thursday?"

She says, "How come you haven't asked me what's bothering me?"

I think, "Oh, God, here we go again with the huge knockers," but I hope for a miracle and say, "Okay, what's bothering you, *my love*?"

She screams, "You shouldn't have to ask!"

Now, wasn't that my position in the first place?

If we know and accept the fact that the majority of marriages fail, why do any of us get married? I think part of the answer is the pressure that is put upon us by family, friends, and society.

During the many years I was a bachelor (and, oh, my God, was I a great bachelor, which, unfortunately, is the book I'll never be able to write, unless I outlive every female I've known since age seven), I was constantly facing off with my married male friends who badgered me to get married. I knew they were jealous of my freedom and especially of my array of gorgeous, sexy women. If there is such a phenomenon as heaven on earth, there was a time that I was its happiest resident. Whenever I momentarily left my home in heaven to spend time with some of my "Mr. and Mrs." friends, my salivating married male friends attacked me individually or in horny wolf packs. Their arguments always took the same tack.

"Come on, Brenner, we're married, everyone is married, why don't you get married?"

It was as if they wanted me to suffer along with them. "Come on, Brenner, we've got hemorrhoids, everyone's got them, why don't you get some hemorrhoids?"

Then there were the intellectual arguments. "Brenner, did you know that married men live on the average eight years longer than bachelors?"

"For what?"

Relatives could be more insistent. I had one uncle who, at every family get-together, would hunt me down and corner me to have the exact same conversation over and over.

"Yo, David, how's it going? (He never waited for an answer.) I know. I hear. I see. You date a lot of different women. I understand. I was in the army. (I never figured out what the hell that meant.) But you know, David, you've got to settle down, get married."

My answer was also the same. "Yeah, you're right. I should settle down. So, how's your wife?"

"Oh, that bitch! Someday, I'm going to seal her mouth shut with Krazy Glue. I'm gonna . . ."

"Excuse me, Uncle; a great-looking woman just walked in. See you later. Give the Mrs. a big hug and kiss from me."

But regardless of the reasons why we get married, the bigger question is what can we do to survive this strange and basically nonworking phenomenon and who am I, a three-time loser, to give marital advice? Obviously, I don't have a clue how to make marriage work, but I've got two suggestions for how to make married life tolerable, even fun. It's the always reliable duo, themselves the world's most perfectly married couple—Mr. Humor and Mrs. Laughter.

It is said that laughter is the best medicine, so now, like good little husbands and wives, let's take the following spoonfuls of medicine. If you or your spouse or both of you are not feeling better in the morning, don't call me; keep taking your medicine and call a marriage doctor or a marriage lawyer. Good luck.

Loving Spoonful One: We all hear about couples breaking up. Just the other day, a friend of mine left his wife for a younger woman. A pretty common occurrence, but what struck me as odd was how many people were upset because it was a younger woman. Come on, how many guys cut out for an older woman? What man comes up to his wife and says, "I'm leaving you, Babe. I met this chick. Glaucoma, a plastic hip, stretch marks across her ass and out the door. I'm leaving you and I've got to do it right now. I have to wheel her back to the home by eight."

Loving Spoonful Two: If married people don't split, they often cheat, and cheating is no longer a man's game. Women are cheating in increasingly greater numbers. I saw a survey in which it was stated that out of the 77,000 married women studied, 27 percent claimed they cheated on their husbands. Another finding in the study revealed that 29 percent said that they faked having an orgasm. So, the good news is that if your wife fakes having an orgasm, there's a 27 percent chance it's not with you.

Loving Spoonful Three: Men and women are worlds apart when it comes to sex, which might explain why sexual problems have replaced money as the number one cause of divorce. Dr. Ruth, the noted sexologist, suggests to men that if you want to be a better lover, before you get into bed with your wife or before you start being amorous, you should recite an erotic poem to her. Come on; is there one man in the world who knows one erotic poem that doesn't have the word "Nantucket" in it?

Loving Spoonful Four: Another sex expert suggests that married people should talk dirty to each other while having sex. This is a concept for today's generation. I can't imagine my grandparents doing that; can you imagine yours?

"Come on, honey, put on that faded terry cloth robe, the sexy one with the holes in the back. Yeah, that's it. Now, roll your stockings down to your ankles. Ooh. Get the rubber enema bag off the hook on the back of the bathroom door and whip me across the ass with it."

After reading all this, you may be wondering why any sane, rational person would consider marriage. If men and women who hate hassles and arguments, who love the freedom to go where they want, when they want, who desire to do what they want, when and where they want, who live to squeeze every joyous drop of experience out of life's sweet fruit, who like the person they are and don't want to change, especially not be forced or coerced into changing by someone of the opposite sex—if these particular people would admit all this, especially to themselves, then they would act accordingly. For these rare human beings who can be that honest with themselves, marriage is like a meal. No matter what you eat, whether it is ballpark hot dogs and sauerkraut or beluga caviar and pheasant under glass, in the end, it turns to shit.

Millions of articles and tens of thousands of books have been written giving advice on how to make marriage work. I never read any of them. I doubt they would've saved any of my marriages. Marriage is not for me. So, I don't have any idea of how to keep a marriage working. My only advice is to view every facet of marriage with the eye of humor.

If you really can't, then find a divorce lawyer with no sense of humor and have him get you the hell out of the marriage. And good luck, especially with the lawyers, because hell hath no fury like that of the lawyer of a woman scorned. Come on, laugh; it's a joke. Sort of.

Work

If you love your job, you are blessed. If you hate what you do for a living, you are cursed, but you're among the majority. Either way, your job is a major part of your life, because it consumes a great portion of it.

I know that most of you assume that I am one of the lucky few who really loves his job. Well, you're right. Being a stand-up comedian is one of the greatest jobs in the world. I don't know what could be better than getting paid to make people laugh. But if anyone assumes that loving work is what I have always done, you couldn't be more wrong. Before stepping on a stage, I had just about every shitty job and shitty boss you could ever have. But I had a secret weapon in my back pocket: a nurtured ability to find the laughs, which started with my first job as a butcher's assistant when I was eight and a half years old.

Not Everything in Life Is as It Appears

My first boss, Mr. Sobel, the butcher, was an alcoholic. My first chore when I got to the butcher's department of the supermarket was to go into the freezer, lift Sobel's face out of the slab of liver he had been slicing before passing out, and drag him out to the heated floor.

More frightening than his staggering, slurring, falling down, and the reeking smell of whiskey on his breath was the way he looked. Sobel looked just like Moe of the Three Stooges, except he had the smallest head I have ever seen on a human being. Even when he was close to you, he looked like he was far away. On top of that, he was an amateur inventor and had invented one of the earliest, if not *the* earliest, contact lenses, except his had tiny wire frames which made him look like a frog being tortured. In addition to his staggering staggers, Sobel was an out-and-out *gonif* (Yiddish for "cheat").

One of the most ingenious ways he cheated his customers was to install magnifying glass in the meat display counters, so everything on the trays inside looked bigger than life, and by secretly brushing them with Mazola oil, so they also looked better than life. To the customer looking through the glass, the veal chops looked like tennis rackets and the steaks looked like Utah Meat Mesas. And Sobel had the uncanny ability to quickly wrap everything to look as big as it looked in the case. Whenever any customer came back to complain about the sudden shrinkage, he always offered the same excuse, "It's the humidity." Unbelievably, most fell for it.

Sobel's magnifying scam came to an abrupt and tragic end, and I was to blame. One day, with the liver stain still on his cheek, Sobel looked up from the sawdust on the floor and yelled at me to empty all the meat out of the case and clean the magnifying glass with a rag and ammonia. He pointed to a small bucket and passed out. There were very few customers in the supermarket, so I let him sleep it off.

I emptied the case and climbed inside. Now, Sobel never told me that I was supposed to pour just a little bit of ammonia into a bucket of water, so I poured the entire bottle of ammonia into the bucket. As I was wiping the glass, the fumes made me dizzy, and I started to pass out. The last thing I remember hearing was women screaming, because, from outside, through the magnifying glass, I looked like a twenty-foot-long boy stretched out in there.

As a result of the customers' pandemonium, the police and firemen were called. A fireman pulled me out of the case and another smashed the magnifying glass with an ax. Sobel's scam was revealed and the police called the Health Department, which demanded that Sobel close shop. He was pissed off at me, of course, and refused to give me the $6.00 he owed me. Now I was also pissed, so I went in the back to where we kept the live Thanksgiving turkeys in cages. My family could never afford a turkey, so we never had one for the holiday. I was determined that we would that year, and being hosed out of my $6.00 motivated me and gave me the justification for anything I might do to seek justice.

I stuffed a turkey into the mackinaw coat that was a hand-me-down from my big brother, so there was plenty of room. I put one of its claws down a sleeve. It protruded, but I was more concerned about a much more serious problem—what to do with the turkey's head and neck. I solved it by slipping the head and neck down the back of my polo shirt. Then, looking like a pregnant little boy with a withered left hand and a hunchback, I walked out of the store and home.

As soon as I got on my porch, I took the turkey out, opened the front door, and made a grand entrance, calling out, "I've bought the Brenner Family's first Thanksgiving turkey!" My mother laughed and clapped. My father looked at me suspiciously. I knew he knew I stole it, but I also knew he would never rat on me.

It was the perfect crime, except for one miscalculation. No one had the heart to kill the turkey. My father, I am sure because he knew of the criminal connection, suggested that I keep it as a pet. I had no choice but to do so. I named him Tommy and used to take him for walks through the neighborhood with a leash around his neck. I told my friends that he was an ugly dog. I even taught him to lift one leg.

For all the years of her life, my mother always loved to tell the story of how her "baby" saved his money to buy the family our first Thanksgiving turkey. Even when, as a fully grown man, I confessed to stealing it, my mother would only giggle and not believe me. She never did. I don't know if there is a heaven, but if there is, and they get my book—Mom, I swear to you that I stole Tommy, God rest his soul. Has He, Mom?

You've Got Mail—Sort Of

Another horrible job with an idiot boss was working for the post office after school, during summer vacations, and over Christmas and New Year's. Even before the advent of anthrax, working at the post office was a shitty job.

I started as a mail sorter, which is exactly what it sounds like it would be—you sorted the mail. You sat on a wooden stool in front of a huge box of cubbies, read the address on the envelope, and put it into the cubby for the corresponding town or city. Actually, you tossed it into the cubby. Government workers back then, not now, of course, were known for being slackers. They'd go to almost any extremes to get out of working, which often demanded more energy than if they had just done the required work in the first place. To ensure that you were actually working, the post office, as you physically tossed the mail into a cubby, made you call out the names of the towns and cities. The noise made by fifty or so men yelling out the names of towns and cities was grating on already grated nerves.

I had to do something to escape this tedious and constant assault on my nervous system. I worked the New Jersey case. I don't know why, but I fell in love with the name of one town, Boonton. Such a funny name, and the more you said it, the funnier it got, so for my entire eight-hour shift, I tossed every single letter into its cubby, screaming the name loudly: "Boonton! . . ." Here's this town of about 2,500 people with every resident getting about 150 pieces of mail a day.

The calling out of Boonton was a magical remedy. It still is. Sometimes, when I hit a bad bump in my life today, I go into a room, sit on whatever most resembles a stool, flicking my wrist into the air, throwing invisible letters toward an invisible cubby, and screaming a series of Boontons, which makes me feel so much better. Create a mechanism for your job. If you can't come up with one, you have my permission to use "The David Brenner Boonton Job Therapy." You can even give it a trial run right now. I suggest you first make sure no one is within earshot. I have found that most people lack understanding.

The obvious, and well-trodden way, of slacking off on the post office job was the tried-and-true cigarette and/or toilet break. Of course, I added my own innovation. The boss in my section was one of the toughest. He drove us like we were slaves in an oceangoing ship, minus the whippings, of course. In addition, he was a human bloodhound, able to sniff out a slacker at the distance of a football field. He was the Sherlock Holmes of the 30th Street Post Office in Philadelphia and, like the Canadian Mounties, he always got his man. His perfect record was a challenge I couldn't resist. After all, a number of my teachers called me "The Artful Dodger."

The first thing I did was give him human proportions. His name was Vincent Jerome. I nicknamed him Vincent "Mad Dog" Jerome, after the infamous gangster Vincent "Mad Dog" Coll of the 1920s. (I gave every boss I had a funny nickname. It really helps. Do it.) The next thing I did was to wait until he was as far away from me as possible before taking a break, giving me a three- to five-minute leeway. I would ask my fellow workers to say I had just left, but they weren't sure if I went for a smoke or to the bathroom, but thought I went to have a cigarette. The smoking lounge was closer, so he would check there first, adding about two or three extra minutes to my break. My last move was to keep an eye on the smoking lounge, and as soon as I saw Mad Dog enter it, I would run to the lounge and lean against the outside wall, so when he opened the door to leave, I would be behind it unseen. As he headed for the men's room, I'd duck into the smoking lounge. Eventually, he'd return to the lounge where I'd tell him I had been the whole time and he probably had trouble seeing me through all the smoke. I would time my last-minute return to my stool, where he'd find me working away. I'd smile and wave to him, and he would scowl.

Of course, the best-laid plans of mice, men, and sorters . . . One day, I was hiding in the men's room for my tenth time or so, when, instead of heading toward the smoking lounge, Mad Dog came whipping around the corner only yards away from me. I ducked into the men's room and charged into a stall, only seconds before he entered, screaming "Where the hell are you, Brenner? I know you're in here!" I thought the next thing he was going to yell was "Throw out your gun and come out with your hands up! We've got you surrounded!"

I called out from inside the stall where I sat on the toilet with a magazine across my lap, "I'm in here, Mad . . . Mr. Jerome."

I heard his Gestapo boots getting closer. I knew he was peeking under the booths for my high-top canvas sneakers. I moved my feet so he would find me.

"You've been on a break for twenty goddamn minutes! I timed you this time, you little son of a bitch," he bellowed. Workers on the other toilets flushed and got the hell out of the men's room. It was just Mad Dog Jerome and me.

I initiated a couple of my talents developed and perfected in school: Disarm and bluff the enemy. "I think it must be longer than twenty minutes, more like thirty. I have a terrible case of the runs." I delivered the lines convincingly. I was brilliant.

The next thing I knew, Mr. Jerome's head was peering down at me from the top of the stall door, which he had used to lift himself up. I smiled at him warmly.

"So, you got the shits, Brenner?"

"I think my head is going to fall out of my ass."

"Can I ask you a question, Brenner?" he asked softly with a never-before-seen little friendly smile moving across his face.

Returning the smile, I replied "Of course you can, Mr. Jerome."

"Well, Brenner, when you take a shit, do you always keep your pants pulled up?"

My one mistake. In my hurry, I had forgotten to drop my pants. I knew telling him that I didn't have time wouldn't work. Instead, I went for the laugh.

"I knew this time it felt different."

Jerome did laugh, heartily, but a few minutes later he was escorting me to the elevator and telling me to take the rest of the week off without pay.

The Dumber They Are, the Harder They Fall

After my bathroom stall run-in with my post office boss Vincent "Mad Dog" Jerome, he had me transferred to dumping bags. Dumping mail and packages out of large, heavy, duffle-like bags onto a moving conveyor belt is one of the most difficult, tiring, and dirtiest jobs in the post office. There were four of us. The other three looked like death row inmates. Two black guys and one white guy, each with tattoos on top of tattoos, and muscles on top of muscles. They each weighed in at 200 pounds or more and looked even bigger and meaner with the sweat glistening on their skin and soaking their tank tops. I was six feet two inches tall and weighed in at 145 pounds. and had a muscle cramp in my left leg.

Mad Dog must've gotten to these guys, because they busted my balls from minute one. First of all, as they lifted bags that had to weigh 150-plus pounds over their heads, flipped them over, and dumped the contents on the belt, they would yell at me to move faster as I rolled the bag onto the belt and shook it.

I showed up the second day so stiff and in so much pain, it hurt me to even lift my eyebrows, but I wouldn't let these bully assholes and Mad Dog beat me. I used every bit of knowledge I could remember from Physics 101 about leverage, managing to get a bag in position to be dumped and then shoveling out the contents with my hands.

I was convinced that when the supervisor, who was a nice guy, but not nice enough to intervene, wasn't looking, these three surviving Neanderthals were going to beat the shit out of me. I had already scoped out a two-foot pipe under the conveyor belt that I could use to cut it down to two against one instead of three, which would mean an extra two or three seconds of life. Whenever I moved, I kicked the pipe along with me.

The tension between us was growing and the attack was imminent. I could tell from their furtive glances at the supervisor, their body language, and a little bit from their verbal language, like "Your ass is gonna belong to us, punk." But Lady Luck kissed me on the cheek. Actually, on the wrist.

I wore a wristwatch that looked like a very expensive Rolex but was actually a rip-off piece of shit. It never showed, because I wore extra large sweats to hide my puny body. One day, while trying to scoop out a big package from the bag, something caught my stretch wristband and my watch slid off and fell onto the conveyor belt among all the letters and packages that my intended killers were dumping. I darted along the side of the belt pushing everything around, in hopes of finding my watch, before it slid into bins on the floor below to be separated into mail and packages and then sent on to the sorting rooms, my former place of employment.

Right before the big plunge, I spotted my watch. I lunged and snatched it up. I checked it for damage, which it didn't have, and slipped it back onto my wrist, covering it with the sleeve of my sweatshirt.

My enemies had watched the whole thing happen. When I got back to my spot, and went to continue emptying the bag I had been working on, the biggest and dumbest of the three said, "Hey, man, you're not allowed to keep anything you find on the belt!" Another one chimed in, "It's against the law." The Speak No Evil one spoke: "They'll put your sorry little ass in prison."

Pop! A lightbulb went on above my head. I had found my way out of my predicament. As I continued dumping my bag, I said casually, "I don't know who told you that crock of shit. Why do you think I transferred here? According to Rule 184, Section 16, Article 9, of the Post Office Code of Conduct and Law, and I quote: 'Any article of value, regardless of said value, that is found outside of a letter or package, that cannot be identified as belonging to a specific envelope or package is deemed public domain and can be kept by the finder.'"

"Bullshit!" yelled Hear No Evil.

"Okay, I'll prove it."

I walked over to the supervisor, who was close enough to be seen but too far to be heard by my three "fish." Showing him my watch and explaining what had really happened, I pointed to the conveyor belt as I detailed how I almost lost my watch. The supervisor listened and accepted my watch, looking at it closely and then toward the belt when I pointed at it. I ended by saying, "So I'm pretty damn lucky, right?" The supervisor nodded in agreement. I shook his hand and returned to my position, only saying, "Told you."

Without hearing the words spoken and by watching the supervisor's reaction and where he looked, including his final nod and handshake, these three muscle-bound idiots were convinced that the supervisor had confirmed the Federal Finders Keepers Law. They were so busy searching for treasures, they lost interest in maiming or killing me. Thanks to a costume jewelry store in my neighborhood, over the next couple weeks, among the fakes that I faked finding were an "18K gold" pen, a "ruby-and-emerald-studded" bracelet, a pair of "platinum and sapphire" earrings, and a "diamond"-faced Rolex watch. They found a ski mask, a ballpoint pen, an army belt buckle, a pair of Mr. Potato Head's shoes, and a bag of granulated coffee—all authentic.

I knew when I complained of not knowing anyone to sell my treasures to that they would volunteer to "fence" my finds for 50 percent of the gross. I got them down to a 60/40 split with a "good faith" $500 up front to me. They agreed. I gave them the goods and collected my $500, coincidentally on my unannounced last day in the employ of the post office. My only regret was not being a fly on the wall the next day, when these muscle-bound schmucks searched every nook and cranny for me.

A few years ago, I took a nostalgic walk through the workrooms of the Philadelphia post office where I had spent so much time in my youth. The sorting tables were gone. The package belts weren't manned. Everything was computerized or automated. At one point, I was recognized from TV by a group of workers who came over to say hello and shake my hand. I asked them if Mr. Jerome was still around and one of them, one of the younger workers no less, answered, "No, Mad Dog Vincent retired a few years ago." There was something so gratifying in learning that the nickname I gave him stuck to him like shit in a pair of pants. I guess I got even after all.

Toying with Toys

Another nightmare of a boss was Mr. K., owner of KC Wholesale Toys and Novelties Specialty Company, where I worked as a young teenager. I can still hear his Billy Goat Gruff's gruff voice booming up the elevator shaft and bouncing off the cold cement walls of the huge storage space. "Get me one gross of Number 2805 stuffed, blue bunny rabbits and hurry, goddamn it!" He was always hurrying and "goddamning" us, and, in general, treating us like indentured servants. I loved my fellow workers and it was through them that I found the key to survival.

Alex was in his late thirties and hadn't graduated from high school, but he had a photographic memory for numbers and things like the exact spot the one remaining Barbie Goes on Vacation doll was located among the thousands of cartons. Harry was a black guy in his mid-thirties who had a strong back, a rippled, muscular body, and could climb, swing, and leap around the stock like a sleek jungle cat. The third member of the stock boy inventory team was Bill, a Merchant Marine in his fifties who worked at KC whenever he was unable to get work on a ship, who could catch a carton thrown through the air like it was a Ping-Pong ball.

Where did I fit in with this incredible three-man team? Mr. K. was a neighbor of mine. He had more than enough money to move out of the neighborhood, or, for that matter, buy the neighborhood, but he was a cheap bastard. The only thing in life he hated more than spending money was driving a car. One summer Sunday, when I was walking by his house on my way to work at the post office, he asked me if I wanted to work for him. My main job would be to drive him to and from work. In between, I could work as a stock boy. When I went back to school, I would keep my position as stock boy and drive him home from work. He would pay me more money than Uncle Sam, but the part of the offer I couldn't refuse was to drive his car, because he had a classic 1946 Buick convertible with whitewall tires. He had bought it new and drove it only to and from work.

All the pieces were in place. I had three cohorts and a plan to make the boss appear less frightening and to add laughter to the workplace. Every day, somewhere in the salesmen's cubby offices, on the toy display shelves, or in the freight elevator, which was also used to take customers up to see the actual stock of the items they were buying for their retail stores, we would create sex scenes with the dolls and toys:

GI Joe getting head from the eternal virgin, Barbie, on top of a locomotive.

GI Joe getting head from Ken while sitting on a dollhouse kitchen stove.

King Kong putting it up the ass of Superman, whose head was in a dollhouse toilet.

Tarzan mating with a French poodle in the train set town of Plasticville, USA.

Wonder Woman and Lois Lane getting it on while on the back of Dumbo.

Donald Duck screwing Mr. America inside a Slinky.

Every time Mr. K. would discover one of our X-rated creations, he would throw a fit, screaming at the salesmen and up the elevator shaft to us prisoners in the stock stockade that when he found out who the sicko is who is doing this, he is not only going to fire him but have him arrested and sent away. The afternoon of the first time he threatened us with the police, he found a cop blowing Pluto while getting it up the ass from Howdy Doody, who was getting it up the ass from Mr. Roberts on a Lone Ranger lunchbox. I thought Mr. K.'s neck veins were going to explode right in the customer's face.

Each of us volunteered to help catch the pervert among us. Mr. K. was so upset, his reward was a promotion and a fifty-dollar-a-week raise. We couldn't buy that many laughs with $5,000. Discussing ideas every day for that day's sexual combination had us doubled up and crying. Then there was the actual creation, followed by sneaking it in. On top of that hysterical fun was watching Mr. K. spend the first half hour of his day, every day, searching for the couple of the day, which, of course, we didn't put on display until after his morning search, moments prior to the first customers showing up.

Each of us now couldn't wait to get to work. It was like being ringmasters in an X-rated Cartoon Circus. If all I wanted out of life at that time was fun, I'd probably still be working there, but I knew this was a dead-end job, and I had big dreams, so I quit in my last year in high school to work for a newspaper and magazine publishing company.

Alex, Harry, and Bill were sad to see me go, and I was sad to leave. Imagine being upset about leaving a dead-end, shit job—but that's the power of laughter.

Exit Here

My father was a numbers writer, a bookie, but he had to have a shit job as a front, to cover up his covert operation. I remember so clearly standing in the living room one morning, my brown bag lunch in hand, ready to leave for my part-time high-school job, as my father, lunchpail in his hand, was leaving for his full-time "legitimate" job. He turned to me and said, "Every day when I'm about to go to work, I feel like I have a dead cat in my stomach. Any schmuck can work for a living, Kingy, don't be one of them. Have fun making your money."

Silently, taking small steps, his back bent forward, so unlike the fast strides, normal ramrod posture, and machine-gun delivery of original jokes and ensuring laughter when he was cruising the neighborhood collecting bets, my father ambled out of the house. I swore that once I was a man, I would never have a dead cat in my stomach and I never have. But in the meantime, I have been lucky enough to search for and discover as much humor in each of the shit jobs of my youth as possible and give myself and my fellow workers as many laughs as I could, never dreaming that someday that in itself would be my job, my fun way of making money.

I am so grateful that my dad lived long enough to share in my many years in show business and to share the laughs and fun with me. For both of us, the dead cat was buried forever.

It's not easy to just pack up your job or career and walk away. There are a lot of reasons, some good, verifiable reasons, why you must stay in a bad job, or think you have to stay. There are only two reasons why you must leave: to find your true self and to be happy. No matter how bad the job was, I always knew two things. One—no matter what, and, hopefully, very soon, I was going to leave. Two—until that moment when I walked away, I was going to find the needles of laughter in the shit haystack. I hope you do one or both, leave and/or laugh. Good luck.

Money

Who hasn't worried about money at one time or another?

I've always followed two philosophies. The first one was an original and the second was an old Jewish saying, or so I was told by an old Jewish man. In order, they were, "If you worry about money, you'll have money worries" and "Instead of spending your time thinking about how to save money, spend it thinking of how to make more." I have spent my whole life following both of these philosophies and found them to be sound.

I started out poor and stayed poor for a long time, much longer than I wanted or expected. How poor? Well, here's a list of clothing dilemmas and how I used my sense of humor to get through them, or as close to getting through them as I could:

If I didn't get hand-me-downs, I got "seconds" or "thirds" or "tenths," that is, rejects. These were articles of clothing that had a little something wrong with them, a design that didn't match, one pant leg a tiny bit longer than the other, some stitches out of line, etc., so they were rejected in the factory by a quality control manager and marked down as much as 90 percent. My problem was that my mother was the worst at buying rejects. Once she bought me a reindeer sweater with only reindeer legs going across my chest and a reindeer head near my left armpit and near my right armpit a reindeer ass. Another time, she came home so proud with a new dress shirt, my first dress shirt. The only problem was that both pockets faced down and it had three sleeves, the third one in the back. I kissed my mom, said thanks, and wore it as though it was perfect, which it wasn't, but my mom was. The weirdest purchase she ever made was her proudest. She came home all excited. She had picked up the bargain of the century—a box of one hundred pairs of shoelaces for five dollars. The only problem was, the metal tips were missing. For years, everyone had to sit on the floor sucking their shoelaces for an hour.

Everything had to be worn for as long as possible and then a little longer. When collars became noticeably frayed, my mother reversed them. When sleeves became too short, my mother converted the shirt into a short-sleeved summer shirt, and, of course, if only one sleeve had seen its better days, I had an unworn spare in the back of my dress shirt. When pants became too short, my mother lowered the extra cloth that was sewn up inside the pants' legs. I had a pair of light brown pants that had faded to a light tan, but somehow, the tucked-up cloth remained the original shade, so I walked around with light tan pants with light brown bottoms. When someone commented about it, I'd tell them it was the way the sunlight was hitting them or the way I was sitting.

When a pair of pants I had worn for a couple years longer than I should have had a hole too big to be sewn, my mother covered the hole with a patch, but the patch was a couple of shades darker than the pants. I looked ridiculous. I asked my mother to sew patches of different colors, designs, and sizes all over my pants. As silly as it sounded, while she giggled, she obliged me. The first day I wore them to school, everyone wanted to know where I got the "cool pants." Knowing that no one would believe they were bought firsthand in a store, I told them something way more believable. I said a "cool cousin" of mine had died in an avalanche in China.

Worse than wearing worn-out, previously owned, and/or weird clothing was never having a store-bought toy and rarely ever getting a hand-me-down one, either. Toys were an extravagance. I had a few action figures handed down from my much older brother but had trouble identifying with Sergeant Renfrew of the Canadian Mounted Police and Tom Mix. Actually, because we were among the very poorest families, my only toy was a dead cat, but I had to share it with my cousin who lived across the street. He was always breaking off the whiskers. Yes, of course, I'm lying. My cousin lived six blocks away.

We had a sofa in our living room that we had bought in a thrift shop. It was okay looking, but it had a problem. Every once in a while a large spring would shoot up through the space between cushions. There was no warning. All of a sudden, you'd hear a loud "bo-ing" and then, like a rocket ship crashing through the clouds, the spring would appear. We got used to it, like everything else that was wrong in the house. When the spring joined the family, whoever was in the living room at the time would get a screwdriver, slide under the sofa like a car mechanic, and force the spring back under the two-by-four board that ran across the base. No problem. The spring was like a family pet.

One evening, we had three female visitors. They were sitting on the sofa. My father was talking, when the spring sprung, scaring the shit out of the women. Without losing a beat, my father pointed to the spring, said, "That's for hats," and continued talking.

From that hysterically funny moment on, I adopted my father's wisdom of looking for the humorous part of everything, even poverty. Being poor was very hurtful to me. There wasn't a night from age eight through high school that my last thought at night before falling asleep and my first thought when I awakened in the morning wasn't, "How do I get the hell out of here?" Getting out of the neighborhood was first on my list of Top Ten Things to Do in Life.

After my family and I were evicted from my maternal grand-mother's house (by my grandmother), I went to work to help bring money into the house. I was eight and a half years old and worked every day, right through high school.

When I was working my way through college, I still lived in the old neighborhood, moving into an apartment above a twenty-four-hour-a-day, seven-day-a-week Laundromat. During the winter months, the heat that invaded my place from the driers below was welcome, but in the summer, the temperature in my apartment was usually 115 degrees and that's only because that's as high as my thermometer would go.

Then there was the elevated train line that ran only feet from my bedroom window, which was blackened by soot and dust so you were unable to see out. You also couldn't put anything on a shelf, or it would walk off, and you had to shout to be heard. The oppressive heat, the invasion of hundreds of silverfish, and the noise were probably what kept my place from being featured in *Architectural Digest*. No big deal.

When I left the apartment, there was no relief, because I had a much more serious problem: no money. I used to steal heads of lettuce (who the hell would ever think that of all the things to steal, someone was going to steal lettuce?) and a jar of coffee.

Every day, and at that time my metabolism allowed me to eat three meals a day without gaining weight, I would prepare the three meals with different arrangements of lettuce: whole, half a head, quarter heads, cut up, chopped, diced, and my favorite, rolled in long strips. Sometimes, I would actually invite a date over for dinner. Thinking of the scene in *The Gold Rush* where Charlie Chaplin boils and eats his shoe, I would laugh while she and I ate our way through my special "Four Forms of Lettuce Au Gratin without the Gratin." It is said that women think humor is sexy, and with the temperature nearing jungle fever levels, forcing one to take off some or most articles of clothing, I had a wonderful sex life thanks to a head of lettuce, a Styrofoam cup of black coffee, and some hot laughs.

The irony of that horrible apartment is that it was there that I made the move out of the neighborhood, never to return, but to always look back at what I had lived through, what I had learned, and the laughter that brightened my lightless life.

My former college professor of mass communications, Bill Seibel, called to tell me that the local NBC-TV station was looking for a writer for a documentary series about crime, corrections, and the judicial process. I had majored in mass communications, hoping to write dramatic scripts for TV and movies. I knew nothing about documentaries except that I loved to watch them.

I stayed up from Friday morning through Sunday night writing a documentary on a subject I knew about, that I had lived through, and that was the transition of a white neighborhood into a black one. I lived on the last white-inhabited street and so I always had black friends. When the neighborhood "changed," I hardly noticed it, but I was aware of what was happening, if only from seeing white people running their asses out of the neighborhood. My father was too principled to move, saying, "No one should run away from other human beings, especially Jews, because we know better than anyone the hate and horrors of prejudice and bigotry." They moved only when my mom got older and the house was too big for her to take care of properly.

Anyway, I finished writing my documentary very early Monday morning, sleepless for seventy-two hours. I showered and met with the executive at NBC. The interview went poorly, because he kept asking me questions about what I knew specifically about writing for, directing, and editing film. I knew nothing and admitted it. Even though I was a good con, there is a time to con and a time not to con, and this was not the time, because the first day I would show up at the studio, my cover would be blown and I'd be fired. I decided to just put the truth on his desk. I stood and said, "Listen, the answer to the next twenty questions will also be 'nothing.' If you want someone with experience, get someone from New York, but if you want someone who is going to learn faster and work harder than anyone you could bring into this building, I'm your man. Here's a sample documentary script I wrote. Thanks for your time."

I tossed the script on his desk and walked out. An hour later I was walking down the same street I had walked since childhood, a street that should have been entitled "Boulevard of Dead Dreams." I let myself into my apartment and called my professor to tell him that I blew the interview and to thank him for trying.

A couple hours later, a woman with whom I had been living came home from her job as a medical technician. She had a great sense of humor. Living there, and with me, she had to have one. I was stretched out on the bed in jeans and shirtless in the above-100-degree temperature. She walked in, smiled, said hello, stripped off her uniform, and paused a moment before speaking.

"David, let's have a financial report on what we're worth."

"Very funny."

"I'm serious. What do you have to your name?"

"Whatever I'm worth is on top of the dresser."

She went over to the dresser and picked up the coins I had thrown there when I came home. She counted them.

"Well, with these three quarters and a nickel and including the checking and banking accounts we don't have, everything in the cookie jar in the kitchen, what is inside the pockets of pants and coats or what has slid down between the cushions of the sofa and chairs in the living room, and what's in my wallet, we are worth a total of [holding up my coins] eighty cents. I spent the last of my money for the subway to get home. So what are we going to do?"

I felt sick. I had reached the bottom of the barrel and there was a big hole in it. I said, "Let me sleep on it," and I turned on my side and closed my eyes, knowing that sleep would take me away from this biting reality. Remember, I was the grown-up version of the kid who always bragged that he was going to be somebody someday and get his family and friends out of the neighborhood, and here I was a nobody and deeply buried in the same streets and alleys of my childhood, the only one not to get out.

I did fall asleep, in spite of the oppressive heat and the oppressive financial report. The phone rang. I picked it up and choked out a hello. It was the NBC executive.

"David Brenner?"

"As far as I know. Who is this?"

"Mr. Riley from NBC. I'll see you tomorrow morning at nine."

I couldn't believe that he was going to give me a second interview. I've always been nocturnal, rarely going to sleep before three or four in the morning, so I asked if I could come in in the early afternoon.

"Well, David, the station opens at nine."

"I understand, Mr. Riley, but I've got a few things to do in the morning and I do better at afternoon interviews."

Mr. Riley laughed. "I don't think you understand, David. You've got the job. See you at nine."

He hung up. I sat with the phone still to my ear, convinced that I had only dreamed the conversation. This was the first time I had gotten my foot in the door that led out of the neighborhood and possibly to the realization of all my dreams. I shook the sleeping woman next to me. She opened her eyes and smiled. I smiled, too, but this was a rare time when I had a real reason.

"Okay, I've slept on it and made a decision. I'm going to start working tomorrow as a documentary writer for NBC. I got the job."

She squealed and wrapped her arms around me. I said aloud but really to myself, "Someday, I'm going to put these three quarters and the nickel on black velvet inside a sterling silver frame with a little placard that reads 'Lest We Forget,' so I never forget where I come from and how poor I really was once and will never be again."

In every place I've lived since then, from a small office space in a corner up to a large, posh home office, there hangs on a wall by my desk a sterling silver frame with eighty cents on black velvet and a placard that reads "Lest We Forget." Fortunately, I've never had to look at it to remember where I come from and how poor I once was. Unfortunately, the statement "and I will never be poor again" was violated, because of a series of financial ups and downs, mostly without my knowledge and out of my control. The downs I have suffered have never been so down as to push me back to the old neighborhood, but if they do, at least I'll know I made my dreams come true, even if not forever, and I'm sure I'll find new laughs in the old place.

Starting with, and thanks to, my first appearance on *The Tonight Show* with Johnny Carson on January 8, 1971, I have earned as much money as I had hoped to in my dreams, and I used it exactly how I had planned in those childhood reveries, and kept all the promises I had made sitting around the family kitchen table and leaning against the brick wall of Moe's Candy Store on the street corner with my friends.

I financially retired my father, brother, and sister. I bought them houses, condos, cars, wardrobes, and whatever else their hearts desired. I paid everyone's bills and sent my parents and siblings on world cruises. I helped out street corner friends. I kept all my child-hood promises before I moved out of the one room I was living in in New York. I had to be the only star in a 20- by 40-foot space who was-n't serving time in a prison. The reason I didn't move was that just in case the bubble burst, I would have kept my childhood promises. It's a street corner value.

But please understand that once those promises were paid off, and in order to fulfill them, for the first nine and a half years of my com-edy career, I worked every night, without a night off except to travel. Once I knew that everyone I loved was okay, I started to toss the bills and coins my way. I bought, gutted, and rebuilt a four-story town-house on the Upper East Side of New York with a live-in housekeeper and an executive assistant. I bought a stretch limousine and hired a full-time driver. I bought a power boat and traded it in for a sailboat, which I kept on Lake Mead in Las Vegas. I chartered sailboats and sailed the oceans of the world twelve weeks a year. I traveled to most of the places in the world I had on my childhood list of "Places to See." I rented houses in France and Spain and treated my family, rel-atives, and friends to European holidays. With those I loved, I shared the good life I had created in my mind when all I had in life were a few hand-me-downs and lots of firsthand dreams.

Life gives and life takes. You've got to learn to roll with the punches and when you get knocked on your ass, you've got to get back on your feet and start swinging to take back what life took from you. And along with faith in yourself that you can do it again and again and again, if necessary, you've got to find the laughs that will help you force open the valve so you don't blow up and lose everything forever.

I've been flat on my back on the canvas a few times. The first knockdown happened in December 1984. At the time, I had a net worth of $5,000,000. It was the goal I had set. I was going to quit show business six months hence on June 9, 1985, exactly sixteen years to the day I first stepped on a stage or held a microphone.

I figured I could live off of about $500,000 a year from interest and investments. My plan was to spend at least two years sailing the world, during which I would take notes about the places I had visited, keeping a list of my favorites. When the day came on which I decided to stop cruising the world, I would live in each of my favorite places for a year or so, my call, my freedom. If I were lucky enough to outlive the countries on my list, I would design a new adventure. I had dreamed of doing this since I was a little boy and now I was about to do it. How perfect is life?

For the first time in my career, I had decided not to work over the Christmas and New Year's holidays, as a sort of prelude to my imminent retirement. I decided to visit Sydney, Australia. Since I was a little boy, Australia fascinated me and I had an inexplicable feeling that something I would find there was going to change my life. It did, but in a way I would have never expected.

I asked a friend to join me for a three-week exploration of this mysterious and wonderful country. He had enough frequent flyer miles for a ticket. I paid for his junior suite, which was connected to my huge one overlooking Sydney Harbor, which, in my opinion, is the most beautiful harbor in the world.

Sydney was magical. The hotel was fabulous; the discos and nightspots were fantastic, the beaches were gorgeous, the Australians were fascinating, especially the women, who were truly magnificent—and it is with one of them that this tale appropriately begins.

My friend and I made daily trips to the pulse-pounding discos, the flashy nightclubs, and the wondrous beaches. We were having a blast of a time. One evening we were invited to a party at a mansion overlooking the entire bay. It was the Australian version of *The Great Gatsby,* which just happens to be my favorite book.

For a while, we circulated, consuming delicious petite sandwiches, drinking champagne, and enjoying conversations with strangers. There was a large patio overlooking the landscape, and dancing by herself to the pulsating rhythms of a small band was one of the most physically gorgeous, magnificently built women I had ever seen. I handed my drink to my friend and joined her on the dance floor. It was the beginning of an unbelievably exciting affair.

On December 24, I got a call from my business manager. Now, everyone who worked with me, as well as my entire family and closest friends, knew not to call me with bad news, unless there was something I could do about it. I describe my philosophy in one simple sentence: "If the dog dies, bury him."

My business manager sheepishly admitted that he had goofed and we owed the IRS $80,000 more on my tax return. After I asked him how he could have goofed that much, he confessed he had no excuse or explanation. It was a screwup, that plain and simple. What are you going to do? Everyone makes mistakes, otherwise O.J. wouldn't be free and playing golf. I took a deep breath and told him to send the IRS a check for $80,000. He informed me that that was the problem. He said that I didn't have $80,000. When I asked him about the $5,000,000, he informed me that the tax shelters he and others had put me into were being challenged. When I asked him for the bottom line, he said that instead of having $5,000,000, I was probably about $400,000 in debt.

Take a break. Stop reading this book. Imagine that you have been told that you have $5,000,000 and are all ready to pull the plug on work only to discover that instead you are $400,000 in debt and your dream to retire and sail the world is as remote as having sex with a frog on Mars. After you throw up, come back and read the rest of this saga.

So what do you think I did? Maybe you think, like my friend, that it was time to pack my bags, check out, and head for the airport. I already told you that I had always wanted to go to Australia and I was seeing the woman of women, so why would I leave? No, what I did was call for my car, tipped the valet handsomely, drove to Sydney's shopping district, and entered a terrific men's boutique. I tried on a summer suit. When it's winter in the USA, it is summer in Australia. I asked how many shades it came in and ordered all four and started checking out sport outfits. As soon as the salesman walked away, my friend turned to me.

"What the hell are you doing?"

"What do you mean, what am I doing? I'm buying my spring and summer wardrobes. You won't see anything like this in the States."

"How the hell can you shop? You just lost all your savings. It'll take you years to get that sailboat and sail . . ."

I interrupted him to tell him about something I learned from an old John Garfield movie I had seen as a kid. It was during the Great Depression. Garfield had a dream and a scheme. He spent years studying about a banana business and had finally arranged to have bananas shipped to the States, but somehow the deal fell through and he lost all the money he had saved and invested. He told his wife to take a shower and put on her best dress, while he ran across the street to a bar to borrow money to take her to their favorite Italian restaurant.

When she asked Garfield how he could go out, after losing his money and, more importantly, his dream, he answered something like this: "You don't have to celebrate good news. You're already happy. But you should always celebrate bad news, because it'll make you feel better."

In other words, "Don't worry about money or you'll have money worries," which is why I bought a fabulous wardrobe that day, had the best Christmas and New Year's of my life, and went back to New York, whereupon I met with my new business manager and told him to forget about 1985, because I was obviously playing a losing hand. I suggested we spend all our energies on 1986, which we did, and it was the first of several financially fabulous years. I got back up on my feet, only to be knocked down eventually, again and again and again, mostly by blindsided sucker punches.

In spite of all my financial setbacks, there was one constant factor present every day of every year—laughs! I had tons of them, and you might be able to say that during these rough times in my life I've given you a few pounds of laughs, as well, right?

Does this mean that I don't think about and miss my old dreams and the lifestyle I used to live? Of course I do, a lot, but I truly believe that I'll get another chance to live my dreams and lifestyle again. Until then, or even if it never comes to be, the jokes will be on me.

Political Correctness

One of the things that seems to be lodged tightly in America's throat, choking us, is our drive, our absolute need, to be politically correct about *everything*. This is stifling our ability to totally protect our homeland from terrorists. It has polarized our people, messing with our traditional melting pot approach, which has always been the keystone of our strength as a nation and a people. Being just an American or just a human being is no longer enough. Now you have to belong to some kind of group, fighting for your group's personal agenda, often at the expense of another group that is also fighting for their own agenda. Somewhere down the line we forgot that "united we stand, divided we fall." Nowadays, it is "we'll stand over here; you stand over there." We are no longer a people seeking solidarity, striving for what is best for all of us, but have sliced ourselves up into a myriad of different groups, emphasizing our differences and seeking what is best for only ourselves, our group, our cause, and our agenda.

To me, television best exemplifies this separatism. We used to have three networks and then a handful of cable stations dealing in one way or another with all our people and having all of our people watching. Of course, it was not a utopian world. There weren't enough blacks, Hispanics, or gays (known ones, anyway) on the air, and the same was true of lots of other invisible citizens. The industry was trying to improve and it was, but instead of continuing to make it better and fairer, we decided to each go our own separate way.

Various cable networks target specific viewers, leaving the rest of

---

Americans to search out their group. It is sort of like "find your own kind." TV zeroes in on one target, one group or kind of viewer. We have channels only for blacks, whites, Hispanics, Mexican Hispanics, Puerto Rican Hispanics, South and Latin American Hispanics, Japanese, Chinese, Vietnamese, Koreans, Muslims, women, children, teens, etc. We had a talk show hosted by four women, so of course we had to have a talk show hosted by four men. God forbid we all worked together and learned about each other, especially learning and accepting our differences, all of which would be our similarities. One for all and all for one.

Even in this new world of separatism, I have noticed that not every group has its own separate but equal individual representation on TV. I haven't seen a channel just for Eskimos, although I've had my suspicions about Maury Povitch, or for the elderly (only 3 percent of all people appearing on air are age fifty and above), or, of course, for only Native Americans, which will probably not happen until there is a channel for the descendants of General Custer.

Then there is the political correctness of being certain that no network, cable, or local TV station will have only one race and/or ethnic group anchoring and reporting the news and the weather. Oh, you'll still see all-black or all-Hispanic newscasters, but only on the all-black and all-Hispanic channels. Otherwise, no group must be left out.

"Okay, we have a Caucasian man, a black woman, and a gay Asian. Does anyone know a butch Hispanic from the Deep South or an overweight lesbian weatherperson?"

"No, but what about an asexual Jewess sportscaster or a Protestant Irishman with a learning disability to be our White House correspondent?"

I saw a front-page story not too long ago showing all of our governors under the headline, "These Are America's Governors. No Blacks. No Hispanics." I thought, why stop there? What about no Jews, no Italians, no Greeks, no Asians, no Jamaicans, no Cuban Americans, no Portuguese, no Icelanders, no Vikings, no midgets, no jugglers, no flamethrowers, no comedians (not professional ones, anyway), etc.? We have over two hundred nationalities living in the USA,

so it is arithmetically impossible to have every one of them represented in a political body that has a total of only fifty members. To put
it in the vernacular, you can't put two hundred pounds of shit in a
fifty-pound bag.

And why stop with only nationalities and ethnic groups? How
many gay and lesbian governors do we have and who represents the
disabled, those with a stutter or a lisp, and name one governor who
represents one of the largest minority groups—name one governor
who is poor. Miraculously, we do have one Native American governor,
have even managed to slip in one wrestler, and have always had governors who represented crooks, maybe not when they were elected
but certainly while they were in office.

I believe in fair representation and treatment of all people regardless of the color of their skin, nationality, religion, political leaning, or
sexual orientation. (God, I hope I didn't leave anyone out!) I just think
we have carried it too far, so far that it is slowly and increasingly rip-
ping apart the great American fabric—"one nation under God . . . a
nation of the people, by the people and for the people." Not a nation
of separate channels and separate agendas.

So far, I have written about this subject only in a serious way.
Now I'll show you how I find the humor in it, so it doesn't choke
me—and you.

First, a personal observation of the plague of political correctness
that I have seen as a live performer, live in the sense of working on
the stage versus TV, not in terms of breathing in and exhaling. About
ten years ago, I started noticing that audiences were changing, and it
has gotten progressively worse. We have become so politically correct
that sometime during my ninety-minute show, someone in the audience is going to be offended by something I say and send me a nasty
note backstage. I could say something as harmless as . . . "I don't like
asparagus," and I'll get a note sent to my dressing room like, "My
brother is an asparagus farmer, you Jew bastard!"

Here is another personal example of overdone political correctness. I had the good fortune to play in a card game in which one of the

regular players was Jack Lemmon. It was a cheap game, quarter, half, but it was the players that made it a fantastic game. I came in, sat down, and, as I was buying my chips, one of the other players said, "Jack, you have to tell David your joke." Jack told me a joke that was so damn funny. Now, I can't do an Irish brogue, and Jack Lemmon, like everything else he did, spoke with a perfect Irish brogue, but, since this is a book, you can imagine that I write in a fantastic Irish brogue and read it that way. Here's Jack Lemmon's Joke.

"In Dublin, two Irishmen walked out of a pub. It could happen."

Now, that's about as funny as it gets, but you can't do that joke onstage, not in today's America.

How about when Carroll O'Connor died and they were showing clips from his old show, *All in the Family,* the most-watched situation comedy in the history of television. I saw one in which Archie Bunker comes running into his house in a complete panic and calls out to his wife, something like, "Edith, jeez, did you hear the bad news? A spook family is moving in next door to us. That's almost as bad as a kike or a wop."

You can't do a joke on TV like that today. America has gotten rid of all the spooks, kikes, and wops. And, if you remember, *All in the Family* was on one of the three networks back then, so it came right into your living room or bedroom. You could switch channels or turn off the TV (few Americans did either), but you couldn't censor it or get it pulled off the air. Some tried even then, when we Americans were a people who wouldn't tolerate that kind of bullshit. We were so open-minded, free-spirited, interwoven with one another, regardless and maybe in spite of our differences, that most of us were able to poke fun and laugh at ourselves and at and with each other. We knew it was a joke. We knew it was just for fun. We also knew that programs such as *All in the Family* fostered understanding, even if it was subliminally. As always, laughter was an important bridge that connected us.

In my opinion, not only is *The Sopranos* the best TV show ever, it is the most realistic in its use of language. Did you know that *The Sopranos* was first offered to all three major networks, ABC, CBS, and

NBC, and each turned it down because, in their infinite creative judgment, it was not a quality show? Now you know why there is such shit on network TV. But thank God they turned it down. Can you imagine watching *The Sopranos* on CBS, instead of HBO? A Mafia boss would get shot and clutching his chest he'd say, "Golly, gee whiz, this stings like heck. I'm gonna get you, you poopy head!"

Now I'll give you an example of uptight political correctness from my personal life. My sons love Las Vegas and love going to the hotels. The two youngest are only three years apart, ages five and eight, so I never have them in the same place at the same time. I hate war. As a matter of fact, until a few months ago neither one knew he had a brother. If you're a parent of two sons close in age, you know what I'm talking about. They love each other to death and try to prove it by killing each other. I'm much more worried about either or both of them getting hold of weapons of mass destruction than Iran and North Korea.

Anyway, on this particular day, it was Slade's turn to go to a swimming pool in one of the famous hotels. Slade had recently turned six and was just learning how to read, so he was reading everything he could get his little eyeballs on. Sometimes it was a major pain in the ass, but it was so wonderful to watch the world opening up to him. What's better than books?

We were sitting on the edge of the hotel pool, dangling our feet in the water, and Slade was reading all the signs around the pool area: "No Running," "No Jumping," "No Diving," "No Glass," etc. There was one sign embedded in a low wall, a finished sign, and Slade read it aloud, " 'No Solo Bathing Permitted.' " He read it perfectly, so I said, "Wow, Slade, you just read a three-syllable word—per-mit-ted. That was great!"

"Thanks, Daddy, but what does the sign mean?"

Having been reading for many years, I quickly replied, "It means exactly what it says. The word 'solo' means 'alone.' Therefore, 'No Solo Bathing Permitted' means . . . What the hell does it mean?" Surely it doesn't mean that if you're swimming in the pool and your wife starts to get out, you start to panic.

"Where the hell are you going? You can't leave me in here! Read the sign!"

You have to answer your children's questions, plus I was so damn curious myself that I signaled over one of the pool attendants.

"What does that sign mean? 'No Solo Bathing Permitted'?"

He leaned over very close to me and whispered, as if God forbid someone floating by in the pool might overhear him. I felt like I was a CIA operative and wanted to say something like, "The Blue Fox will not jump tonight." Anyway, he whispered, "We don't want to offend anyone. That is management's way of saying 'No Skinny-Dipping in the Pool.'"

First of all, would you figure that out in less than a million years, give or take a day or two? And secondly, I'm talking about Las Vegas. In the "old Vegas," I remember seeing signs in the casinos like "No Bare Tits at the Blackjack Tables." And back then, no one obeyed them, thank God. To the "boys" who used to run Vegas, I'm sorry, it's a different Las Vegas and a different America.

This reminds me of another example of political correctness that crept into our children's world.

The Cartoon Channel decided to air an extensive retrospective of Bugs Bunny cartoons. Who didn't grow up loving Bugs (Bunny, not Siegel)? I thought showing all those old cartoons was a great idea. A whole new generation would be turned on to this great American icon.

Since years of being on shelves might have damaged some of the cartoons, they screened them and repaired those that needed it. While looking at the cartoons, they found a bunch that were not politically correct in today's America and refused to air them. One that was nixed was a cartoon in which Bugs Bunny calls an Eskimo a "big baboon." So you knew we were never going to see the one where Bugs called Porky Pig "dick head."

Let's move up in age and down to our southwest border. When we increased the border patrol in 2001, the number of illegal aliens sneaking into our country from Mexico dropped 22 percent! An organization in Mexico filed a formal complaint against our border patrol charging them with getting the illegal aliens lost. What the hell is their job?

"Psst, señor, you're going the wrong way. L.A. is that way. I'll close my eyes. Have a nice day and come back to see us real soon, you hear?"

Did you know that the legislature in New Mexico ratified a bill that a person cannot be turned down from serving on a jury only because he or she doesn't understand any English? How would you like to be on trial in New Mexico for a murder you didn't commit, and as your attorney is addressing the jury, pleading your innocence, you see jurors sitting there with dumbfounded expressions on their faces or saying, "Que es 'alibi'?"

According to the latest census, which, in my opinion, was the worst one ever . . . Did you fill it out? It was like writing a book. There were so many personal questions. They had the standard question that I always hated, "What race are you?" This time, they added a whole bunch of boxes for "mixed races." Poor Tiger Woods; he had to check fourteen boxes. Originally, the only thing the census was interested in knowing was how many Americans there are and where do we live. Why don't they go back to that? Stand on a street corner and count us as we pass, and then simply ask us where we're going.

Anyway, in the last census they did a whole study of immigration. Why, I don't know, because the story of immigration in this country has always been basically the same. People have always immigrated to the USA in waves from a particular country, because of problems in the mother country, like the potato famine in Ireland in the late 1800s, or they came here because of opportunities like the Chinese did, helping build the railroads. These waves of immigration swept in from all over the world. The Swedes came over, followed by the Italians. Then the Jews came over, followed by the Germans, who were following the Jews.

When each wave crashed on our shore two things happened. One was that we did something that no other country in the world had ever even come close to doing. We assimilated. People from over two hundred countries around the world became something, one thing that the world had never seen before. Something brand new and wonderful. Something called Americans!

The other thing that happened was that in our homes, we held on to some of the old country, like the cooking, holidays, traditions, customs. We even spoke the native tongue, but only inside. Outside the home, we all learned and spoke English. There are 172 languages and dialects spoken in homes in New York City alone, but only in the homes. In the streets, stores, schools, and in the workplace, everyone was determined to learn the language of the new country that offered them freedom and the opportunity to carve out a better life for themselves, for their children, and for every generation to follow. In some way, learning English was their way of expressing their thanks, appreciation, and respect.

Nowadays, for the first time in our history, one group of people won't learn English. They want the rest of us to learn their language or we'll be left behind in our own country, not them, us. Afraid to be politically incorrect, we give in, even encourage it in a lot of ways by becoming more bilingual in everything from street signs, billboard ads, and safety instructions, to our schools. We've even agreed to accept a bastard combination of the two languages called Spanglish. We never had Frenglish, Italglish, Chinglish, Yiddglish, or any other glish. What does not learning the main "glish"—English—lead to?

Well, for one thinglish, a small thinglish but indicative of bigger and worse thinglishes to come, it leads to something I read in a front-page story with the headline: "Police Learning Spanish as Latino Population Grows." In other words, let's say there is an altercation in a Hispanic neighborhood, guns being fired. Nowadays, the cops pull up in their patrol car, jump out, reach inside their jackets, and pull out a little translation dictionary. As the bullets are flying, they duck and one of them calls out, "Donde es . . . su casa . . . señor . . . por favor?"

Now, let me tell you something. I moved more times than probably anyone reading this book even thought of moving. As a kid, we sometimes moved three or four times in a month. I told you that my father was a bookie, a numbers writer, so every time a number hit, we moved. The benefit to me was that I lived with every nationality and ethnic group you could name. I lived with all Greeks, Armenians,

Irish, Puerto Ricans, Sicilians, Arab Americans, Gypsies, Jews, Dutch, Spanish, Russians, and Slavs. I was the only white kid in a black neighborhood for years. You name the people, and I lived with them.

In every ethnic ghetto in which I lived, when there was an altercation, the police came in, drew their guns, and yelled, "Get the f— outta here! Now!" And everyone understood; even the guy who just got off the boat that morning. He might not have understood the word "hello," but he knew to run his ass off.

I guess what I am trying to say is that right now, today, and maybe for all our tomorrows, in light of what happened to us on September 11, 2001, this is the time for each of us to draw the line and say: I'm not going any further. I am not going to continue being a party to the great divide of the American people. Enough separation. Enough politically correct bullshit. We are one people. And for anyone who doesn't like it, we Americans can tell you to go screw yourself in over two hundred languages, including Spanish.

The other thing I am trying to say is that maybe this problem is very serious and calls for people of goodwill, who came from all corners of the world to live here together as one people, to do something to make certain that political correctness does not overshadow or destroy human correctness, for if we continue down the road on which we have been racing blindly and silently these past years, there will be less about which to laugh—and that alone will be an American tragedy for all people.

Religion

I'm asking for big trouble, aren't I? There's an old saying that one should never discuss politics or religion. Here I am doing both. But I have to do it, because religion and politics are two areas that sometimes give people a lot of concern, or grief, or angst, and this book is about how to make it easier to deal with just that. It isn't that I know a lot about religion, although I've read the Old Testament, the New Testament, the Koran, and the teachings of Buddha and Zen. I gleaned from each some things that I thought might be of value in guiding me through life, and they have.

I am not a religious man, but I believe I am a spiritual man and, more importantly, a good man. Most importantly, I am a tolerant man, believing that every human being has the right to practice freely whatever religious belief he or she wants, or no religion, as long as the practice of such does not hurt another human being.

I am also supposed to be a funny man, so let me tell you a brief anecdote that might help you think and laugh through the personal questions, concerns, and worries you may have concerning religion.

Let's warm up a little, ease into it, so to speak. Here are a couple of minor theological questions for which I have never found the answers.

There was a TV evangelist. I won't mention his name, but I'll tell you that he was one of the top five. After two went to prison, he moved up to number three. He was not only an evangelist; he was a faith healer. He could put his hand on people and heal their physical ailments. I saw him touch a man who couldn't walk, who was confined to a wheelchair for decades, and just from a hand and a few words to God, the man got up from his chair and walked to the back of the auditorium to the thunderous applause of the thousands who were there. Another time, I saw him put his hands over the eyes of a blind man and when he took his hands away, the man could read any eye chart in America.

Here's my theological question. The evangelist was bald. If he could perform miracles on the deaf, blind, and crippled, why couldn't he put a few extra hairs on his own head? That should be a breeze compared to the other miracles. He could go to sleep with his hand taped to his head. I don't get it.

Another time, I drove past the palatial headquarters of a different evangelist/healer. In his employees' parking lot, there were spaces for handicapped parking. Did he hate his employees so much he wouldn't whip a hand on their legs or wherever and cure them? Or maybe, like in TV game shows, all employees are disqualified from winning.

Pope Paul II has made nearly five hundred saints, which is more than have been made in the four hundred years preceding him. He's saint crazy.

"Poppa, the pizza is here."

"I like that pizza boy . . . He's been on time twice. That's two miracles. I dub thee Saint Pepperoni."

Sainthood is something I never could understand, even though I grew up with a lot of Catholic friends. Before we ran a play in football, they would kiss their Saint Christopher medals, the Protector, and then they'd get the shit knocked out of them. I used to ask them if it was because Saint Christopher liked the tackler on the other team better. Then, saints get fired, booted out, end up standing in unemployment lines. I knew it was going to happen to Christopher. Not because of football, but whenever there was a real bad car accident in the neighborhood, there'd be a Saint Christopher on the dashboard with a broken arm or his head missing.

I hope I am not offending anyone. It is not my intention at all. I know this is a sensitive area and have stepped over bounds a couple of times, the most recent of which was when the American cardinals met in Dallas in 2002 to discuss the problem of priests molesting young boys in their congregation. I ad-libbed two lines that night that have never been uttered by me again:

"You know what I don't understand? The cardinals are staying in Dallas in a Holiday Inn where children stay for free." (Help!)

Instead of stopping there, I continued, "And why don't they pass a strict no tolerance law like the courts have—three tykes and you're out." (Help! Emergency airlift!)

I thought it was interesting that the Pope has appointed the first Asian American as a bishop. He is going to be at the San Francisco archdiocese. His name is Monsignor Wang. No comment. I've learned my lesson, thank God.

Now let's move on to a more substantive and safe theological question. Ever since he was nominated and confirmed to be our attorney general, John Ashcroft has been taking it on the chin because of his religious beliefs and practices. He's a minister's son and belongs to one of these minor sects, small in number but usually long in name. You know, something like "Fourth-Day Adventist Say Hello to Jesus, Wave to Mary." The followers of this religion are not allowed to drink alcohol, smoke, gamble, or dance. This is what the media jumps on almost every time they report anything about John Ashcroft, regardless of subject content. Typically, you might hear a TV anchorman say the following on the evening news:

"Thirty-two al-Qaeda terrorist suspects were arrested this morning in Buffalo, New York. It was announced by John Ashcroft, the attorney general who is not allowed to drink alcohol, smoke, gamble, or dance. The arrest was made at . . ."

Enough already! Let the man do whatever his religion tells him to do. He isn't hurting anyone. Besides, the truth is that it isn't just Ashcroft's religion that seems a little strange to those not of his faith. The truth is that every single organized religion in the world has a bunch of weird things you're not allowed to do.

For example, I'm Jewish, and on our Sabbath, which runs Friday night at sundown until Saturday night sundown, instead of the Christian

Sabbath, which begins Sunday morning (because Jews don't like to get up early), we are not allowed to do any work, perform any labor. This doesn't just mean going into the office Saturday afternoon to catch up, or typing away at your desktop at home. There's a long list of things you are not allowed to do, many of which are really weird. For example:

You're not allowed to turn on a stove, oven, or microwave to cook. Even the barbeque is off limits. Cook everything before the sun goes down and let it simmer on a low flame or enjoy your bologna sandwich—but don't cut it!

You can't turn on a light switch in a dark room, which is why every Jewish family hopes someone in the family gets palsy. "Uncle Sam, go in the kitchen. Keep your hand near the wall. That's it. No, God must've turned it on. Now, go into the children's bedroom."

You cannot push an elevator button. That ever so slight, almost indiscernible movement is considered labor. So you have to stand in the lobby and hope a Gentile comes along. Then, once on the elevator, you have to hope the Gentile is nice enough to push your floor button. Otherwise, you hear PA announcements like, "The Jew is still riding up and down in elevator three. Will someone please go in elevator three and push nine for the Jew, and don't push a four and a five like the last guy. It's not funny."

So as I was reading one of the media attacks on John Ashcroft's religion, I flashed back to a Friday night when I was fourteen years old and was hanging out on a street corner with four of my Sicilian friends. I saw it in my mind's eye as clearly as the night it happened.

I said, "I'm hungry. Let's get some hamburgers and —"

"Are you crazy, or what?" my friend interrupted. "It's Friday night. Fuhgehtahbowtit."

Back then, Catholics were not allowed to eat meat on Fridays.

I said, "I don't get it. Let's say we get the hamburgers and eat them, what's going to happen?"

"Oh, you want to know what's gonna happen, Brenner? I'll tell you what's gonna happen. I'm gonna get a sin. How's that for what's gonna happen?"

Now, I already told you that I'm Jewish, so I don't know anything about sin. What's so funny? I'm serious. We don't have sin. It wasn't in the original Bible. The Christians rewrote it and put it in. What a lunatic concept.

I said, "Okay, I still don't understand. Let's say we get the hamburgers and eat them, and you get one of those sin things, so?"

"Sin thing? I'll tell you what'll happen if I get a sin thing. I'll go to fuckin' hell! That's what'll happen."

I can remember what I said next, as clearly as if I said it five minutes ago.

"Okay, let's say we all go get some hamburgers and eat them, and you end up in hell, and the Devil shows up one day in your district of hell, and he points to some guy and says, 'What is your name and what did you do that ended you up in hell?'

"The man stands up and says, 'My name is Hannibal. I conquered the world, and I did it with elephants, so I crushed to death anyone who was in my way, and that's why I ended up down here in hell.'

"Then the Devil points to another guy and asks him the same question and the man stands up and says, 'My name is Adolf Hitler. I killed more than twelve million innocent people and that's why I'm in hell.'

"Then the Devil points and says, 'Who are you and what did you do that sent you to hell?' The guy stands and replies, 'My name is Tony Raggazino and one Friday night I ate a hamburger with David Brenner . . .'"

I put my hands out like the dishes of a scale and weighed the imaginary world conqueror and murderers in one and Tony and his burger on the other. Where's the balance? Where's the sense?

"Excuse me, Devil. My name is John Ashcroft, and I danced."

"You danced? What the heaven is wrong with you? Sit with Hitler!"

Yeah, I don't get it.

I remember a little piece of philosophy from my childhood. It went like this: "There are only two things to worry about in life—

whether you are going to live or die. If you're going to live, you have no worries, but if you die, you'll have two worries. Are you going to heaven or are you going to hell? If you go to heaven, you have no worries, and if you go to hell, you'll be so busy shaking hands with everyone you know, you won't have time to worry."

There's a line in an old blues song, "Everyone wants to go to heaven, but no one wants to die."

Recently, I thought of something. It might be an epiphany or just a simple thought. In heaven there are no churches, no synagogues, no mosques, no Buddhist temples, and no religions. God Himself knows which of the thousands of man-created religious dictates and rules you must and must not obey, so not one of earth's religions has it completely right while all the rest have it wrong, or each religion has a few things right and a few wrong, or maybe none of the religions has a damn thing right. So what is the intelligent reasoning for believing that your religion has got it right and all the others are wrong, and why isn't the intelligent thing to do not to belong to any organized religion, except the one that beats in your own heart and then just be a good person? Maybe this is just too simplistic and with too little finger-pointing and hate to be true or accepted. No one would go to war, try to conquer the world, or die over anything so basic, which might be what is wrong with it for mankind. Oh, well, it was just a thought.

Here's something else to think about. A young boy in Russia goes to the old rabbi in the small town and asks him, "Rabbi, please explain the Talmud (the basis of all laws governing Jews and all the teaching in Judaism) in one simple sentence." The rabbi takes a switch and thrashes the boy, saying, "How dare you ask for the Talmud to be reduced to one sentence?"

The boy travels to the next town and asks their old rabbi the same question and gets the same response and words. The boy goes to the next town. There is a young rabbi. He asks again, "Rabbi, please explain the Talmud in one sentence."

The rabbi looks at the boy and says, "Do to another person as you would want the other person to do to you—everything else in the Talmud is merely conversation." This is my religion. It causes me no worries and causes no other human being any grief. It isn't funny, but it allows life to be.

I am not a praying man, but if I were, I would pray that God has a sense of humor.

Crime

The subject of crime has always been a major part of my act. On my first appearance on national TV, *The Tonight Show* with Johnny Carson, I closed my monologue with a routine about crime that not only brought down the house, it launched my career.

I'll tell you how I thought of the routine, which I called The Dead Man. I was walking on the Upper East Side of Manhattan at the height of the evening rush hour, heading to do a set at the Improv on West 44th Street. The streets were jam-packed with pedestrians, thousands of them. I wanted to cross 57th Street but the crowd physically pushed me across Third Avenue.

I was pissed, so when I went onstage that night I vented my anger in the opening moment by telling the audience what had happened to me earlier. I said, "It is so crowded in Manhattan that you have to actually announce to a crowd where you want to get off. 'Excuse me, could you push me into the next building? I work there.'"

The audience screamed. I wasn't trying to be funny. I was just trying to get something off my chest. I then said, "You could commit the perfect murder in New York. All you have to do is take the body with you and slip it into the crowd. They'll take him for the next week."

Again, they screamed, and I continued by becoming the dead body, moving around the stage like a cadaver being pushed and manipulated by an oblivious, hurrying mob. In your mind now, picture me, at that time a tall, skinny, young man with a big nose, bouncing and sliding across the stage floor, waving arms, making jerky movements, acting like a corpse in wild motion and calling out the words, as I fly around. And, now, ladies and gentlemen, we go back in time to witness The Dead Man Routine:

"The body goes into Macy's, through women's lingerie.

"Boom! The body is carried up Madison Avenue, into Cooke's Funeral Home, where a few people say he looks like he's sleeping.

"Boom! The body shows up at the army recruiting office and is classified 1-A.

"Boom! It gets swept into Central Park, where it gets raped twice and mugged once.

"Boom! It gets thrown into traffic, where it is killed three more times.

"Boom! A class trip picks up the body. The teacher: 'Okay, who's talking? Is it you, the blue boy in the back?'

"Boom! The body is carried up Broadway to Radio City Music Hall, where it does twenty minutes with the Rockettes. [This was the most fun to do.]

"Finally, the body shows up on a subway. A cop sees it. 'Look at that weirdo, Bill, holding a strap with his foot. But we can't do anything unless he spits, smokes, or carries a lighted pipe.'"

That's exactly the way I performed it that first night, verbatim, and I never changed even one word of it for my national TV debut. I owe an entire career to one minute and thirty seconds of ad-lib madness about a crime, the perfect murder.

I've continued to find the humor in serious crime news. I want to share with you some of my favorite jokes that are derived from true crime stories. My objective is to train you to look for the humorous side so that you can find some levity in news that normally brings you down. Okay, here we go. Put on your seat belts and . . . excuse me for digressing, but whenever a flight attendant demonstrates how to close your seat belt, I always think that if someone is so stupid that they can't figure out how to secure a seat belt, they should be thrown off the plane, preferably while it is taxiing. Okay, for all the intelligent passengers, let's take off for Laugh Land.

News: According to the latest FBI statistics, crime is down in every metropolitan area of the United States with one exception—Honolulu. Crime is up there.

Punchline: It's easy to understand why. They can't apprehend the criminals. I'll tell you what I mean. Let's say a police radio dispatcher calls a cruising police car in Honolulu.

"Come in, Car 29; Car 29, come in. Over."

"This is Car 29. Over."

"There's a robbery in progress at the corners of Wahalahalulu and Hehouhanahannanah. Did you copy? Over."

"Was that the corner of Wanahalaunihuli and Heekulanihanolookie? Over."

"Negative. Make a left on Heekulanihanolookie to Wakiwakihanluki. Over."

"Was that a left on Heekulanihanolookie or Heekulanihanolookielooie? Over."

By the time the police get there, if they ever do, the robber has already bought himself a Mercedes Benz and is raising hell in Tijuana.

News: Crime is way down in Malaysia, and it is being attributed to the broadcasts on their TV network of videotapes of actual canings. This is where they strip a prisoner and whip his ass with a long bamboo rod.

Punchline: Malaysia is a different culture than ours. It wouldn't work here. In San Francisco alone, crime would go up about 800 percent.

News: A man who beat a young gay man to death said in the courtroom that the reason he did it was because the gay man was making sexual advances toward him. He got sentenced to life in prison.

Punchline: Well, he solved his problem.

News: In Pat Buchanan's latest book, he states that homosexuality is a crime and is addictive.

Punchline: Where are they going to put the patch?

News: Bank robbers are getting dumber. We used to have great ones like John Dillinger, Willie "The Actor" Sutton, and, possibly the most interesting of all, Bonnie and Clyde. The modern version: A man in Miami, Florida, robbed a bank at gunpoint, shoving a gun in the teller's face and demanding all the money. He took the two bags of money, shoved them down the front of his pants, and ran out of the bank. He forgot that tellers put paint bombs in with the money. They exploded.

Punchline: Now Clyde is Bonnie.

News: A man in Canada robbed a porno shop of over $1,000 worth of sex toys.

Punchline: Police say he is armed and very satisfied.

News: Tom Green (not the brilliant and bizarre comedian) is a Mormon who believes in the old ways of the Mormon Church, which allow a man to marry as many women as he wants. Green has five wives and recently became the father of his thirty-first child. He was arrested on charges of bigamy, put on trial, found guilty, and sentenced to many years in prison, which he has begun to serve. At his sentencing, the judge said, "This man must be punished!"

Punchline: What do you mean "must be punished"? This poor bastard has five wives and thirty-one children. What's worse than that? You want to punish him? Send him home."

News: A boy of fourteen went to Chicago and forced his elderly grandmother to withdraw money from an ATM machine. After getting the money, he got into a shootout with police and used his grandmother as a human shield. She got shot three times, all superficial.

Punchline: If she were Jewish, she would've said, "At least, he visits."

News: A woman arriving in Montreal, Canada, was given a complete cavity search by airport security because they suspected her of trying to smuggle in African parrots.

Punchline: Now either those are the smallest parrots in the world, or this woman has an ass bigger than Wyoming.

News: In New York City a man urinated out of the window of his hotel room right on the head of a man walking on the pavement six floors below. No matter how much the victim ran or ducked, the peeing perpetrator kept hitting his target right on. The police arrested him.

Punchline: Arrested him? They should've given him a medal. Most men can't stay inside the bowl. They should've made him an instructor.

News: A woman in England was arrested for stealing her husband's sperm.

Punchline: How sound a sleeper was this guy?

News: Michael Skakel was convicted and sentenced to twenty years to life in prison for the murder twenty-seven years ago of Martha Moxley. The jury deliberated three days, before bringing in the guilty verdict. When asked what the factor was that tipped the scale over to the conviction, they said it was his alibi. Skakel's alibi was that at the exact moment the girl was being murdered, he was up in a tree masturbating.

Punchline: This guy had twenty-seven years to come up with an alibi, and the best he could do was that he was whacking off in a tree. Even if he's innocent, just for the alibi, they should've given him life.

News: I was in some small town watching TV, when the chief of police interrupted the broadcast to announce that someone stole an Oscar Mayer Weinermobile, and then he gave the license plate.

Punchline: He gave it so you wouldn't confuse it with the other large hot dogs that are whipping around your neighborhood. (By the way, that's a father's nightmare: to see your daughter's date drive up in the Oscar Mayer Weinermobile.)

News: Police said that one of the best pieces of evidence they have against the Beltway Sniper is a brown glove that appears to match the one found at the scene of the last killing.

Punchline: Here we go again! Where's Johnnnny?

Side Note: There are two amazing aspects about the Beltway Sniper. One is how the FBI overnight turned the suspects' white van into a green Chevy, and the other is that since the beginning of this nation, except for the serial killer serving time in Atlanta, who a lot of people think is innocent, every serial killer in our history has been a Caucasian man. This is the first time that it has been a black man. Think about it. First, they took over baseball and basketball, then football and golf, and now they want to be the serial killers. We have to draw the line somewhere or else they'll also want to start all the wars, and that is a white man's job!

News: Did you read about the man who was visiting a prisoner and the guards wouldn't let him, the visitor, use the men's room, and he ended up urinating in his pants? Well, he sued and was awarded $10,000.

Punchline: He got $10,000 for peeing on himself just once? Do you realize how many men are riding NYC subways that have no idea how rich they are?

News: I saw this headline in a Los Angeles newspaper: "California Legislature Demands Tougher Death Penalty."

Punchline: What does that mean: a "tougher death penalty"? What are they going to do, put the electric chair on Amtrak? I like how Amtrak keeps bragging about their Acela high-speed train that goes 137 mph. You know what that means? A longer walk out of the woods. Before I get on an Amtrak train, I check the sides of the cars for grass stains. One little bush, I walk.

News: Some states have adopted the "Three Strikes and You're Out" law. If you commit your third criminal offense, you are automatically sent away for life. Period, the end, zero tolerance. It looks good on paper, except it doesn't always work as expected. A case in point is the man who had never committed a violent offense, but did commit his third crime, which was stealing videotape movies from a store. Under the Three Strikes law, he was given life in prison.

Punchline: This poor guy has to show up in prison and join all the other lifers whose crimes range from raping and killing a farmer's wife and daughter and then raping fourteen cows, to a bank robber whose escape routes were littered with the dead bodies of witnesses and law enforcement officers. Now imagine the first day the serial video thief shows up among these "illustrious" killers and is asked, "What are you in for?"

"Have any of you guys ever seen *The Little Mermaid*?"

News: Some leading penologist has suggested that the way to make the most violent criminals less violent is to castrate them, because they have an imbalance of testosterone.

Punchline: If anything would make a guy less violent, relax him, turn him into a mild-mannered pacifist, it would be telling him, "Hi, Harry. Good news. After lunch, we're going to cut off your balls." Not as effective, I might add, as telling him that you're also going to sew his dick on the back of his neck.

News: A man who shot and killed an airman was sentenced to die, but then it was discovered that he had an IQ of only 59. The prosecution said that he was bright enough to know how to operate the gun and the defense claimed he was too dumb (in layman's terms) to know what he was doing was wrong.

Punchline: I suggest as an alternative, you get him a job in airport security, so he can be with his own kind.

News: A woman showed up in a Chicago police station with testicles she bit off of a boyfriend. Police questioned her for one hour.

Punchline: I'll bet you the first question was "Would you like a mint?"

Before we leave the subject of crime, I'd like to give you some random thoughts and even, if I may be so bold, my suggestion for a solution to the existence, if not the rise, of crime, the inequities of the judicial system, and the omnipresent problem of overcrowded prisons. These are areas of great stress for law-abiding Americans, and also for many criminals. To eliminate the problematic areas is indeed a very tall order, one that all the experts have been unsuccessful in solving, but, ego aside, I, your neighborhood comedian, have the answers. Let me dazzle you.

First off, the jury system does not work. I'll prove it with two letters: Give me an O. Give me a J.

Let's take another famous case and its illustrious jury of peers, which are more often more like a jury of pears. When both sides rested their case in the Jeffrey Dahmer trial, the jury spent three days arguing whether Dahmer was insane. Three days to argue whether a man who killed young boys and made sandwiches out of their body parts was sane or insane. I can hear one of those idiot jurors arguing:

"Well, I have a cousin who likes to eat liverwurst, onion, olive, chicken, and peanut butter sandwiches, but that doesn't make her insane. Most people have strange tastes."

I'm not going to drag this on any further. I'm sure you get the point. The jury system sucks and has to be eliminated. My plan, which I'll describe in detail, does exactly that, and it also solves another serious problem—overcrowded prisons. We can eliminate every single prison in America.

My judicial and prison reform and my idea of how to end crime as we know it, are simplistic and effective.

Prison is a joke to most criminals. They can do hard time on their heads. They spend their prison time bodybuilding, making weapons, dealing and using drugs, learning how to be better at their trades, designing tattoos, and enjoying same-sex sex.

Then there is the matter of no uniformity in our laws and, therefore, the resulting inequities in punishments. If you rob a store in one state, you get up to twenty years, while a few miles away, across the state line, for the same exact crime, the maximum is five years. In one state, having oral sex with someone of the same sex is a crime, while in another state it is called fun. We need a uniform judicial system in all fifty states.

Here's my plan of how we can eliminate jurors, judges, prisons, the inequities in the law—the whole shit and caboodle. (Don't ask me what a caboodle is.)

My Plan

We develop a uniform code applicable in every state with automatic uniform punishments that covers every possible crime that could be committed. This uniform, universal code is placed in a large book and given to someone who merely has to be able to read and follow directions. He or she can choose to wear a black robe or blue jeans. After a person is arrested, he is taken before this Person of the Book, so to speak, who questions him:

"What did you do?"

"I committed robbery, your honor."

"Don't 'your honor' me, you piece of shit. Just answer my questions and call me Sidney."

"Yes, Sidney."

The P.O.T.B. opens the "book" that has every crime possible listed and thumbs through it. "Okay, let's see . . . jaywalking . . . spitting . . . tearing the label off a mattress . . . whacking off in public . . . whacking off on Sunday . . . whacking off in a sundae . . . here it is—robbery. Okay, what did you rob?"

"A 7-Eleven."

"You can say 'This is a robbery' in Hindi? Amazing." *(Thumbing again.)* "Let's see . . . robbing a poor box . . . robbing a poor man . . . robbing a pure man . . . robbing a robber . . . robbing a rubber . . . robbing a ribber . . . robbing a rabbit . . . rubbing a rabbit . . . robbing a 7-9 . . . a 7-10 . . . Ah, here it is, robbing a 7-Eleven. What time did you commit this crime?"

"About two in the morning."

"What's the matter? Trouble sleeping?" *(Thumbing.)* "Okay . . . before breakfast . . . after breakfast . . . around brunch time . . . before dinner . . . during dinner . . . after dinner . . . after a dinner mint . . . before six . . . before sex . . . during Letterman . . . after Koppel . . . after copulation . . . late at night . . . one . . . two. Okay, two in the morning. Did you have a weapon?"

"A gun, Sidney."

"Don't call me Agunsidney. I hate that name. Call me Yendisnuga, which is Agunsidney spelled backward. Now, did you or did you not have a weapon?"

"Yes, I had a gun, Sid . . . a gun Yendisnuga."

"What kind of weapon is a gunyendisnuga?"

"I had a . . . a pistol."

"Why didn't you say so in the first place?" *(Thumbing pages.)* "Let's see. A knife . . . a rope . . . a baked potato . . . a baked potato with sour cream and chives . . . a frozen chicken . . . ah, here it is—a pistol sometimes called a gunyendisnuga. Now, did you threaten anyone?"

"The owner, Sidney."

"Same name as I. Coincidence, I am sure. So, you threatened an owner named Sidney." *(Thumbing pages.)* "Here we go . . . threatened a cashier . . . a clerk . . . a duck . . . a dick . . . a duck's dick . . . a duck named Dick . . . a dick named Duck . . . a duck named Clark . . . a dick named Clark . . . a Dick Clark . . . Dick Clark's duck . . . here it is . . . threatened an owner.

"Okay, let's compile your crime and see your automatic, uniform punishment." *(Compiling data.)* "You robbed a 7-Eleven at two in the morning with a gun and threatened an owner named Sidney. Okay, here is your automatic, uniform punishment." *(Reading from the code.)* "Every morning for six straight months, at exactly two o'clock A.M., a bull elephant will shit on you. Just thank your lucky star that you didn't have two guns. Next case!"

Now, there are a lot of guys who can do hard time as easily as sitting on a beach, but I never met anyone, no matter how tough, who could take six months of that shit.

"No, it can't be two already. Does Jumbo still have diarrhea? Can I wear a hat? Please."

Crime statistics would drop off the charts and eventually disappear. There would be no use for prisons, only holding areas and dump rooms, no judges, and no juries—voilà!

If you're smart, you'll get on the phone or your computer right this second and buy stock in every company that manufactures shovels and buckets. You're welcome and may you enjoy my crime-free world.

Cloning

Talk about a sensitive, touchy subject, let alone put words about it in print; cloning has got to be near the top of the list. So you know I'm not about to put my neck on the chopping block or my balls in the meat grinder over this one. If you want to get someone worked up to the point where steam hisses out of their ears and veins bulge in their neck and maybe even on their nose, open up a discussion about the religious and/or moralistic aspects of cloning. Cloning now ranks on the Shit Hit Parade of top subjects best never discussed, along with Abortion, Religion, and Politics.

Hell, the government has made it a mandatory $1,000,000 fine and ten years in prison if you get caught, in any scientific level, from rudimentary to expert, trying to clone a human being. I don't know about you, but as soon as I heard this, I charged down to my basement workshop and destroyed every piece of cloning equipment I had, including my box of two hundred various-colored Crayola crayons.

However, because cloning is one of the most difficult pills for people to swallow, I feel obligated to deal with it, to find the humor in it, to remove its hot edge and deliver all sides to a compatible, friendly, and even playing field.

Without getting into the inflammatory religious or moral issues, but, rather, from a very basic and obvious position, I can state categorically that I am 100 percent against cloning human beings. The next time you're in a crowded restaurant, sports event, movie theater, concert, or wherever large crowds gather, look at the people around you and ask yourself if you would want to see two of each of them. I rest my case. I'd like to qualify this a bit. There is one human being I'd like to see cloned, Mike Tyson, because I'd like to see him get in the ring with someone as crazy as he is. What a fight that would be. Maybe I ought to try salvaging my cloning equipment.

When it comes to cloning animals rather than humans, I am completely on the other side of the fence. If the world were to outlaw all cloning tomorrow, the benefits to man and animals already derived from this science have been tremendous. Because of the necessity, prior to the actual cloning, of studying down to the smallest, microscopic detail all we can about the DNA map, we have also learned more about the animal kingdom and mankind than we could've possibly learned in tens of thousands of years, if ever. I'll get into this shortly, but first let's discuss the history of various cloning activities that have been conducted around the world.

Animal cloning began in 1997 in Scotland with a sheep named Dolly. I was happy for Dolly, one day something in the gleam of a scientist's eye and test tube and the next day all fuzzy and running around on four legs—the sheep, not the scientist. But I felt so sorry for the group of scientists who pulled off this near miracle. I'm sure they truly believed that the world would beat the proverbial path to their door. Instead the world almost tore down their entire laboratory and beat the shit out of them. Why? Because, they hit a religious, moralistic chord, and it didn't help matters when the head scientist, not realizing the inference of his words, defended his creation by holding Dolly in front of him and saying "I stand behind her." A real baaaad choice of words, and so much for all the months of lonely nights in Scotland's cloning facility.

Scientists have also cloned goats, cattle, and mice. You might ask "Why mice?" I understand why. I was just saying to myself the other day, "There aren't enough mice in the world." The most recent animal to be cloned was a cat named CC, who was created either to go after the mice or, more likely, because the scientists found out there were only one billion cats in the world and they panicked. What are next—locusts and cockroaches?

I am glad they're trying to clone gorillas, because just a few weeks ago, I was at a zoo waiting in front of the gorilla cage for my little boys to come out of the little boys' room. There were three gorillas who starting throwing shit at me and I remember thinking, "Why can't there be forty of them?"

In England, they are cloning pigs, lots of pigs. You would think that in England they would clone dentists first. Aw, come on, have you ever been to London? Everyone looks like a hockey player. These people once conquered the world. You'd think with all the herbs and teas they brought back, they would've included some toothbrushes or, at least, some false teeth.

Now, let us discuss the knowledge gathered and gleaned from the new science of cloning. There has been so much. From cloning pigs, scientists learned that a female pig has an orgasm that lasts for thirty minutes! When I read that, all I could think was, "How does a female pig fake it for thirty minutes?"

This is my whole point. No, not pig orgasm, but that, when it comes to the question of cloning, if you put aside any religious or moral objections you might harbor—which really only cause you to become angry, uptight, and/or unhappy, anyway—and concentrate on the noncontroversial aspect of cloning, that is, the knowledge gleaned, you might develop a new perspective, and, if not, almost certainly a few laughs.

For example: I'm going to pose a question about cloning and then, after offering you enough time to think about it, I'll give the answer. The purpose for doing this is to guide you on how to find the humor and laughter about this sensitive subject. Actually, the pig orgasm would have worked here, but you never repeat a joke. By the way, you can research all this stuff on the Internet to check its validity. What follows was discovered while intensely studying the genetic blueprint prior to attempting cloning.

Which animal in the world, including man, makes the most noise and screams the most while having sex? . . . Give up? Okay. The answer is—da da da dum de dum—the monkey. I would've bet on the porcupine. You know what else the geneticists learned that was unknown prior to the cloning breakthrough? The answer to "How does a male monkey entice a female monkey to have sex with him?" The answer is with a banana. So I guess if a female monkey says to a male monkey, "Are you happy to see me, or is that a banana in your pocket?" it could be both.

So did I get you to laugh? I hope so. Now, one of my many comedian clones will read these jokes and do them on a stage somewhere in America this weekend, which is another sound reason to be against human cloning, for me, anyway.

Cloning is and will probably always be one of those controversial issues, like should the Dodgers have moved from Brooklyn to Los Angeles or are Britney Spears' tits real? It will continue to create debates among nations and individuals and, at times, red hot arguments and white rage. Put all this aside. I don't mean that you should give up your point of view or not fight for what you believe is right and just. All I am suggesting, regardless of your stand, is that you look at the funny side of this subject that really screams out for jokes and laughter. If you are so uptight about cloning that you can't find anything humorous in it, let someone clone you with the insertion of the good humor gene.

By the way, the original David Brenner doesn't know that I, his clone, wrote this. I think I'm funnier. What do you think?

Politics and Politicians

On every national Election Day, my father wrote in his name for president of the United States. One time he returned home from voting and announced to the family "I think I got a damn good chance this time." Of course, we all laughed. My father didn't. He just looked at us as though we were a group of foolish doubting Thomases and left the room grumbling to himself.

When I was still a little boy, I asked my father why he always voted for himself for president. He answered, "Because every politician is a crook. I am, too, but if I get elected, at least I'll know how and where I'm cheating me." I laughed. He continued, "Everyone cheats at something, Kingy [his nickname for me]. One guy cheats on his income tax. Another guy steals paper clips from his office, cashiers shortchange you, fruit vendors slip a bruised peach into the bottom of the bag, big businesses overcharge, cops take bribes, and kids cheat on school tests, right, Kingy?" I didn't answer. I didn't have to. My father knew his youngest apple hadn't fallen far from his tree.

I took the line about every politician being a crook with a barrel of salt, because my father thought everyone on earth was a crook. It was just a matter of degrees. Then while doing a one-day-a-year job that I had first gotten at age nine, I started having second thoughts about the invalidity of my father's philosophy.

Every Election Day, local and national, I sat outside a polling place on a wooden box whittling a piece of wood with my switchblade knife. The boss of the polling place would come outside with a voter next to him.

"Yo, kid, do they teach you how to vote in school?"

"Yeah, in Social Studies."

"Good. How about being a good kid and helping this man to vote?"

I'd say sure, close my knife, put it in my pocket, and go into the voting place. The one in need of assistance would differ from person to person. It was someone with bad eyesight or blind, very short, physically infirm, a new citizen, a very old person, a first-time voter, or someone just plain stupid. I would go into the voting booth with them, close the curtain, and show them how to vote a straight ticket, how to split their vote, and how to vote on the ballot issues. I'd ask them if they wanted me to stay while they voted. If they did, I stayed; if not, I left. It didn't matter and neither did their vote, because I had pulled all the levers and voted the way I was told by the political party paying me. If I left the booth, I threw open the curtain and cast my vote; If I stayed, I'd slip open the curtain just enough to register my vote.

I never got one letter of thanks from any of the political candidates for whom I had cast hundreds of votes. Thieves and ingrates. But I got twenty-five cents a vote, plus tips sometimes from the suckers I helped. I sometimes made as much as $50. My day job paid me $12 a week at age nine. I loved the democratic voting system, well, for at least one day a year, anyway.

My conscience didn't bother me for the same reason I thought politicians were schmucks, because a lot of kids worked outside of most of the polling places doing exactly what I was doing. We worked for the Democrats or the Republicans. It didn't matter. I knew that for every vote I cast for, say, the Republicans, some kid at a polling place nearby was casting his votes for the Democrats, so it was probably a wash or close to it. Thieves, ingrates, and schmucks.

I know this colored my opinion of politics, and as I grew up I always wondered if my father was right. Was every politician, or even most or many, a crook? I still don't know, although I have my personal leaning. Don't ask me what it is, but let me ask you a question. Would you work for an organization of over five hundred employees if you found out the following facts about them?

Twenty-nine have been accused of spousal abuse.

Seven were arrested for fraud.

Nineteen have been accused of writing bad checks.

One hundred and seventeen were directly or indirectly involved in bankruptcies.

Three served hard time for assault.

Seventy-one can't get credit cards because of bad credit.

Fourteen have been arrested on drug-related charges.

Eight have been arrested for shoplifting.

Twenty-one are currently defendants in lawsuits.

Eighty-four were arrested in 2000 for drunk driving.

If your answer is no, then you would have turned down the opportunity to be one of the 535 members of our prestigious 107th Congress of the United States of America.

So where's the laugh? After all, that's what this book is all about. Okay, here's the laugh. This Congress passed over one hundred laws to keep us in line. It's a riot, isn't it, or it may be someday.

A noted psychologist has suggested that politicians should work meager jobs, such as McDonald's, on occasion, in order to keep in touch with the public. Can you see a politician working at McDonald's?

"Would you like lies with that?"

In spite of their own record of dishonesty, one of the worst displays to me of political infighting, backbiting, and finger-pointing is how the corruption of our CEOs has become a political football.

The Democrats blamed the Republicans for the decline in integrity of our nation's CEOs, citing that George Bush himself had been a CEO who sold his last company's stock shortly before the bottom fell out. Coincidence? Then the Democrats attacked Dick Cheney, reminding us that for over five years before becoming vice president, he was the CEO of Halliburton, which is being investigated for creative bookkeeping, the same as Enron and the other companies involved in the CEO scandal.

The Republicans counterpunched smartly and succinctly, claiming that all the blame for all the corruption among all the CEOs can be placed squarely on the shoulders of one Democrat, former president Bill Clinton, because "President Clinton created an immoral climate in this country."

In other words, all the CEOs were watching TV and said, "The president is getting a blow job? Let's screw the people!" I know that the night I heard the news, I went out and robbed a diner.

As you probably know, former president Bill Clinton has been given the largest book advance in the history of publication to write two autobiographies, the first to be called *Wham Bam* and the second *Thank You, Ma'am*.

Okay, let's talk about presidential sex, for a little while, anyway. It's not yesterday's news, because the odds are pretty damn good that sometime in the future, it's going to be news again. Bill Clinton was not the first and only nor will he be the last president to do a lot of his thinking from the waist down. The history of sex in the White House is well documented; only of those who got caught, of course.

Thomas Jefferson had a wild love affair in his home, Monticello, with one of his slaves, who even gave birth to his offspring. If you flip over a nickel and look real close, you can see them doing it in the top right-hand window. President Harding got caught shtupping a woman in a closet in the Oval Office. No man has ever been so fearful of coming out of the closet. Woodrow Wilson was a serial shtupper. He was in a league of nations all by himself. President Franklin Delano Roosevelt did not let polio slow down his escapades. He had naked women sitting on him on his chair doing wheelies through the White House. "Spin, Franklin baby, spin!" There was never a truer campaign slogan than Dwight Eisenhower's "I like Ike." We all heard about (and many of us envied) the extracurricular activities of JFK. When George Bush Sr. was asked by a reporter for the identity of the female CIA secretary who very often "traveled with him," he answered, "It's none of your business."

The only thing that bothered me about the Clinton Scandal was his choice of women. Paula Jones? Please. If the best the governor of Arkansas could do was Paula Jones, what was the busboy from IHOP taking home at night? And Monica Lewinsky? She still had the marks from the ten-foot poles. Not even with yours.

What bewildered me the most about the entire incident was that Monica Lewinsky was a twenty-three-year-old woman at the time who had landed one of the plum jobs in the universe, working as an intern in the White House with the president of the United States of America, meeting the most influential world leaders, being an eye-witness to history being made. Why'd she blow it?

You see, I believe George Bush Sr. was right. What goes on behind presidential flies is none of our business, only what the president does behind the Oval desk . . . well, not in Clinton's case, anyway. I guess what I am saying is that, as far as I am concerned, I'd rather have a president who does it to a woman once in a while than a president who does it to the rest of us 24/7 for four years.

One of the most annoying aspects of politics to me is the political convention. I had to go to the Democratic Convention in 2000 to appear on TV shows, because all the shows were being broadcast from the venue. The policemen and police barricades were far away from the convention hall, so you had to walk a great distance to get there. Being curious, I asked a high-ranking officer why. He said it was to keep the hookers from embarrassing the delegates. It made sense. We wouldn't want to embarrass a delegate from Iowa with no teeth, wear-ing a red, white, and blue diaper with a donkey hat.

Did you ever watch a political convention on TV? Did you ever look at the delegates? Do you know one person who looks like that? Where do they find those Americans? I think they shake a state and every asshole that falls out, they hand him a straw hat. "Here, act like a total schmuck for a week."

I was raised in a strange way. My mother told me when I was a kid that I was a citizen of the universe. She did not approve of any-thing that separated human beings from one another, including coun-tries and states. Therefore, I grew up believing there was no difference or importance as to where anyone was born or raised. Besides, our birthplace is no more than an accident. I was born and raised in

Philadelphia, Pennsylvania, a very nice city and state but it was only by accident that I'm from there. To be truthful, if my father had an extra five dollars for gasoline, I'd be from New Jersey.

The worst display of stupid state pride takes place at a political convention, when, after their caucus, the head delegate stands to announce their nominee for president. Before he tells you the name of their choice, he spends twenty-five minutes bragging about the wonderment of his home state.

"The gorgeous, splendiferous state of Louisiana, famous for the manufacturing of pillowcases, national leaders in barnyard dancing and pocket weaving, birthplace of the 1976 National Thumb Wrestling Champion, first in the nation in the consumption of cashew nuts . . ."

I'm always hoping some delegate from New York will jump up and, pointing his thumb at his crotch, yell, "Yo, I got your nuts over here!" There's a good chance of this happening in 2004, when the Republican National Convention is held in Madison Square Garden. The muggers, hookers, and con artists can't wait.

Every state does the Big Brag and no state tells all the truth. You never hear any leader of any caucus say, "My fine state is also first in syphilis and gonorrhea and has given birth to more rapists and serial killers than any of the other states. We nominate . . ."

Worst of all, these thousands of assholes decide who should run for president. I wouldn't let them decide which side of my bread to put the butter on, even though they spend their entire political lives knowing exactly who is buttering which side of theirs.

Actually, even bright, well-informed, well-educated, sophisticated Americans would have trouble nominating anyone from the field of losers we are given. Look at the choices from the 2000 election.

Dan Quayle: Did you see him on TV during his campaign, when someone asked him what he thought of HMO and he answered, "Personally, I prefer Showtime"? At least he had enough brains to drop out early.

Donald Trump: Another early dropout. He was so annoying, always talking in the third person. "The Donald is hungry. The Donald wants to go eat." Can you imagine him as the president conducting a press conference? "The Donald thinks this. The Donald thinks that." Great, Donald, and what do Daffy and the other ducks think?

Ralph Nader: The nominee of the Green Party who constantly bragged about his political strength in California. The only reason so many Californians supported him was because they thought they were going to get green cards.

Pat Buchanan: What amazed me about this candidate was that just he and his sister conducted his entire campaign, just the two of them, from a bunker in Berlin.

David Duke: The former head of the KKK now serving time in prison was a possible candidate. What was his campaign slogan going to be—"If you can't take the heat of the cross, get off the lawn"?

John McCain: A prisoner of war in Hanoi for over five years. A good man, but I was afraid that if he were elected president, the first thing he would do would be bomb Vietnam. "I'm coming back over there, you little gook bastards!"

Bob Dole: He did commercials for Viagra. I felt sorry for him. Here he is with the first woody he's had since 1945, and he's on the road campaigning with his wife, Elizabeth, back in Washington. I'll bet he was on the phone every twenty minutes. "Join me on the campaign trail, Lizzy baby; Bob's big boy is waiting for you." Actually, Dole looked like he bathed in Viagra; he was so stiff. After the election was over and Dole lost, he appeared on a lot of TV shows, including *David Letterman* and *Saturday Night Live,* and he was so loose, likable, charming, human, and especially funny, nothing like he was throughout his entire campaign. A lot of people said that if he been that way when he was running, they might have voted for him. I comment on this because it shows you the power of humor and laughter, even in politics and politicians.

Al Gore: Not the smartest campaign ever conducted, but if I were to pick his smartest campaign answer, it would be the one he gave after his opponent, candidate George W. Bush, had responded to whether he had ever tried marijuana, by answering, "Not in the last seven years."

Al Gore answered, "Yes, in Vietnam," and the subject was never brought up again and it seems neither will the question "Will you run again?" He said he's not going to run in 2004 and maybe never again and who can blame him? He got more popular votes than any presidential candidate in American history and lost the election. Let's not rehash it, right? Except, maybe to ask what the hell is wrong with Florida. Every time there's an election you see voter poll workers holding ballots up to lights, looking for holes they call chads. What is it with Floridians? Are they that dumb? Why can't they figure out how to vote? What's the big deal? We could all vote right now. By a show of hands, how many think forty-nine states are enough?

George W. Bush: The only winner, but . . .

Okay, it's time to beat around the Bush, but before we do, I want to prequalify anything that I write by stating that I have rarely been a fan of any president, including those who served even before I was born. It is always said that history will bear out the truth of someone's administration, but research does the job better.

For example, it has been documented that George Washington holed up with his troops in Valley Forge for the winter, before attacking and defeating the British troops who were luxuriating in Philadelphia. Well, it is true that George was freezing his ass off in Valley Forge, although there is no proof that his wood teeth were chattering. Wooden teeth, what a beauty he must've been. How could any soldier take seriously any command yelled through wooden teeth?

"Okay, men, let's go to Valley Forge! . . . Knock off the laughing and who's the wise ass who said 'knock on wood'?"

I really feel sorry for his wife, Martha. What kind of life did this poor woman have?

"Come on, George; take them out for an hour. I've got splinters in my thighs. I'm the laughingstock of the whole neighborhood."

Anyway, historians have come up with many reasons why the general of the British army inexplicably did not attack Washington when he was in Valley Forge, freezing, low on food, and with demoralized troops—and it's only an hour by car from Philly. Well, researchers have uncovered the real reason. The British general was shacking up with a Philly filly. So, if it weren't for a hot piece of ass, we'd all be eating fish and chips and beating the shit out of each other at soccer games.

Researchers have uncovered unknown facts about another one of our greatest presidents, Abraham Lincoln. First of all, Honest Abe was not as honest as he led us to believe. The world's most famous rail-splitter might have been gay. So all this time that we thought he was sleeping with Mary Todd, he was sleeping with Mary *and* Todd. Secondly, it has been factually confirmed that throughout his life, Abraham Lincoln suffered from hemorrhoids. Think of this the next time you are driving through New York City's Lincoln Tunnel.

"Oh, my God, Ralph, what the hell are those things hanging up ahead? Make a U-turn!"

One more revelation. Andrew Jackson suffered from severe diarrhea. How did anyone come up with this one? After all, Jackson has been dead for over one hundred years. It has been validated by scientific studies of his hair. I agree. If it was in his hair, it was severe.

Back to Bush and another personal prequalifier. I admit that before September 11, 2001, I was not a Bush man, politically speaking, that is. Actually, I was not a fan until I heard him speak that night, because there was something I didn't understand about what the president did on that horrific day. I still don't understand, actually.

It has been documented that on that black day in America's history the president was in Sarasota, Florida, about to speak to a public school class of second-graders, when he was called out by Condoleezza Rice and told what had happened to the World Trade Center and the Pentagon. Then the Secret Service told the president that they had "reliable information" that his plane, Air Force One, was "a prime target of the terrorists." Then they said, "Mr. President, get on the plane," and he did.

That's what I don't understand. To me, most of life is a microcosm of the street corner where I grew up. If one of the guys hanging on the corner suggested we get in Tony's car and go for pizza and ended by saying "We think there's a bomb under Tony's car," forty guys would be running their asses off in forty different directions. Yet the president got onboard and flew first to Louisiana, and then, even though there were no other planes in the skies above America than his and the accompanying jet fighters, he flew again, but not back to Washington. He went to Nebraska.

Hearing all this reported on the news, I had two thoughts. The first was why they didn't just hide the president in a condo in Sarasota. Who the hell would ever think of looking for the president of the United States in one of Frieda Berkowitz's Clean and Comfortable Condos by the Sea? My second was about the deadly Nazi V-2 bombings of London. After it was confirmed that Buckingham Palace was one of the prime targets, the queen was asked if her children were going to be removed, possibly even to a safe haven out of London or the country. As I remember it, the queen said something like, "The children will not leave, unless I do. I shall not leave, unless their father does, and the king will not leave under any circumstances whatsoever."

Anyway, the president finally arrived home that evening and was reunited with his wife, who had stayed at home in the White House, in spite of it also being one of the suspected prime targets of the terrorists. There is no record of whether he ate dinner there, or on Air Force One, or stopped somewhere between Sarasota, Louisiana, Nebraska, and D.C. But there is a record of a speech he made to the American people that included some of the most inspiring, uplifting words ever spoken at a time when Americans needed them the most. It was this speech that united a remarkable 82 percent of the people behind their leader. I was one of them. The following are the words that made me join the ranks of the majority of Americans:

"Terrorist attacks can shake the foundations of our biggest buildings, but they cannot dent the steel of American resolve. America was attacked because we're the brightest beacon for freedom and opportunity in the world. And no one will keep that light from shining."

I was so moved; I was so dumbfounded that this was the same man I had found to be so average, at best. I mean wasn't this the guy who couldn't think of a more creative name for his dog than Spot? Wasn't this the same guy who said he was going to take a one-month vacation on his ranch in Midland, Texas, to give him "a chance to sound out the people I represent"? Come on, how many people live in Midland, Texas, and how many of them are Asians, Puerto Ricans, Jews, Vietnamese, or any of the other 220-plus nationalities he represents? Wasn't this the same guy who changed all the art in the Oval Office and put his favorite painting on the wall nearest him, reportedly saying that it was his favorite painting because he could never figure out the mystery of how they got the dogs to hold the cards?

As much as I couldn't believe that I had flip-flopped about him overnight, I was even more mystified how he had flip-flopped over night, too, transforming into a great leader, maybe even the best wartime commander in our history. How the hell did it happen? With the words ringing in my ears that he had spoken to describe the White House Rose Garden in which he stood, "Such a beautiful, beautiful part of our national . . . our national . . . really our national park system. I guess you would want to call it," I began my search for the answer as to how both the president of the United States and the American Comedian had flip-flopped overnight.

I thought about the words he had spoken that made me take the first step in the flip-flop and had united 82 percent of the citizens, and I thought about other words he had used in the near past in an attempt to unify us: "Our nation must come together to unite" and my favorite, "I think we all agree—the past is over."

Other pre–September 11 words only confused me more in my search for the answer. Such words as the following:

"I know how hard it is to put food on your family."

"It is clearly a budget. It's got a lot of numbers in it."

"I believe we are on an irreversible trend toward more freedom and democracy but that could change."

"We are ready for any unforeseen event that may or may not happen."

"Redefining the role of the United States from enablers to keep the peace to enablers to keep the peace from peacekeepers is going to be an assignment."

"You can't have it both ways—you can't take the high horse and then claim the low road."

"So, Americans, we ought to make the pie higher."

When it came to education, a subject reported to have been always very dear to the president, partially, I am certain, because his wife, our first lady, Laura, has a degree in library science, he passed one of the best education bills in our history, keeping his campaign promises "My number three priority is to put education first" and "We are going to have the best-educated Americans in the world."

The president spoke often about education:

"Education has to be discussed about."

"Quite frankly, teachers are the only profession that *teach* our children."

"If you can't read, it's going to be hard to go to college, so when your *teachers* say 'read,' you ought to listen to *her.*"

"Rarely is the question asked, 'Is our children learning?'"

Well, Mr. President, is they or isn't they and is you or isn't you?

At this time, I was certain that if I were ever to meet the president by himself and asked him, "Mr. President, do you have any idea of what the hell you're talking about?" he would have answered, "No, but I slept in a Holiday Inn last night."

With the words spoken in the past, I was shocked and more confused when President Bush stood before Congress on September 12, 2001, and buckets of pearls of wisdom poured from his mouth and into our idolizing ears and the ears of foreign leaders who previously had thought he was an idiot and who now responded to his clarion call for an international coalition of world powers to fight terrorism and free Afghanistan by force.

In that speech, he said, "This isn't just America's fight. This is the fight of all who believe in progress and pluralism, tolerance and freedom. We ask every nation to join us."

Was this the same world leader who only months before had put his arm around the French-speaking premier of Quebec and said "Mi amigo?" Was this the same guy who had to have the foreign leaders' names spelled out phonetically, like "Toe-Knee Blah-Air of Ing-land," and the same man who said, "We must keep good relations with the Grecians," which I guess is true, if you use it on your hair?

How did George W. Bush become so intelligent, wise, and articulate overnight? Here he was, standing before the Congress of the United States and before us, saying what had to be said in the most effective and yet poetic way.

"I know there are struggles ahead and dangers to face, but this country will define our times, not be defined by them."

A few months before this, he had declared, "Most of our imports come from overseas."

"Tonight, we are a country awakened to danger and called to defend freedom. Our grief has turned to anger and anger to resolution. Whether we bring our enemies to justice or bring justice to our enemies, justice will be served."

How damn much better could it have been said? Not at all and by no one, and yet, a short time before this night, this same man had said, "If we don't succeed, we run the risk of failure."

Come on, is this the same guy, and if so, how the hell did it happen?

About the future, the new President Bush said, "This will not be an age of terror. This will be an age of liberty here and across the world." Speaking of the future a short time before this, he had asked, "Will the highways of the Internet become more few?"

What words could have been more inspiring about a great challenge facing our nation and our people—a great threat to our freedom—than these, spoken by our president before Congress and the American people? "Our nation, this generation, will lift the dark threat of violence from our people and our future. We will rally the world to this cause by our efforts, by our courage. We will not tire, we will not falter, and we will not fail."

What words could have been less inspiring about another challenge facing our nation and our people—the great threat to our environment—than these, spoken by our president before the press and the American people prior to September 20, 2001? "It isn't pollution that's harming our environment; it's the impurities in our air and water that's doing it."

Same person? Same brain?

In his State of the Union speech, 2002, possibly the best one ever given, certainly the best one I had ever heard, the president said, "The United States of America will not permit the world's most dangerous regimes to threaten us with the world's most destructive weapons." And then he pinpointed the exact trouble areas in the world, by naming Iraq, Iran, and North Korea, calling them "the axis of evil."

Prior to this time, when he was asked to pinpoint the trouble spots in the world, he had said, "When I was coming up, it was a dangerous world. It was us versus them, and it was clear who them was. Today, we are not so sure who they are, but we know they're there."

So, how did he flip-flop overnight into this brilliant, articulate, knowledgeable, and respected world leader, no, *the* world's leader? A man whose every word and action could decide the fate of millions of human beings around the world in this time of weapons of mass destruction? How did a president gain our faith who, upon learning of the number of nuclear weapons there were in our arsenal, said he was shocked, while most Americans were shocked thinking that he was in charge of them? How did a president who, when it was confirmed that jet lag can cause the brain to shrink, had a nation plead with him to take a bus, turn it around so we cheered his every frequent-flyer mile? Really, how the hell did it happen? After thinking about this so intensely and searching for an answer for so long a time, I have concluded that George W. Bush must be the only human being ever to fall *up* a flight of stairs.

Of course, I know that when it comes to politics, I am jaded, a cynic, a curmudgeon. Maybe I even worry excessively about the problems facing our nation. Right now, on the top of my list is the economy. I felt so sorry for the president the other day. He was speaking to factory workers. They represented all American workers and his speech was about job security, since we have a frighteningly high and constantly rising unemployment rate. The president was trying to allay fear and was brilliant in his approach, which he spelled out so forcefully. The president scanned the room with his eyes and his finger and spoke.

"You are American workers. You are the best workers in the world. You produce American Products, which are the best products in the world. Therefore, you and all American workers have job security."

I felt so sorry for him. I was watching it on CNN and you know how they have news stories move along at the bottom of the screen? Well, just as the president said the above words, across the screen a news bulletin flashed, "101,000 more workers join the unemployment ranks this month." Even the president looked down and said, "What the hell is that?"

One of the president's greatest weapons against the ill economy, besides war, is his tax plan, which worries me almost as much as war. First of all, on a positive note, the way it is written is comical enough to elicit laughs, which is good.

For example: You will get back 10 to 15 percent more if you are single and earn between $6,000 down to zero. Down to zero. Zero is exactly how it is written. Why? As if some homeless guy will be saying, "Bush is better for us."

Then, if you are married and earn between $12,001 and $43,850, your tax is 15 percent, but it goes up to 25 percent if you earn between $43,851 and up, so for that one extra dollar, you pay an extra $4,385.10. Now, we have all worked for bastard bosses. "Hey, John, happy New Year. Here's an extra dollar."

If you boil it down, the typical family of four receives an average tax relief of $1,425, while a rich family of four receives an average tax relief of $9,750.

Come on, what does $9,750 mean to someone who earns millions? "Honey, you want to stay an extra night?" A lot of modern-day Republicans compare the Bush plan to JFK's plan that, granted, was similar, except only 6 percent went to the rich compared to 42 percent.

President Bush's latest addition to the tax plan, no taxes on stock dividends, is even a better deal for our richest citizens: 1 percent of our richest citizens own 49 percent of all the stock, getting an average return of $89,000. To personalize and bring it closer to home, if this plan were in effect in 2001, Dick Cheney would have gotten back $80,000. Poor guy would have missed reaching the average by $9,000. I guess he would have had to tighten his belt a bit. Life's a bitch, isn't it, Dick? One might argue that it is not being fair looking at only the top 1 percent. They have a point, so let's slide it up a bit, say to include another 4 percent of our wealthiest. Okay, here's the change. The top 5 percent wealthiest of our fellow citizens, rather than just the top 1 percent, would reap nearly two-thirds of all the money. This would leave only one-third of the money for the remaining 95 percent of Americans. That's much fairer isn't it?

Let's get back to the Bush Tax Plan. It will give the American people (remember that it benefits mostly rich people) a total of $1.35 trillion over a ten-year period. It is the Ronald Reagan trickle-down theory of economics and we all remember how well that worked. I say, screw the rich! Why not, they've been screwing the middle class and poor for years? So, my fellow citizens and Mr. Bush, here's The David Brenner Equitable Tax Plan.

There are approximately 80,000,000 rich people in the country. They've got enough. If they don't think so or don't appreciate it, I say, "Go to hell, and let's move on." Those ungrateful bastards are left out of my plan. Period, the end.

Now that we got rid of the selfish, we divide among the remaining 200,000,000 Americans the $135,000,000,000,000. This comes to $6,500 for every man, woman, and child, so instead of a family of four getting $1,425, they get $27,000. Instead of getting it a little at a time over ten years, they get it all in one tax-free lump. They have one week to spend it, and they must spend it in America on American products. So now, instead of a trickle, we have an avalanche! The economy will snap back like it has a spring up its ass. Yes, I will accept a third party's nomination for president.

I think I also found a loophole in the Bush Tax Plan and it's in the

Estate Tax Provision. In case you don't know what this is, it is when a rich person dies and leaves his money to his heirs. They used to have to pay an inheritance tax on the money, but now under the Bush plan the heirs do not have to pay one penny in estate income tax; they keep one hundred cents on a dollar. But here's the loophole. This plan runs out at midnight on December 31, 2010, so you know, that night, all over the country, there are going to be children screaming, "Give me the goddamn pillow! I'll put it over his face! Hurry up, damn it, we've only got four minutes!" I've already arranged to be in Guam, Katmandu, Easter Island, or Sri Lanka that night. Four possible countries for only three sons tracking me down. Smart, ain't I?

But be that as it may, George W. Bush is our leader until 2004, at least, so let us wish him well, if for no other reason than Dick Cheney. Let me say for the record that as a kid I loved all his father Lon's movies, especially *The Wolfman Meets Frankenstein*. But will someone please tell me why we elected a vice president who has a bum ticker? The vice president is supposed to be a heartbeat away from the presidency, not a heartbeat away from another heartbeat. Every time they wheel Cheney out of a hospital, his doctors scare the hell out of me, because they always say the same thing. "He can live his normal lifestyle." Great, his normal lifestyle is to have a heart attack every two or three weeks. You want to know the real reason why we didn't see Dick Cheney for three weeks after September 11? They didn't want to tell him what happened. He kept asking why everyone was running around so much, and all they would say is, "There's a hurricane off Florida. Put the cold compress back on your head and relax."

Actually, the vice president was the president for about three hours, when the president went into the hospital for a colonoscopy. What a momentous day in American history that was. The president of the United States is lying on a table with a tube up his ass and there's a Dick in the White House.

When I read the first article on the narrow-minded and intolerant comment made by Trent Lott at the party celebrating the one-hundredth birthday of Strom Thurmond, I was angered and outraged. I was hoping he wouldn't get away with saying it was a spontaneous slip of the tongue, because I remembered that his tongue had slipped the exact same words some years ago. I was getting all worked up, when, as I looked at the front-page photo of the party and zeroed in on Strom Thurmond, the comedic part of my brain took over the controls and, instead of being distraught, I thought, "Oh, my God, this guy's dick is one hundred years old."

All of a sudden, all I could think about was that I didn't want to get that old. I figured that if I did live that long, I would lie. "I didn't get a dick until I was sixty."

Of course, there would be times I'd have to confess. "Yeah, my dick is one hundred. You want to see it? Hand me that hanger. No, I'm not going to touch it. Would you want to touch a hundred-year-old dick?"

I imagined a scene in a public men's room. "Hey look at that guy. His dick's got to be one hundred years old. Aren't you afraid to shake it? Is it really one hundred years old?" "You want to cut it in half and count the rings? Yes, it's a hundred years old. It's a Strom."

I started to laugh to myself, actually out loud, because I realized that there was a chance that, after forty-eight years serving in the Senate, the longest of anyone, his legacy might be having an old dick named after him, the Strom.

Every time after that first time, whenever I read or heard about the Trent Lott affair, all I could do was think of Strom's Strom and laugh. It made me feel so much better about this dark spot on America's history. I know that a Strom won't work to soften (no pun intended) all national and international problems and to survive the horrors we suffer because of politicians, but until we come up with a better idea for laughter, we can think of everyone who holds a public office as an old dick. Why not? Those pricks earned it.

Airport Insecurity

If you have flown from a U.S. airport since September 11, 2001, you'll understand and empathize with the following. If you haven't flown yet—*don't*! Well, not until the idiots in Washington, D.C., have figured out what to do to truly make it safe to fly. They have done a few good moves, such as replacing a lot of the stupid people who had been handling airport security. If their IQs would've dropped one point, they could have legally qualified to be kitchen utensils or pigeons. It's better, but not by much.

Unfortunately, on my post–September 11 tour, Laughter to the People, I average four to six flights every week, so I speak to you from a position of extensive airport security experience, a position that is similar to my standing neck high in shit and someone vomits in my direction, and, so, my dilemma is—do I duck?

The horrendous stories of airport security incompetence are already legendary, like the eighty-six-year-old man who was held in security so long he missed his flight, because no one in security could identify the mysterious metal object in his carry-on bag nor identify the person who signed the letter that accompanied the threatening object, which was finally identified as the Congressional Medal of Honor, and the signature on the letter that accompanied it was an unknown person named Franklin Delano Roosevelt. No one in security had heard of either. These kinds of stories have already taken their place in American folklore.

Did you hear the one about:

The congressman who was strip-searched because of his metal hip replacement?

The man who wanted to prove to his wife that airport security was anything but, so he went through the screening with seven knives in his carry-on bag?

The man who boarded his flight and told a flight attendant that he just noticed that he had forgotten to take his legally licensed handgun off his belt and leave it in his office? Incidentally, he was arrested for bringing a firearm onboard a plane, or, another way of putting it, for being honest.

The man who went through security with his carry-on bag filled with seven knives, one Sten gun, and pepper spray?

The one thousand passengers in Louisville, Kentucky, who had to go through security again, delaying hundreds of flights, because a security screener was discovered sleeping on the job?

The former vice president of the United States, Al Gore, who was searched in two airports, because no one recognized him? It wasn't in Miami, thank goodness.

The twenty security people at Boston's Logan Airport who were fired and arrested for presenting false social security IDs and forged immigration documents to get their jobs? This might have gotten accolades had it not happened a full five months *after* 9/11.

The eighty-year-old disabled lady who was pulled out of her wheelchair by two security guards who held her under the armpits, dangling like a broken marionette, while her sensible black wedgies were X-rayed? When asked why they were doing this to the elderly lady, one security guard replied that she could have explosives hidden in the wheelchair. When informed that it was an airport wheelchair and asked if they believed that the woman's name was Mrs. AIRPORT PROPERTY, as in the bold letters written across the back of the chair, neither guard replied and kept dangling the woman.*

The six-year-old boy who had the lining of his baseball cap ripped out in order to enable a search for explosives, while adult males, some of definite Middle Eastern origin wearing baseball caps, walked unabated through security?*

The seven-year-old and four-year-old brothers who were made to empty their Scooby Doo backpacks, remove their sneakers, and raise their arms in police arrest and search style, so a wand could be passed over their bodies?*

The famous American comedian who was being searched in security and having his carry-on bags totally emptied and microscopically searched at the boarding gates 50 percent of the time, who since writing a complaint letter to Tom Ridge, the head of Homeland Security, which was publicized in *USA Today,* has *coincidentally* had his searches increased to 100 percent of the time?*

The air marshall who was carrying a loaded .357 Magnum in a locked box in his carry-on bag and presented the proper documentation to do so to the security guard, who checked the papers and the weapon and proceeded to then search the personal belongings of the air marshall, found a fingernail clipper, broke off the pointed file, and handed it back to him? The security guard's rationale obviously was that if the air marshall were to go berserk on the flight and open his carry-on bag, he would have to make a decision whether to attack the crew and/or passengers with a loaded .357 Magnum or a nail clipper.

The uniformed airline pilot who had his expensive mustache trimmer taken away from him and tossed, and when he inquired why, was told by the head of security, "Because you could use it to take over the plane," to which the pilot angrily replied, "I'm the *pilot!* I always take over the plane."

The flight that was diverted to Wichita and grounded overnight because of a "suspicious wire" on a bathroom floor that officials later learned broke off the toilet paper holder?

The ticket area being evacuated, several flights delayed, and the shutdown of the Tampa airport for forty-five minutes when "a suspicious object" was spotted in a coffee can and a bomb squad removed it from a suitcase by using a robot and the object turned out to be a mousetrap? (This occurred a few months after federal screeners were in place, just in case you think security has gotten a lot better since they took over.) P.S.—The mouse was rebooked on a later flight.

The screeners at thirty-two U.S. airports who, during undercover tests, failed to detect 30 percent of the guns, 70 percent of the knives, and 60 percent of the simulated explosives? They probably knew the public wouldn't believe the six A-Bombs, nine H-Bombs, and an Osama bin Laden look-alike, so that was left out of their report.

The nine young men from the Middle East on September 11, 2001, who were given "extra scrutiny" by airport security because of "questionable or irregular IDs or by computer indications to sweep their baggage for explosives" and were all cleared and went on to fly jets into the World Trade Center and the Pentagon?

* You most likely didn't hear those four noted with an asterisk, because I was the one who spoke up for the lady in the wheelchair, the second was my son at the San Francisco airport, the third was my two sons at JFK, and the fourth was me at too many damn airports.

Yes, I have been searched 100 percent of the time. This means, while they are looking through my socks and underwear, the bad guy could be getting on the plane. I'm afraid the al-Qaeda is already telling their people, "Fly with Brenner."

The most ridiculous is when I am called out to be searched by my name. The first few times it happened to me, I asked the security people if they knew me. They always replied that they were big fans and had been watching me on TV for years. When I would ask them, "If you know who I am, then why did you pull me out to be searched?" the answer was always the same—"Random." I remain one of the few celebrities in this country who is still considered to be random. What's really frightening is that this happened to me in Michigan with about ten of the newly appointed federal security guards who had spent fifteen minutes discussing comedy and asking to shake my hand and get autographs. I told them that the only difference between them and the people who used to work there was that they were stupid in English.

Before I get into solutions the government could employ and what I suggest should be done, as well as what I do personally, all of which might help you to find the humor and, thereby, laugh your way through this raging, out-of-hand, escalating airport fiasco, let's look into the very core of the problem.

I don't know about you, but even years before September 11 ever happened, I have been neither happy nor felt secure knowing that the persons working in airport security were only there because they had failed the 7-Eleven hiring test.

"No, no, the *bottom* of the lid goes on the *top* of the coffee cup. No, it doesn't twist on. Push it. That's because you handed the customer the coffee with the lid facing down. Maybe you should consider airport security. We send hundreds there every month."

This helps explain why, sometimes when you are handed back your carry-on bag, the security guard asks, "Do you want fries with this?" Having these idiots as America's first line of defense would be like having dwarfs as the front line of the Dallas Cowboys.

The government has gotten rid of most of the security people who didn't speak or understand English. Gracias! Merci beaucoup. Danka shane. But before they weeded them out, they first decided that not speaking or understanding English was not a major deterrent to performing a job in which a command of English is necessary and that the real problem was that these workers were receiving the minimum hourly wage. Of course, this decision had nothing to do with the airport security companies' lobbyist in Washington. There's no way congressmen would ever put their own selfish interest ahead of national security and the protection of American lives.

Anyway, the government raised every security guard's hourly wage by $5.00. Now, we have all worked with stupid assholes. You give one of them $5.00, you have a stupid asshole with an extra $5.00. He doesn't take the bill and say, "Plato has always been my favorite philosopher. I love his theory on the World of Ideas." So the idea floated around in the toilet, until, finally, the government pushed the handle and sent them swirling out of our airport security system, replacing them with persons who spoke and understood English.

I don't want to be accused of being prejudiced toward persons who have a limited command of the English language, even though there's no chance they are reading this book. There were a lot of stupid airport security people who were born, raised, and educated in the USA and, therefore, understood, read, and spoke English—well almost.

Tucson, Arizona, 6:30 A.M., an early flight, so there were only about two hundred of us passengers waiting in line to pass through security. The head of World Security, an American, born, raised, and schooled right here in the good ol' USA, announced to us *twice*, "All computers must be 'tooken' out of their bags!" I called out, "You're a 'fooken' idiot!" The people in line roared with laughter. He didn't get the joke, of course.

In addition to getting rid of all the non-English-speaking security guards, the government also fired those who were in our country illegally and were felons. It took too long for them to get around to all this, but they did it. Some of their other security measures have been ridiculous.

In a few airports, in order to reduce passenger rage over being searched, as security people were going through our personal effects, the government hired Disney characters to entertain us. Bad enough we had a stranger going through our most sensitive items, we now had to deal with Goofy holding up our underwear for all to see with that stupid voice of his. I hated the bastard when I was a kid.

At O'Hare Airport in Chicago, in order to lower the public's stress level, the government hired white-faced mimes to entertain the long lines waiting to get through the security checks. It worked, too. You wouldn't believe how much stress is relieved when you punch one of those silly sons of bitches in the jaw.

To ease your traveling pain somewhat, I'm going to forewarn you, so you can prepare. I'm talking about what you are allowed and not allowed to carry onto a plane. You can put just about anything in your checked-in bag, including time bombs, because only 10 percent of the bags are checked, but the Transportation Security Administration is very concerned about what is inside the bags you take onto the plane.

Right after September 11 and for many months afterward, there was a lot of confusion and fear as to what would and would not be allowed, because there were safety hazards. This has been resolved. The following items are no longer restricted:

Pets There's nothing more frightening or sickening than a dog or cat exploding.

Walking canes Understandably. It would be kind of scary to see a cane board a plane.

Umbrellas A justifiably suspicious item, since there has never been a rainstorm inside of a plane and very few leaks.

Nail clippers I always took umbrage with this, because I could never imagine a plane full of Americans being held back by four terrorists with nail clippers. "Take one more step, and I am going to clip your nails, including toes, so help me Allah!"

Eyebrow tweezers Growing up in the tough streets, this was always my weapon of choice.

Eyelash curlers I think these should still be on the Verboten List. Nothing can force someone to fall in line faster than the threat of having their eyelashes curled, when they don't want it.

Scissors of any kind I use scissors daily to cut out newspaper, magazine, and Internet articles as possible premises for jokes. While on the road during my tour, before the scissors ban was finally lifted I had to purchase a total of over one hundred pairs of scissors, leaving each in a hotel room, because I couldn't take them aboard my flight to the next town. Using what little business acumen I possess, I told my stockbroker to buy shares in every scissor manufacturing company in the country. For a time, I solved the problem by hiding a pair of scissors in a stun gun. The good news is that blunt-edge scissors are now allowed as carry-on. Just to avoid problems, I taped the government's notification of this on the back of my four-years-to-six-years-old scissor pack. The sad news is that 50 percent of the time, I have had to alert security guards to it to stop them from confiscating them.

I must tell you that I have seen some heartbreaking moments in the security line, when a beloved personal item is taken from a passenger and thrown into the security garbage can. I'll never forget the eighty-year-old woman's face when the security guard removed an ivory-handled letter opener from this woman's pocketbook, and not caring about her plea that it had belonged to her great-grandmother, tossed it on the pile of other confiscated items. She had a choice, as everyone does, of returning to the check-in counter and mailing the item back to herself, but, as with most passengers, she would miss the last flight home.

In this sweet woman's honor, and to make sure that none of you have something that means a lot to you or that you would miss if it were confiscated, I am now going to provide you with the official Transportation Security Administration's latest list of items that passengers may *not* carry on to a plane. You can Xerox this list from the book and keep it in your check-in bag. Do not try to carry any of the following aboard in your hand, on your person, or in your carry-on bags:

You can no longer bring on board as a carry-on a baseball or softball bat. Now, I have been flying my entire adult life, and I have never seen anyone come on board a plane carrying a baseball bat. Not even someone from Brooklyn.

No sewing kits, even the miniature ones that are in baskets in hotel bathrooms. This is a good precautionary idea, because one sight of a thimble and any pilot would turn over the controls to a terrorist.

For whatever reason, the government will not allow you to bring on board ammunition, automatic weapons, axes, bows and arrows, box cutters (I wonder why), bullwhips ("You're in my seat! *Crack!*), cattle prods, crowbars, dynamite (again, why?), fire extinguishers (you wouldn't want to put out a fire, would you?), hand grenades, hatchets and meat cleavers (how the hell do they expect us to go on vacation without them?), plastic explosives (another inexplicable one), and here's a real bummer for anyone who has finished reading his book and saw the movie—no power saws. You can't carry on "religious" knives, so all you have to do is say "This is an atheist knife. We tried to get him to go to church but he won't."

The following verboten items are even more picayune. You can't bring on a plane revolvers, rifles, shotguns, spearguns, or swords. Now, when is the last time you saw a guy walking through the airport trying to put his sword into its sheath?

Finally, no toy transformers. These are those colorful Japanese toys where a racing car can be transformed into a toy gun, and you know how realistic those guns are that are yellow, pink, purple, orange, red, green, blue, and puce and have a car fender for a trigger.

For the latest update on what is and is not allowed to be taken on a plane, check the Transportation Security Administration's website: www.tsa.gov.

Feds began checking bags that are checked onto a plane. They claimed that they would be making sure there were no explosives in the bags checked onto the plane. The American public felt more secure, until it was soon discovered that we only had enough machines to check 10 percent of the bags and the sniffing dogs were too few and too busy and too stoned checking for cocaine in Miami to help. The government admitted to this but countered that the main reason to check all the checked bags is to make certain that every bag goes on the same plane as its owner passenger. A great idea, because if there is anything that would upset a suicide bomber it would be worrying that his checked bag is flying to Anaheim while he's heading for Washington, D.C. He'd be sitting on the plane bemoaning, "Oh, what a shitty day this is going to be."

The government gave the airports until the end of December to install the checked baggage inspecting machines, which they did. Supposedly, they are checking every bag. The only flaw I see in the system is that passengers are not allowed to lock their checked-in bags, which the government says is for security reasons. I'm not worried about some dishonest bag handler stealing something from my bag. I am worried about a terrorist being able to easily slip a bomb into my bag or anyone's bag because it is not locked. Maybe it's just me.

One of the first and most bragged about moves by the government was placing National Guardsmen inside the security gates of every airport in this country. I saw them everywhere. There they were, standing tall in their camouflage uniforms. Camouflage in an airport. So they blended in. Were they waiting for a jungle to come through security? But they did have their automatic weapons slung over their shoulders, ready for action, except, because of a public safety issue, they were not allowed to have bullets in the clip. Man, if anything would have scared the shit out of a terrorist, it would have been being slapped in the face with a National Guard beret.

Then the government told the airlines they could stop asking those stupid questions when you checked in.

"Did you pack your own bag?"

I hate to bother my neighbor. "Come on, Jim; just do the underwear, no big deal."

"Since you packed your bags, have they been in your sight the entire time?"

I don't know about you, but after I pack my bags the night before I go on a trip, I guess it is a quirk of mine, I like to go to sleep. I don't like to stay up all night staring at my bags. "Damn, you walked in front of my bags! You blocked them! Now I've got to tell them at the airport that they were out of my sight for ten seconds."

The reason they stopped asking these questions is even dumber than the questions themselves—they realized that the terrorists could lie and it took them only fourteen years to realize it (since the bombing of Pan Am Flight #103 over Scotland in 1988).

So let's forget the federal government and the airline industry in the search for solutions. This calls for Americans to take matters in their own hands. It's up to each of us to make suggestions and, until things change, to find the humor and laughs to get us through this stupidity. For example, I suggest that the government do a study and publish for all Americans the collective IQs of security workers in every airport. So now you can look up an airport and gauge how long the lines will be. "Let's see, Dallas International's collective IQ is eighty-two, so that should be a two- to two-and-a-half-hour wait, while LAX's collective IQ is fifty-four, which is a three- to four-hour line."

Let's take a short break from the jokes. Think of this as a commercial, or, more apropos, a Public Service Spot. Here are some of my serious suggestions:

If getting rid of non-English-speaking employees, stupid English-speaking employees, illegal aliens, and felons, and replacing them with federal government employees does not improve the person-to-person security in our airports, I suggest we put out a call for American patriotism, as they did in World War II with the volunteer Air Raid

Wardens. Give these good Americans the present pay scale of $12.00 an hour as a token of thanks and ask that they work for three months, six months, however long they can. They can be trained quickly, especially since they all understand English.

Among those who might volunteer their time, intelligence, and common sense abilities could be the following English-speaking and English-understanding American citizens: recent college graduates who can't find work in an ailing economy, retired store owners, office bosses, job supervisors, military officers, professionals (we can skip lawyers, former members of Congress, and ex-presidents, except Jimmy Carter), firemen, and cops.

Talking about cops, how about every cop who is flying somewhere on a vacation be allowed to carry his loaded police weapon in his carry-on bag? Wouldn't you feel safer knowing that a Brooklyn cop might be sitting two rows behind you, trained to recognize criminal behavior and in the use of firearms? I sure as hell would.

I am not a nihilist, tearing down with no idea of how to replace what he has destroyed. I have torn down a good chunk of the security system. Let me now help build it back up with the sole intention of creating a safe America on our homeland and in the red, white, and blue skies above us. The core of the problem is not being able to guard against those who will attack our airplanes or use them to attack us on the ground, so what has to be done is to catch them before they can act.

President Bush put together a blue-ribbon panel to hold hearings and come up with a definitive solution to airline safety. They did. The panel urged profiling at all U.S. airports.

Let me go on record that I am categorically against racial profiling. It is disgraceful that someone is harassed or pulled out of the driver's seat of a car in this country only because he or she is Hispanic or black. I know that some bigots have presented the idea that the way to solve this problem is just to not issue driver's licenses to Hispanics and blacks. The way to really solve this problem is to teach tolerance in the home, schools, and houses of worship and get rid of any cop who practices racial profiling and put him into jail with the minority group he profiled.

I cringe every time I read or think about how we interned over 100,000 Japanese, 70,000 of whom were American citizens, in concentration camps in California during World War II. We didn't do that to the other descendants of our enemy countries at the time, German Americans or Italian Americans. Actually, who would've had the balls to tell Italians they were going to a concentration camp?

"Mr. Benedello, you and your family must —"

"Screw you where you swallow, dick head!"

"Eh, okay, Mr. Benedello. Only kidding. Enjoy the war."

One must also acknowledge that among the more than two hundred different nationalities and ethnic groups that make up the melting pot that is our country, the three groups, in ranking order, who commit the lowest number of antisocial behavioral acts, who have the lowest percentage of alcoholics and drug addicts, and who commit the fewest crimes are Asians, Jews, and Arab Americans. Go into any prison in this country and it is not packed with Asians, Jews, and American Arabs. In this country, the Arabs are law-abiding and peaceful and should be treated accordingly, regardless of September 11.

Because of the prejudice against them, after September 11, a growing number of Arab Americans have changed their names. For example, Mustafa Mohammed Salaam is now Ahmed Abdul Bin Nasser. You know what I would like to see? One of them change his name to Sheldon Horowitz.

All this said, there was one news report that was very disturbing. In spite of the U.S. presenting to the world irrefutable proof that all nineteen of the terrorists on September 11 were Muslims, 61 percent of the Muslims polled in a sweeping poll in the Islamic world said Arabs were not involved in the attacks. Personally, I never heard of a Norwegian named Assam Ahmad Dib wan Albidani or a Mexican called Bashir-Ali Al-Maktawi.

Let us look at a thumbnail sketch of the history of major terrorist acts in this world from 1972 through 2002, only thirty years, footnoting all the Israeli men, women, and children murdered by so-called suicide bombers:

1972   The murder of the athletes at the Munich, Germany, Olympics.

1979   The takeover of the American Embassy in Iran.

1980   Americans kidnapped in Beirut.

1983   The U.S. Marine barracks blown up in Beirut.

1985   The *Achille Lauro* sea-jacking and murder of a disabled, American citizen onboard.

1985   The skyjacking of TWA #847 and the murder of an American sailor who was a passenger.

1988   The bombing over Scotland of Pan Am #103, killing all onboard.

1992   The bombing of U.S. Embassies in Kenya and Tanzania.

1993   The car-bombing of the World Trade Center.

2000   The first of many suicide bombings in Israel.

2000   The bombing and murder of U.S. sailors on the USS *Cole*.

2001   September 11.

2002   The murder of reporter Danny Pearl.

2002   The kidnapping and murder in the Philippines of a nurse and a missionary.

2002   The bombing of the U.S. Embassy in Pakistan.

2002   The murder of an American diplomat in Jordan.

2002   The bombing murders at the nightclub in Bali.

2002   Fill in all the blanks yourself, ad infinitum.

Every single terrorist act from 1972 into 2002 has been committed by an *extremist Muslim* between the ages of seventeen and forty. No exceptions! One hundred percent!

You can suggest Timothy McVeigh. Yes, he was an American citizen but he was not a member of any terrorist organization but, rather, was acting alone against his own definition of "the enemy." Or, I thought, the claim bit the dust when I read the headline in the *New York Times:* "Britain Charges Venezuelan Who Had Grenade in Airport." Immediately, I thought, "Oh, no, now we've got to worry about

Venezuelans." I read the article, which named the Venezuelan, Hasil Muhammed Rahaham-Alan, a Spanish family name dating back hundreds of years.

To reiterate, every single terrorist act from 1972 into 2003 has been committed by an *extremist Muslim* between the ages of seventeen and forty. No exceptions! One hundred percent!

Now, if every single store robbery in the world over the last thirty years was committed by a man wearing a bright blue rubber shower cap with a red feather sticking out of the top of it, a pair of Groucho glasses and fake nose, floppy clown shoes, and carrying a dead pigeon on the end of a pool cue, walking with a limp, and you saw a man wearing a bright blue rubber shower cap with a red feather sticking out of the top of it, a pair of Groucho glasses and fake nose, floppy clown shoes, and carrying a dead pigeon on the end of a pool cue, walking with a limp, about to enter a convenience store—wouldn't you want him searched?

If every mugging in this world over the past thirty years was committed by a six foot two, 165-pound Jewish man with dark brown eyes, brown hair with a shock of silver in the front, a large nose, and a Philadelphia accent, and the police stopped me, I would understand. Why would they question a bowlegged, fat, bald, blue-eyed, mute Chinese dwarf?

Because we Americans have become so uptight about doing anything that is politically incorrect, except canceling the TV show by the same name, we go out of our way not to offend anyone. Here's an idea of how to test the validity of my premise. The next time you have a flight, show up at the airport dressed as an Arab sheik and see if they pull you out of line. It's a good way to have fun, too, only I suggest you have a notarized invitation to a costume party.

In my opinion, this is not the time to be super politically correct. This is a time to be super smart and save our country and our asses. Now I'm going to tell you what I do, not because I want to save the world, but because I want to save me, so that I can look in a mirror every day and be proud of the person I see. When I am pulled out to be searched at airport security, from the outside pocket of my carry-on computer bag, I pull out a card on which I have Scotch-taped the faces taken off the FBI website of all the suspected terrorists living here, or thought to be traveling here, and the FBI's Most Wanted known terrorists, including Osama bin Laden, and I show it to the security person, saying loudly: "This is who you're supposed to be looking for, not an American Jew comedian!" Of course, if you decide to voice your protest in a like manner, you'll have to delete "Jew comedian" and tailor it to whatever you are and do.

Has it worked? Well, one federal frisker said, "What do you want me to do? Write your congressman." A few security people have threatened to arrest me, but hurried me on the plane when I said I would love to show this on network and cable TV. Most security people had no idea what I was talking about. Why would they? They work in airport security. But every traveler within hearing range laughed loudly, and this is the sidebar of what I am trying to accomplish—to get people to find the humor and laughter. So in this sense, yes, it has worked great, but if some of you reading this start to protest, too, in your own way, then maybe something will be done about this horrible but correctable situation.

Terrorists and Terrorism

What could possibly be funny about terrorism? I'll show you in a moment, but a far more important question is why it is important to find something funny in such a god-awful subject. I'd say that it is far more important that we find and communicate the humorous side of terrorism than it is for more than 90 percent of all other areas of life that need comedic relief. Otherwise, the terrorists will succeed in their intention, which is to make us fear them and change our lives to accommodate this fear. So far, they are succeeding. We can't let them do what no other enemy did, including the Nazis and Japanese Imperial Forces. We Americans must do what we have done throughout our past—face the monsters head-on and kick their asses and, while we do that, we have to make fun of them and ourselves. For example:

After September 11, 2001, a breakfast media conference was held by Peter Gross, the House Intelligence Committee chairman (please remember the word "intelligence") and his counterpart in the Senate, Bob Graham. Everyone in mass media was represented, the three TV networks, all the cable TV news shows, talk radio stations, national magazines, and most newspapers.

At one point, during the discussion of America's ability to ward off future terrorists' attacks, Peter Gross said, "I'm surprised we haven't had an attack yet at our seaports . . . they are much more vulnerable areas than our airports—those tens of thousands of containers that come into America every day from around the world with only a miniscule number of them being inspected."

As if this wasn't enough, Bob Graham added, "Our bridges and museums could be leveled with truck bombs."

What the hell is wrong with these guys? Don't they know that the terrorists watch our TV and read our papers and magazines? I'm sure, at that very moment, some terrorist somewhere in America was on the phone, whispering: "Salem Alechem, this is Abdullah, the White Camel; I just got a couple of great ideas from CNN."

In this War on Terrorism, which I think we'll win exactly one week after we win the War on Poverty and two weeks after we win the War on Drugs, the president ordered the initial deployment of a national missile-defense system, at a cost of about $238 billion, which is designed to shoot down ballistic missiles before they reach us. It has a testing failure rate of three in eight or 37.5 percent. It is then announced by our military and printed in the media that the missiles will be positioned in Ft. Grealy, Alaska, and Vandenberg Air Force Base in California, with accompanying, detailed maps.

Now, thanks to our freedom of press and equal opportunity of stupidity, all the enemy has to do is direct a bunch of their missiles at Ft. Grealy and Vandenberg AFB. Even if only 37.5 percent of their missiles get through successfully, our Star Wars shield will be turned into junkyard metal shavings. And how about this question—besides us, who else has such weapons of mass destruction capabilities? The answer is two countries: our good buddies, the Russians, and China, a semi-friend kept at arm's length. What about our enemies, especially in the Middle East? Colin Powell announced before the U.N. that we had proof that Iraq has missiles capable of flying a little more than seven hundred miles. The last time I checked my world map, we're a little further away than that by a couple thousand miles. This is a missile; not a skimmer rock. The missile doesn't hit the Atlantic Ocean, bounce a few feet above the surface, land again, skim again, and keep doing this, until it bounces on top of Stamford, Connecticut. Also, it has been predicted by our best scientific minds and military experts that Iran won't have long-range missile capability until 2010, and Iraq until 2015. I don't know about you, but I am a little more concerned about something a little closer in time, say next week.

So, it boils down or up to this, according to how hot under the collar you get from seeing your tax dollars tossed into the toilet. We are going to invest a fortune in something that is going to take years to build, that has a shitty success track record, to ward against enemies who are more likely to shoot goats at us than missiles. There's an idea. How about goat shields? I think they go for $39.98 at Wal-Mart. Or else, let's take all the money we save by not building the Missile Shield, gather those same best scientific minds in this country, and ask them to develop mustache- and long-beard-seeking missiles.

President Bush didn't only push for the Missile Shield Program and let it go at that; he established the Office of Homeland Security with Tom Ridge, former governor of Pennsylvania and an ex-marine, as its head. Then the Senate overwhelmingly approved the counterterrorism bill that will cost us about $31.5 billion, which is approximately $11 billion more than it would cost us to buy most of the countries in the Middle East. There are two minor questions I have concerning some of the "protective measures against terrorists" that are included in the bill:

1. $2,500,000 is allotted to map the coral reefs off Hawaii. Why? Are the terrorists going to disguise themselves as fish and float up on our beaches with bombs?

2. $2,000,000 is allotted to the Smithsonian to construct a new building in which to store their stuffed birds, bugs, fish, and frogs. This is war! I say screw the frogs!

Now, let us address the actual attacks that may occur on our homeland. One warning from our government scared the shit out of a lot of New Yorkers, who are the toughest and least intimidated Americans. They were warned that there was reliable information that "dirty bombs" were going to be activated in their subways. It never happened. New Yorkers, not being our silent citizens, wanted to know why nothing happened, thank goodness, why no terrorists were caught, and what the hell is a dirty bomb anyway. The first question was answered with some mumbo jumbo about a mix-up in intercepted intelligence. The next question was answered by explaining that a dirty bomb is highly potent because it has no odor. Most New

Yorkers who ride the subways said the bomb would be just as tough to detect if it smelled like urine and vomit.

But most Americans are having problems trying to live even close to their normal lives. How can we, with the government constantly scaring the shit out of us with possible attacks? Finally, in order to reinstate confidence and a feeling of security, the government came out with a color-coordinated alert system. It was designed to communicate threats to the nation and advise communities and individuals what to do. Not only didn't it achieve its goal, American cities and Americans individually ignored the alerts, because no one knew what the hell they meant and still don't. I don't. Do you? Who would? Let's look at it.

The alerts don't come in packages or sizes, but they do come in five basic colors: green for low, blue for guarded, yellow for elevated, orange for high, and red for severe. Personally, I would have preferred a nice lavender and puce and maybe some stripes and polka dots, but one can't have everything one wants, especially during a war. So what do the colors mean? What are we supposed to do? Here's the way I interpret it.

Green Alert: You can visit your cousin, have a piece of fish, and get home ASAP.

Blue Alert: You can go to your cousin's house, but you can't go in; wave to him and get the hell home.

Yellow Alert: Stay at home but feel free to send your mother-in-law out for groceries—we've got problems.

Orange Alert: Pray and/or throw up.

Red Alert: Get the hell out of your house and out of the country. Major terrorist shit is about to hit our fan!

In February 2003, Tom Ridge put the nation on Orange Alert and Attorney General John Ashcroft announced that they had very reliable information that the terrorists' prime targets were revered American symbols, hotels, means of mass transportation, and Jews. There I was a Jew sitting in a hotel room in Washington, D.C., about to leave for my flight home. I was dead meat.

Of course, like all the other beautifully colored alerts since 9/11, nothing happened. It turned out to be another false alarm, this time based on our eavesdropping on terrorists who were lying over their cell phones. Right away I thought that the terrorists could beat us without ever attacking us again. All they have to do is get on their toss-away cell phones and make up stories.

"Schtumof, go enjoy a Hollywood premiere."

"The footballs will not bounce this weekend."

"What has eight sides and lots of brass?"

"Soon, we'll stop beating around the bush and get a dick."

We Americans have been given a barrage of warnings about possible terrorist attacks, causing us to close the Golden Gate bridge, empty airports, increase guards at our nuclear plants, etc., but, thank goodness, none of the attacks came. The warnings came over and over and over, until they had the same effect as hearing there was a 10 percent chance of light showers. We are giving new meaning to Cry Wolf.

Even when the head of the CIA put the risk of the next attack at the 9/11 level, we continued to go to movies and ball games. When a report warned us that "the USA today is in grave danger," we merely muttered an unconcerned "Uh-huh" and continued reading our *USA Today* at tables in outdoor cafés. Americans paid no attention when the vice president of the United States, Dick Cheney, announced in the press that he "expects further attacks." Many Americans brushed it off by thinking he was probably talking about his own health issues. It turned out to be something even dumber. He was warning us about a plot to blow up apartment buildings. Apartment dwellers were told to report anything suspicious. Like what—neighbors getting on elevators with arms filled with plastic explosives or rocket launchers slung over their shoulders?

This was when the FBI was being accused of having allowed lots of information to go unnoticed or slip through the cracks that might have prevented some or all of the events of September 11. The FBI countered that had the public reported the suspicious things they had seen, their agents might have been able to take preventive action. One of the examples they cited was Mohammed Atta, the ringleader of the 9/11 terrorists, who was staying in an apartment in Venice, Florida, and was evicted by his landlady because he had body odor. Now, really! Does the FBI really believe this woman should have reported this to them?

"Hello. Is this the FBI in Washington? . . . My name is Frieda Gittlestein, I own a little apartment complex here in Venice, Florida not Italy, I only wish, which was left to me by my late husband, Saul, may he rest in pieces, the cheating bastard, but anyway (lowering her voice), in 12F, a lovely, breezy room, I have a tenant staying by me who smells like shit. You'd better get over here right away."

The FBI chief calls suicide bombers "inevitable" and warns us that "nobody is safe anywhere." We are told to report anyone acting nervous in a public gathering who is wide of girth, which is ridiculous when it is followed by a health survey confirming that 26 percent of Americans are obese and 65 percent overweight. So most Americans look like suicide bombers. Actually, I've always been afraid of them blowing up.

In my opinion, it doesn't matter who didn't do what or should have done what. September 11 happened and uncovering and debating the possible reasons why is not going to undo what happened or prevent it from happening again. We have to be on guard, a realistic one in reaction to facts, not loose suspicions and inaccurate tips, and we must know exactly what we can do to truly prevent more attacks on our homeland. And every minute of every day, we must strive to identify everyone who is funding terrorism, every terrorist, and all their leaders and then go get every last one of these bastards, starting with Osama bin Laden.

In the past two-plus years, hardly a day has gone by without picking up a magazine or a newspaper and seeing the question—"Osama bin Laden: Dead or Alive?" Rumors and analyses flew like pigeons after a car backfire. The rumors ran from the more ridiculous to the most ridiculous.

One of our leading FBI terror chiefs said that he believed bin Laden was dead, because he was a victim of genetic imperfection. Bin

Laden is the offspring of first cousins and, as a result, had kidney problems which led to his death. Isn't the cultural difference between our two societies interesting? In the Middle East, if your parents were first cousins, you become the supreme leader of the people. Over here, in America, you get on *The Jerry Springer Show*.

Then there was "reliable information from an unnamed source" that bin Laden had escaped by dying his hair red and taking a bicycle into Pakistan. Sure, a six foot four Arab with red hair pedaling a bike—who would notice?

Even more bizarre was a report from another one of our "reliable sources," that bin Laden was alive, but had been hit by shrapnel during our bombing raid on Tora Tora. He was treated in a hospital in Pakistan and released. Sure, I can see the hospital receptionist in the Emergency Ward getting on the public address system. "Will patient Osama bin Laden please raise his hand . . . thank you, Mr. Laden, the doctor will see you now. Do you have insurance and ID?"

In February 2003, another audiotape turned up and scientists once again confirmed that it was really Osama bin Laden talking, proving once again that he was alive.

Some time ago I read a lengthy article in *USA Today*. It was primarily an interview with a gentleman named Ned Livingstone, who is one of the leading antiterrorist authorities in the country. The federal government has been picking his brains since September 11.

Livingstone says that we have been and continue to approach the problem of bin Laden and the most wanted nineteen al-Qaeda all wrong. Excuse me, seventeen. We killed two in fifteen months. Israel kills five a week. Different tactic. Anyway, Ned Livingstone suggests that what we should be doing, in antiterrorist jargon, is "target them," which, when translated in everyday talk, means, locate them, aim at them, and blow their brains out.

This I understand. I was raised in the inner city streets of Philadelphia's slums, where everyone was taught "an eye for an eye and a tooth for a tooth," so personally I'm all for killing all those bastards, wrapping them in pigskin, and burying them. The reason for the pigskin is that pig is verboten to a Muslim. If he has anything pig on him, he cannot go to heaven. He cannot meet Allah.

Yeah, personally, I say kill the bastards. "Bastards." Say, wouldn't it be great if just once, President Bush took advantage of the First Amendment's right of freedom of speech, as we comedians do? I mean, wouldn't you love to see the president look directly into the TV camera and say, "Bin Laden, we're going to get you, you cocksucker!" Just once. After all, during his campaign he called a reporter an "asshole." Even asshole is better than "Evildoer." What the hell is an evildoer anyway? It sounds like something out of a Spider-Man comic. Can you imagine hanging on the street corner and someone runs up and says, "The evildoers are coming to get us"? Everyone on my corner would have pointed his thumb at his crotch and said "I've got your evildoer right here. Evildoer this."

So I totally agree with our antiterrorist expert Ned Livingstone's advice that we should blast these guys, but there is one thing he said that I don't understand. Livingstone said that the reason we should target Osama bin Laden and the other terrorist leaders is "because this is why God made the .50-caliber sniper rifle." I would've gotten that wrong on a high school test.

"Psst, Jimmy. Psst. Number six. Who invented the sniper rifle?"

"God."

"Psst, Jimmy. Screw you."

It would be great to know Osama bin Laden and the other top dog shits are dead, but it's not going to end terrorism in this world. Only when we track down every last one of them and then deal in an honest manner with the problems that created them will we end it. Until then terrorism and terrorists have become a horrible way of life in today's world. We must be on guard, but we've got to do something about improving our early warning systems. Almost every day we continue to hear about horrible things that are about to happen. You can't pick up a newspaper or magazine, watch TV or listen to radio newscasts, or surf the Internet without reading or hearing about a horrible terrorist act that is going to be perpetrated against innocent

American men, women, and, worst of all, our children. But then nothing happens and no plots are discovered or dismantled, no bad guys are caught.

Still, something very serious manifested and not from terrorists. The constant "cry wolf" alerts and warnings turned public apathy into public fear; Americans became afraid to live their lives.

The federal government has defended all their false alarms by claiming that they didn't want something horrible to happen and have the public wonder why they weren't warned. The problem is that we are warned continuously and nothing ever happened, not that we would have wanted it to, but we certainly would have wanted to see these master plans foiled and their culprits arrested and brought to justice or killed on the spot.

Instead we are being told constantly by our government and leaders—"Americans, be on the alert. Be vigilant. Keep your eyes and ears open. Report anything suspicious . . ." Okay, we Americans can do that, maybe even better than any people in the world, but do you mind telling us what the hell we're supposed to be looking for? Fear can quickly turn into panic and in some instances it has, not in displays of mass hysteria but individually. Americans are going into malls, which the government had told us were on the top of the terrorists' hit list, and panicking.

"Oh, my God, look, a midget!"

"Watch out! He could blow up!"

"Run for your lives!"

"Stop! That man is eating a sweet potato!"

If we don't get a grip on ourselves and put all this in perspective, we are going to see terrorists everywhere.

"Waiter, call Homeland Security immediately! I think there's a terrorist in my soup!"

No wonder some people are panicking. How long can we take the pressure put on us, not by the terrorists, but by the fear of them that emanates from our own government and the lips of our own leaders? There was a period of a couple weeks during which the government continued announcing in the media, "All Americans, be on the lookout for a Yemeni man."

I'm sure there were a lot of Americans like myself who asked, "What the hell is a Yemeni man? Does he look like a Neanderthal Man?"

The terrorists present a real danger to our physical being, and, in a very real sense, to the wonderful American way of life. Our fears are founded, although our panic isn't. It is true that other than Pearl Harbor in 1941, we have never been attacked on our soil with the magnitude of September 11, but, regardless, it is not the American way or nature to panic, to allow any nation, any group, or any individuals to destroy the remarkable country we have built and defended for over two hundred years. It is our style to fight back and a part of our fighting spirit and our remarkable fortitude has been our uniquely special sense of humor, our ability to laugh at ourselves and at our problems regardless of how big or serious.

We laughed at Adolf Hitler, Mussolini, Emperor Hirohito, Tojo, and every other master terrorist who has threatened our way of life. We laughed and we were victorious. Well, our opponents might be playing by a new set of rules today, but it is still the same ball game and no one plays ball better than we. So, come on, Americans, let's roll back our heads and laugh and roll back our sleeves and beat the shit out of these bastards! Then let's have a few drinks and some peacetime laughs. The jokes will be on me, and the drinks will be on you, of course.

Anthrax

This is one of those life-threatening problems no one has ever heard of, and then suddenly everyone has not only heard of it but is scared to death about it. People will remember forever the day that anthrax entered our lexicon and our lives.

A photographer for the *Globe* newspaper headquarters in Florida was the first to get it, and he died. His fellow workers might have also been infected and in grave danger. Then anthrax moved north and struck in our nation's capital, first prominent politicians and then post office workers. A few more deaths. The nation's capital emptied and all Americans were put on alert about opening their mail, for it was in letters that this killer was hidden, waiting to sneak out and attack without warning. Immediately, almost every American and law official feared another terrorist attack, this time in our very homes.

The antibiotic Cipro became another new household word. It was given to government officials and postal workers and the public flocked to doctors for prescriptions.

America was under attack. The FBI stepped in and took over the investigation. This killer had to be stopped and the people behind it had to be brought to justice, quickly.

I'd say that is a pretty good capsule of the anthrax story, a story that was horrifying and unbelievably frightening. But you've got a choice, as you always have with every problem in life, whether it originates from inside of you or comes crashing in from the outside world: You can dig around for the funny bones inside this terrifying monster and go on with your life. Let's do exactly this. Instead of an anthrax letter, let's open the funny envelope and shake out the laughs.

We'll start where anthrax started. When anthrax first struck in Florida, our government immediately sprang into action. Who will ever forget the picture on the front page of every newspaper in the country of the Health Department medical teams that were rushed to the scene? The workers from the *Globe* were lined up to have Q-tips shoved up their nostrils for a nasal swab. The medical team doing it reassured every person that there was "absolutely nothing to fear," that this was "merely a precautionary measure." Reassuring words spoken by men wearing *biohazard suits*! If one of them ever approached me, I would've ripped off his protective hood and kissed him flush on the lips, driving my tongue down his unprotected throat.

When addressing the U.N. with "evidence" that warranted a war with Iraq, Colin Powell held up a small vial that was filled with some kind of innocent powder to demonstrate how little anthrax was needed to empty the U.S. Senate. He forgot to make reference to the House of Representatives standing on the steps of Congress that same day blocks away from where the anthrax was discovered, appearing on live TV to tell us, "My fellow Americans, we, your 359 elected Congressmen and Congresswomen, are here today to assure you that there is nothing to fear from anthrax. We'd like to reassure you some more, but we have to get the hell out of this town." And then every single one of them took off for the airport like their asses were on fire and flew 35,000 feet above the homes of the brave.

Fear gripped a large portion of our population that was still shaken up from September 11. But many people were irrationally panicking over anthrax. I was on one of the flights that had to turn back, because a woman panicked. Unfortunately, it was the flight that was taking me home for my one day between gigs.

A passenger ripped open his packet of Sweet'n Low to put into his coffee. Unfortunately, some of the powder spilled on the aisle rug. A woman saw it, panicked, and screamed, "Anthrax!" The woman then screamed, "I need oxygen!" I yelled out, "Throw her out the fuckin' door! It's filled with oxygen out there." My suggestion was not taken, I don't know why, and the pilot made the decision to return to the airport, guaranteeing that I would miss my connection to get home to my two small sons.

Anthrax is a real problem, if only in the mind. So I have done extensive research. I am going to do what the government has failed to do and that is, reassure you that there is little, or nothing, to fear from anthrax.

First of all, it is not nearly as deadly and frightening as the Tylenol scare of a few years back. Someone (never caught, by the way) was lacing Tylenol with poison that killed quite a few people. Maybe it was especially frightening for me because I am allergic to aspirin. So if I got a headache, you know what I had to do, right? I had to take out a couple Tylenol, give them to my dog, and wait a few hours. "Here, Bruiser, another meatball and you don't have to beg for it." I'm only kidding, folks. I had a cat. (Joke!)

Secondly, the chances of you dying from anthrax are one in five hundred million! To offer you a comparison, so you are able to put this in perspective, the odds are one in three hundred million that you will die on a roller coaster. The odds of being killed by a shark are one in one hundred million and being struck and killed by lightning one in three million. So compared to dying from anthrax, you have a better chance of being struck by lightning while a shark is eating you on a roller coaster. Feel better? A little reassured? Good. Here's some more reassurance.

In the last two years, eighteen people have been infected and five people have died from anthrax. Five in two years in a population of 285,000,000! Meanwhile, every thirty-three seconds an American dies from cardiovascular disease. Just in the time you have been reading this, three people have died. Maybe within feet of where you are right at this moment. Am I still making you feel better and more reassured? Good.

Repeat—the odds that you will die from anthrax are one in five hundred million. The odds that you will die of heart disease are one in four hundred, not one in four hundred million, one in four hundred. The odds that you will die of cancer are one in six hundred. So if you are fat and you smoke, you might as well sniff anthrax. Now that you are feeling way better and are totally reassured, let's go on to another aspect of the anthrax scare.

The FBI investigators have taken a pounding in this case. Well, this criticism might be well deserved. First of all, after the first few weeks of the anthrax scare, the first official statement they issued to an anxious public was that they had concluded that "the anthrax outbreak is unlikely to be the work of the hijackers." I should add that my grandmother is also dead and not responsible.

Then the FBI warned that the anthrax letters could have been sent by terrorists living in this country. At least this time they were not dealing with dead suspects. The terrorist theory seemed to make sense but not for long. One day while alternating my thoughts between buying a package of gym socks and anthrax, I started adding up the government's two and two and was getting zero.

Think about it. The anthrax attacks began with a photographer at that schlock rag sheet, the *Globe* newspaper. Right here, you've got to ask some questions. You can understand why they would attack such national figures as Senate minority leader Tom Daschle and network news anchor Tom Brokaw. Why would they start with a photographer for the *Globe*? Did the terrorists have a meeting and one of them stood up and said, "You want to really scare the living shit out of the American pigs, then let's send the first anthrax letter to that photographer at the *Globe* newspaper. You know who I mean. He took the pictures of the woman kidnapped by the Martians and taken to Mars. You remember. They sewed her vagina on her forehead."

Realizing their shortcomings, the FBI finally put out a plea for help to thousands of microbiologists. The public was kind of stunned that the FBI made so little headway. I know I was. It was difficult to understand why the FBI, who had all the anthrax letters, plus the anthrax itself, couldn't nab the culprit in a second. You can't blame us for our disappointment. After all, if you watch *Chronicles of the FBI* on TV, *CSI,* or documentaries on the Discovery Channel, they show how the FBI agents go back to the scene of a crime three years after it has been committed. They find a dab of snot on a windowsill.

"He's Canadian, six foot five, wavy blond hair, hates raisins, has a tattoo of the Brooklyn Bridge on the right cheek of his ass, and is impotent."

All this from a three-year-old dried-out piece of snot. But, finally, the FBI came through with flying colors, announcing that they had made a major breakthrough in the case. Their "experts" had "puzzled out the clues" offered by the anthrax letters and, thereby, had narrowed the field of suspects.

The first clue was that the dates are written with the day first, the month second, and the year third. We Americans write it month, day, and year. Then in between the numbers of the date, there are dashes; we Americans use slashes. All of the large English words are spelled correctly, but a lot of the small English words are terribly misspelled.

So from these important clues, the FBI has narrowed the field of suspects down to two possibilities: The person sending these anthrax letters "is a foreigner pretending to have mastered English or a native English speaker pretending to be a foreigner." Wow, either or, that narrows it down big time. I feel better already. Thank you, FBI.

Now, let's see what the health and welfare arm of the federal government is doing for us, the public (who, by the way, are their employers). The media and the public have been crying out, demanding to know what to do to assure their safety when opening their mail. Although the number of persons who have been infected with or have died from anthrax is small, it has the potential to be catastrophic, because it is delivered silently and unseen in the mail, something every person in the USA handles. God forbid Iraq took the anthrax viruses we sold them under President Reagan's administration and used them to make weapons of mass destruction; we could be in real trouble. So what can we, the everyday person, do to guard against an anthrax attack?

Finally, the media's and our pleas were heard and answered by the Centers for Disease Control and Prevention. It suggested the following "anthrax precautionary measures":

1. When opening your mail, wear gloves. They don't mention what

kind of gloves. You know a lot of Americans have the intelligence of lawn furniture. I know there are some schmucks somewhere in this great country of ours who will put on ski mittens. "I can't open the letter, honey, and I'm late for my security job at the airport."

2. After opening the mail, wash your hands. Hands? Why not feet?

3. Keep the mail away from your face. I don't know about you, but when I open a letter, I like to rub it all over my face.

4. Be suspicious of any mail that's bulky with a brownish discoloration and a strange odor. Are the al-Qaeda sending us their soiled underwear? Besides, this one is really stupid. Think about it. If you received in the mail a bulky box with a brownish discoloration that stank, would you open it? "Sweetheart, bring the kids down. I want them to see me open this shit box we got."

5. Wait until you hear number five. Okay. Let someone less at risk handle your mail. "Your mother's coming Tuesday, right, darling? Here, put these letters on her bed."

I'll give you one tip. You know that the government has raised the reward for the capture and conviction of the anthrax mailer to $2,500,000. Don't try to collect it, because they will mail you a check in a brownish stained box that smells like shit.

I've had a thought about this whole anthrax business. The mailing of the letters after September 11 could just be a wild coincidence. You know the inefficiency of our mail delivery service. These anthrax letters could have been mailed during the Vietnam War and are just arriving here. The point is, you can't count on the federal government to protect you from anthrax, anymore than they protected you from other national health threats, such as how to avoid the West Nile Virus, when all they could do was advise us, "Do not play with a dead, infected bird." I don't know about you, but sometimes after dinner, I like to take a walk around the neighborhood, scoop up a dead sparrow, and swing him around a little. No more; the fun's over. Anyway, you've got to protect yourself and the best way to do it is to realize that, unless you are one unlucky son of a bitch, you're not going to die from anthrax, so forget about it. But be careful walking, because the chances of dying from falling down are only one in twenty thousand. The other way to protect yourself is to start with a smile and let it grow into a wonderful, sincere, hearty belly laugh. Don't laugh too hard, though, because according to the federal government and the FBI, belly laughs cause chronic abdominal hemorrhoids and ringworm. Should we believe them?

War and Peace

It seems ludicrous, at best, and cruel, at worst, to imagine there is anything funny about war. Yet if you were to ask any combat veteran if there were any laughs, he would tell you that not only were there plenty, but that laughter was critical to get through it all. I'm lucky. I spent two years in the army but never saw any action (other than in the local bars and brothels), so I cannot speak firsthand about foxhole humor. However, I have made some humorous observations about our current and pending conflicts that have and are causing great consternation for a lot of Americans, including yours truly. Maybe a chuckle here and a laugh there, and, hopefully, even a big guffaw, might take a little bit of the war worry away. Let's try.

There is no doubt that we kicked ass in Afghanistan and kicked it hard, driving the al-Qaeda and Taliban troops of Osama bin Laden into the mountains, proving that our former pals, Osama and his band of merry, bearded men, didn't remember the training we gave them when they were fighting our former enemy, and our present friend, Russia.

Every day, we Americans sat in front of our TV sets, watching the success of our bombing missions in Afghanistan played out for members of the press and an anxious public. People cheered the pinpoint accuracy of our bombs. I didn't, because, and maybe it was just my TV, all I saw was how we were turning big dirt into little dirt. The whole country looked like dirt. I couldn't imagine any Afghan child running out of his dirt house to join his friends on the dirt street to play dirt ball ever hearing his mother call out, "Don't get dirty!"

Then there were the Northern Alliance Troops. Without a doubt, great and dedicated fighters. One American army general was quoted as saying, "These Northern Alliance soldiers are brave. They have been seen attacking tanks and armored vehicles on horseback." Brave? They're schmucks. What American soldier would listen if told, "Okay, Private Blecksoe, I want you to get on that horse, the old one with the sagging back and the limp who has the word 'glue' written all over him, and attack that armored vehicle out there. The big one with the two machine guns in the front and the forty armed troops standing in the back. Trot back and report your kills to me. Hey, come back here, Blecksoe! That's an order."

Talking about "kills," what was the story behind our pursuit of Osama bin Laden and his thousands of troops into the mountains of Tora Bora? We hit them with everything we had, the latest in modern-day technology—smart bombs, Rhodes Scholar Bombs, Albert Einstein Bombs, Water Bombs, Bad Joke Bombs, everything but the Kitchen Sink Bomb—and after the smoke cleared, we found twenty-five dead bodies. Only twenty-five! Of course, the government came up with a logical explanation. According to the dictates of their religion, Muslims must bury their dead quickly, as is true also for Jews, ironically. The American public bought the religious reason for the sparse corpse turnout.

First of all, we have to make the assumption that the twenty-five that were left above ground, or sand, in this case, were either disliked assholes and everyone said, "Screw them. Let the vultures have a feast," or they were just unlucky that burying time ran out and running away time began. Let's say the latter was true and hundreds were buried before the run-your-asses-off-bell sounded. Did you ever dig holes in a beach as a kid, and at the end of the day, your mother told you to fill in the holes so no one would trip and break an ankle? Did you ever notice that the sand under the soft, sun-bleached surface sand is thick, sometimes damp, and always darker? Did you ever notice, when you left the beach and looked back, you could see exactly where your holes used to be because of the darker sand?

Okay, now imagine you are leaving the beach after having buried a few hundred guys and you turn around to pay your last respects, do you think that you would not be able to spot any of the graves? Your honor, I rest my case. Your witness, government.

There is no denying that the Northern Alliance did the job in Afghanistan, but what was it with their battle gear? They didn't wear helmets like our guys. They wore pancakes. The way I figured it out from seeing them in our media was that the enlisted men wore one pancake, officers wore a pile of two pancakes with butter, and warlords wore a three-high pile with butter and a rasher of crisp *beef bacon,* optional. The reason I emphasized the words "beef bacon" is because Muslims are not allowed to eat pig. Wait, that's what we should have done. Instead of dropping bombs, we should have dropped millions of pigs.

"Allah damn it, pigs! Run, everyone! Pigs!"

And we should have dressed our soldiers as giant pigs.

"Th-th-th-th-th-that's all folks!"

Although our fighting men don't wear any breakfast foods as headgear, they are great soldiers, the world's best! Every American should be proud of these young men and women. Every American should be appreciative. If you love and honor our great nation, you must love and honor those who protect it, often with their blood and too often with the ultimate sacrifice, their lives.

One of the fighting teams we heard a lot about during the recent action in Afghanistan was our Special Forces. We were never told exactly who they were or what they did. All we knew was that they did whatever they were assigned and did it successfully to the maximum, and, maybe, that's all we really needed to know, but we Americans are a curious lot. Along with the help of the press, we pressured the government to give us the scoop on these special fighters. Finally, the government gave in a little, offering us a hint.

"These men could go and drop out of the night, stay on the ground an hour or two, and leave nothing behind but holes and screams."

Now, where I'm from that's crack dealers. Don't laugh. This is actually a brilliant idea on the government's part. While fighting the War on Terrorism, we are doing something about the War on Drugs. Maybe in our next war on something, the government will drop in people on welfare to help us win the War on Poverty. Wow, we could clean up two old wars and one new war by adding a few droppings, as in bird.

When I was writing this book, there was a strong possibility that we were going to go to war with Iraq, maybe even North Korea. I didn't feel like laughing when I read and thought about this horrible prospect in which so many lives, mostly young, would be lost on both sides. It is because I was distraught about this that I *needed* to find the humor in it, somehow, and make myself laugh. And take the reader with me.

I wrote the following in the present tense, according to the present time. If by the time this book was written and published, we were involved in a war or two, I ask you to merely think back to when the fighting in Afghanistan was over and we weren't dropping bombs or shooting at anyone else in the world other than each other in our city streets. Okay, folks, come on; let's go back in time to the post-Afghanistan, pre-Iraq-Iran-Korea-Lichtenstein wars laughs. America is at peace but on the brink of war with Iraq . . .

For starters, we've been told by President Bush that the reason we have to go to war against Iraq is because "it'll ruin the economy if Iraq attacks us first." This was said after 101,000 Americans lost their jobs in *"peaceful"* December 2002, a horrible retail buying Christmas, and two years during which our government magically and unbelievably turned the largest surplus in our history, $174 billion, into a $159 billion deficit and rising. Neat trick, boys, but I wish you would've just pulled some rabbits out of your hats. On top of all this, our government estimated that the war with Iraq would cost us, *not earn us,* as much as $2 trillion! But let's not confuse ourselves with the facts.

Even ignoring the government's mumbo jumbo accounting, there are other reasons why I don't understand why we have to attack Iraq at all, let alone first. I just can't fathom why a country only as big as California would want to attack us. Secondly, I can't figure out how they would do it, because all we have to do is extend the "no fly zone" that has been in place for over a decade and Iraq wouldn't be able to fly a hummingbird out of the country. There's something else that it seems our government never thought through. Iraq doesn't have a navy, no battleships, no submarines, and no canoes. Maybe it has something to do with the fact that they are surrounded by land, not water. Maybe it also explains why they have only attacked neighboring countries. So the question I am waiting to hear asked by someone in the press and answered by someone in the White House is, "Without airplanes and ships, how the hell are they going to get here to attack us?" Are they going to take a very, very long march or are they going to rent some buses in Canada and Mexico and drive up and down our highways tossing grenades out the windows, or risk their own lives by using Amtrak?

The government suggested that this possible preemptive "attack" would include Iraqi terrorists who might already be here. Although all the terrorists we know about in the past thirty-some-odd years have come from countries in the Middle East other than Iraq, I thought there might be some validity to this when, in January 2003, days after warning us about these preemptive Iraqi terrorist attacks, members of the government, including the president, asked all Americans to help look for five Middle Eastern men who were suspected of entering the United States illegally from Canada.

Their pictures appeared on our TV screens, on the front pages of our newspapers, and on the covers of our magazines. First of all, maybe it was me, but they looked like quintuplets. Then, a few days later, a jeweler in Pakistan called authorities in his country to express his shock at seeing his face as one of the five terrorists being hunted in the United States. So for a few days we Americans were looking for a harmless jeweler who was in his homeland of Pakistan selling his handcrafted hoop earrings and gold-plated goat pins. We also had been warned by our government that the names the men used might be fictitious, as if we would be thrown off the track if Abid Noraiz Ali was really Mohammed Azi bin Ackbar, but more important to our search, the government said nothing about their faces being phonies. Personally, I spent two weeks of my life looking for Azu Jamal Bitafu who was actually Zimi Ahmed Mohabi and, instead of being a terrorist hiding in America, he turned out to be a Lebanese proctologist living in a houseboat in Oman. The whole deal turned out to be a fiasco based on a phony tip.

But let us say the government is right and there are Iraqi terrorists already hiding in our country ready to strike when given the word. Now, let's guess what might make them come out of hiding and strike. Would it be (A) if we didn't attack their homeland or (B) if we did attack their homeland? If you answered (A), then how come they didn't attack even before or when we first started messing with them? If you guessed (B), then why the hell would we want to provoke them? If there was a bully living down the street who would attack anyone who walked on his lawn, would you put on the biggest boots you could find and stomp the shit out of his dandelion patch or just avoid the asshole?

We have filed charges against Iraq for having weapons of mass destruction, which is in spite of the fact of our having more of them than all the countries in the world put together. No, sir, no country in the world can match our capability of destroying the whole world several times over. If the world has to be destroyed, we Americans can do it as easily as falling off a log. But we didn't want Iraq to have even one of these destructive beauties, so our president appealed to the United Nations to either join us in an ass kicking or, if they wanted to seek a peaceful solution, to allow us to do the ass kicking all by ourselves, maybe with the help of England and Monte Carlo.

The U.N. suggested we hold back our bugle call to arms, while it sends inspectors to Iraq to find these weapons of mass destruction. Iraq said they would welcome them with open arms and totally free access to any place they wanted to go to look for the weapons and to test the air, water, and ground for signs of nuclear and/or biological weapons. President Bush, backed by a majority of our Congress, objected and wanted to bomb the shit out of them ASAP, but as world opinion became more and more in favor of sending the inspectors, our government canceled the October 2002 surprise attack we had announced publicly back in August. (Can you imagine sending word to Tony Bellafookio, a bad guy you intend to beat the shit out of, that on Friday night, at 8:15, you are going to surprise him by climbing in the far left bedroom window and kicking him in the balls?) War was avoided, for the time being, anyway.

The teams of U.N. inspectors went to Iraq, and, as you know, they didn't find any smoking guns but they did find a knife which caused a lot of excitement when it was thought to belong to O.J. Simpson, but it turned out to belong to Saddam's butcher who was rumored to have been subsequently butchered. As the U.N. kept reporting finding nothing in over three hundred surprise inspections, our president kept saying he had proof of Iraqi weapons of mass destruction. The condemning document was probably being kept in the Oval Office safe along with Senator Joe McCarthy's list of communists in Hollywood and Washington and Jimmy Hoffa.

We did declare that according to our intelligence (the branch of government, not our mental abilities), Saddam Hussein had mobile chemical labs. We, too, have had and still have chemical laboratories on wheels, only we called them the Grateful Dead's and Rolling Stones' tour buses.

The U.N. inspectors did find twelve empty canisters that could have housed chemicals for biological warfare. My first reaction was to feel sorry for the Iraqi who forgot to clean up.

"Mustaf, Saddam wants to see you. You can leave your head; you're not going to need it."

But the thought of biological warfare has kind of scared us a bit. We started making gas masks and protective uniforms for our armed forces. To allay our fears, Secretary of Defense Donald Rumsfeld announced a new policy created in the Pentagon called "Psyops," whose aim is to persuade Iraqi weapon handlers to disobey orders Saddam Hussein issued to launch chemical or biological weapons, if we invade Iraq. The plan calls for the dropping of leaflets which warned Iraqi soldiers that we would be keeping a list of everyone involved in releasing biological and/or nuclear weapons. And, after our obvious victory, they would be put on trial as war criminals and for crimes against humanity, and if found guilty, they would be hanged just like the Nazis found guilty at the Nuremburg Trials after World War II.

Let's take a moment to think this through. First of all, what are the odds that the story of the Nuremburg Trials is taught in Iraqi schools? Keep in mind that most of the crimes against humanity were about the killing of Jews, not exactly the most popular people in Iraq. I think it is safe to say that appealing to the humanity of the Iraqi soldier would work just as effectively as it did in the 1940s in Germany. I don't remember ever reading or hearing about thousands of Nazis who refused to fire the V-2 rockets on the civilian population of London or removed the poisonous gas from the death camp showers. Then there is a matter of common sense. Wouldn't you think that Saddam Hussein would have only his most loyal followers manning those weapons? I doubt very strongly that there would be guys saying, "Saddam Hussein? I can take him or leave him. Don't push the button. Here, wave the Stars and Stripes I have sewn in the inside of my battle jacket." Excuse me, Mr. Rumsfeld, would you please whip up a different policy? Maybe one that has at least a snowball's chance in hell of working?

We prepared our armed forces for war and allowed the media to show the public the "war games" our military was conducting to show the efficiency of our fighting men. In a front-page spread in *USA Today*, complete with color pictures and continued on page two, there was an eyewitness account of simulated street fighting in a town named "Shughart Garden" in the country of "Cortina." This was a brilliant move on the part of our government so Saddam Hussein would not know we were practicing to fight in the streets of Baghdad and would let his guard down.

The war game was described in great detail, and I mean *great detail*! Under a photo of soldiers attacking a tank, the caption read: "Enemy attackers leap onto an Abrams tank and lay powerful explosive charges on top near the turret where the armor is the thinnest and the Abrams tank is the most vulnerable." How many war rooms in Iraq do you think have this nailed up on the wall?" Can you imagine letting Tony Bellafookio know that one punch to your left rib cage would send you crashing to the floor in a pile of your own vomit and shit?

Without any substantive evidence, world opinion was more and more against our attacking Iraq and the consensus was that our president was trigger-happy. To counter this accusation, a member of Congress took the fire out of the president's rhetoric by saying that the government's position actually was not haphazard and dangerous, because what they were *actually* saying was, "Significant provocation is needed to justify an invasion of Iraq." In other words, the head of the CIA would have to go to the Oval Office and tell the president something "significant," like, "Mr. President, we have very reliable information that Saddam Hussein said your father is a pussy. Yes, the army, navy, marines, and air force are already on their way to Baghdad."

If we really have substantial and reliable reasons to attack the sovereign nation of Iraq—and forget the overused bullshit "to free an oppressed people," or we would be attacking a lot of countries in this world—then I have a suggestion of how we could avoid the loss of American lives and save the trillions of dollars. Remember my idea of killing bin Laden and his followers by having our best scientific minds develop long-beard-seeking missiles? Let's just add mustaches. The only fly in the ointment is that there is a chance that Saddam Hussein could still escape, because our intelligence reported that he had five identical look-alikes—and two are men.

Then an elephant jumped in the ointment. Right in the middle of us telling Iraq they'd better divulge and divest themselves of all their weapons of mass destruction, North Korea announced to the world that they are going to fire up their nuclear reactor that had been closed down in an agreement in 1994. They kicked out the U.N. monitors, quit the Nonproliferation Treaty, and started working on developing atomic bombs.

I was kind of surprised at first that we got so bent out of shape about this, especially the president. I thought he would consider it the highest form of flattery, believing that they were imitating him, since it was he who broke our Nuclear Testing Ban with Russia and withdrew from, rejected, did not join, or broke the Bans on Biological Weapons and Land Mines, the Global Warming Treaty, and the International Criminal Court.

Disregarding that President Bush publicly called North Korea part of the "axis of evil" and made speeches about stopping any "rogue nations" from developing weapons of mass destruction, we responded by saying that we can put this on the negotiating table rather than on our bombing targets, stating that it is more important that we deal with Iraq because it can turn into North Korea. To me, that's like letting Jack the Ripper off and going after his son, because he might become a butchering murderer like his father, rather than a butcher like his uncle. There was a bit of a public groundswell after this dichotomy was announced. Many people were still confused why we were going to war with a country that might have atomic weapons in a few years, instead of a country that confessed to the entire world that they already had a couple atomic bombs and were going to start making more. To some, the answer was simple and obvious—unlike Iraq, no Korean leader ever called our president's father an asshole.

Another reason for our reluctance to attack North Korea is our fear that China might join in on the side of North Korea. Lately, we've had poor relations with China, beginning with the accidental collision over China between one of our surveillance (spelled s-p-y) planes and a Chinese fighter plane, in which the pilot was killed. Our plane was confiscated and the crew detained. After a lot of tension, China finally released the crew and then allowed us to cut our plane up in little pieces and mail it back home. You know our mail service. We still haven't gotten all the pieces. I'd bet that next week in a farmhouse in North Dakota a husband will be calling out to his wife, "Say, honey, did you order a fuselage?"

Another move that further chilled our relationship with China was the president's announcement that we were going to "sell" (as in, "Here's a few million that I know I'll never see again") military equipment to Taiwan, our friend and China's archenemy. The deal consisted of four guided-missile destroyers (at a cost of $1 billion each), as many as eight diesel-powered subs, a dozen P-3 submarine–hunting planes, four Kidd-class destroyers, and possibly a few M-1 tanks, plus another $350 million worth of other weapons, the specifics to be determined later.

The reason the president gave for justifying the sale was to maintain a balance of power between China and Taiwan. I don't care if we sell Taiwan guns, swords, knives, slingshots, or even nail clippers. What I do care about is someone trying to bullshit me about doing it to maintain a balance of power between these two countries. Taiwan has a population of 20,778,000. China's population is 1,277,558,000. So for every Taiwanese there are six hundred Chinese. Therefore, an attack against Taiwan by China would be exactly the same as if all the armed forces of the United States joined ranks with all the military might of Canada and Mexico and the three of us simultaneously attacked Reno, Nevada. Instead of weapons, what we should do is sell Taiwan 20,778,000 little white flags to wave, made in China, of course.

There's hope that all of this will be academic, that there won't be a war in that area of the world, because we have agreed to negotiate our grievances with North Korea. I believe in negotiations, as I believe in peace talks. Only dialogue between or among nations can possibly lead to a true and maybe even an everlasting peace. I do have one criticism and a suggestion. I believe that negotiations and peace talks take so long or fail for one simple reason: where we hold the talks. We always hold them in wonderful places like Paris, Oslo, London, Washington, or Zurich. No one on the negotiating or peace-talking team is going to give up a job working in these glamorous spots. The negotiators are eating delicious Swiss chocolate, buying Swiss watches real cheap, attending the Follies de Paris, sitting in the stands during a Redskins game, touring the fjords, or hanging out with the Rolling Stones. If we want a quick and fair settlement, we should hold the talks in a place like . . . well, like on a subway in the South Bronx.

"Okay, we'll give you Boardwalk and Park Place for the green and yellow monopolies. Now, let's get the hell out of here!"

Seriously, and I am entitled to be serious for a moment or two, aren't I? Did you ever stop to wonder why it is that America is always in the forefront of almost every military conflict in the world? Is it because we became a world power after World War II and, therefore, feel an obligation to protect, especially the downtrodden, the oppressed, and other underdogs? Is it because we are so moral that we must right every wrong? I'm sure it is a little bit of each of the above, but we are the red, white, and blue, not the all-white, as pure as the driven snow. We're more like a day or two after the snowfall, when cars, buses, and trucks have driven on it and plows have piled it up along the pavement sides of the street. Still white but with different shades of gray and black interspersed.

I love this country. I have believed since childhood that I was living in the greatest country in the world and having traveled through about two-thirds of the world, I believe it now more than ever. However, there was a time not too long ago that I wondered whether I had been fed a few crocks of bullshit by my history teachers, and now I worry whether my three sons might be being fed the same in smaller or even larger amounts.

We advertise ourselves as the world's most noble believers in peace and, therefore, the most adamant enemies of hostile aggression. I'm not a history buff, nor am I a war maven, so I have a few questions about these claims and whether true history provides support for them.

Our nation started out with a few ships landing on our eastern shore where they deposited a couple hundred men, women, and children. My question is how did we manage to get our hands on all the land between Plymouth Rock and the Pacific Ocean, between Canada and the Gulf of Mexico and the Mexican border, as well as a few places off our shores in the Atlantic and Pacific Oceans. After all, my family and I moved into a small house and we never took over other houses on the block. If we had tried, we would have had to fight like sons of bitches to toss out the people living in them, unless, of course, we would have bought them out. Since America keeps claiming that we are a peaceful, nonaggressive people, we must have bought all the land we moved into, right?

It seemed that we used our checkbook, because I remember learning in history classes about one of our biggest land expansions—the Louisiana Purchase. I also remember learning in math classes that in all purchases, money or property of value must be exchanged. That is what constitutes a purchase. Thinking back to my history lessons, I don't remember hearing about anyone walking into a store, laying money or a cow and two sheep on the counter, and saying, "I'd like to purchase Louisiana." Did I sleep through that day's lecture or were there a lot of people already living in Louisiana who didn't get bought out but kicked out? If any reader has a copy of the check we wrote or the receipt we received for our purchase, please send me a copy of your copy, so I can copy it and send it to others who question the legitimacy of this purchase.

I also remember studying the "Spanish Cessation," which was when the Mexicans ceded the land that now includes such states as Colorado, Arizona, and California. This territory comprised approximately 40 percent of their country. Looking back, I question why any country would cede, which means to surrender or relinquish, almost half of their nation, unless, of course, someone was shooting at them and chasing their asses, but our ancestors would never have done that. They, like us, were peace-loving. After all, didn't we, their descendants, free the people of Granada from the Cuban airport construction workers, in a war that many thought would end in the defeat of our nation, or, at least, Little Deer Cay? So I guess the Mexicans just decided they owned enough land and left.

And what about the rest of our vast country? How'd we get it all? We were only thirteen colonies on the eastern seaboard. Was the rest of the land uninhabited? It must have been, because there is no way we haters of hostile aggression would have ever attacked or killed other human beings, especially if they were there first, were outnumbered, and had inferior weapons. This would be as lopsided as China attacking Taiwan, and we know how much we are against such inevitable butchery.

My guess is that after we laid claim to every inch of the land, we must have noticed a whole bunch of people who had been living there a couple thousand years. Oops! At first, we called them savages, then Indians, and now we call them Native Americans. It is our way of acknowledging and apologizing for not noticing them, as we took over the place. On the little land that we doled out to them, the descendants of the accidentally overlooked peoples opened casinos. Now, night by night, card by card, dice by dice, and slot by slot they are collecting the money owed to them for the "purchase" of their land.

I wanted to also question how we got the Philippines and Puerto Rico, but I was already confused enough. What I did do was research how we got Alaska and I was so glad that I did, because, I discovered that we actually purchased it peacefully from Russia, with money, mind you. Although we didn't call it the Alaska Purchase, it was a validation to me of America's claim to being noble believers in peace and the most adamant enemies of hostile aggression. I felt so much better after learning this.

Most importantly, I now believe, and will continue to believe, our president and our government leaders whenever they say we have a moral obligation to kill people in order to save them and bring peace to their country. I am ready to rally around the flagpole, boys! Count me in! Where's my old uniform and slingshot?

I don't blame our president or any world leader or any country for not being able to establish a long and lasting peace, because I am not certain that human beings can live in peace. It's as if it is some unknown mechanism inside each of us that, if provoked or conned, can turn us into warriors.

Countries are always fighting countries. Sections of a country fight each other in what is called a civil war. How's that for a misnomer? Then cities hate other cities in a country, because of religious preferences or just because. In my hometown of Philadelphia, the guys from South Philly were always fighting the guys from North Philly and in South Philly the kids living on Fourth Street were always fighting and throwing things at the kids from Sixth Street, usually the kids from Fifth Street, and on my block the family living in the house at 1435 South was always fighting the family living in 1452 South, and in my house my brother, sister, and I were fighting. World peace? I have a feeling sometimes that there is a monk sitting all by himself in a mountain cave beating the shit out of his own leg. But I continue hoping and laughing at the ridiculousness of war, which brings me to a confession.

I do know one foxhole joke and this may be the perfect time to tell it.

In World War II, an American foot soldier is ready to go into battle, but he doesn't have a gun. He tells his sergeant, who takes a sweeping broom, breaks off the straw, and hands the soldier the broom handle.

The soldier asks, "What the hell am I supposed to do with a broom handle?"

The sergeant answers, "When you go into battle, you point the broom handle and go 'bangity-bangity-bang.'"

The soldier says, "But what if we get into hand-to-hand combat? I don't even have a bayonet."

The sergeant grabs the broom handle out of his hands, ties a little piece of rope around the end, and hands it back to the soldier, saying, "Now, when you get into hand-to-hand combat, you point the broom handle and say 'Stabity-stabity-stab.'"

The battle begins and the soldier runs in with his broom handle, yelling "Bangity-bangity-bang, stabity-stabity-stab." He looks around. There are dead soldiers everywhere, except for one German soldier about thirty feet in front of him.

The soldier goes, "Bangity-bangity-bang," but the German soldier keeps coming. The soldier points the end of his broom handle at him and says, "Stabity-stabity-stab," but the German soldier keeps coming, walks into him, knocks him down, steps on him, breaking his leg, ribs, arm, and head, and, as the German soldier is walking away, the American soldier hears the German soldier saying, "Tankity-tankity-tank."

Sports

I have loved sports all my life, but I much prefer being proactive to being a spectator. I'd rather play a sport than be in the stands watching it live; be sitting live in the stands over watching it on TV; watching it on TV over listening to it on the radio; listening to it on the radio over reading about it in the papers or a magazine; reading about it over listening to some boorish asshole tell me about it.

It was especially difficult to be a professional sports fan growing up in Philadelphia when I did. Every professional sports team was always in last place. We used to read the sports page upside down, just to get an idea of what it was like to have a team in first place. Of course, all this has changed over the years and Philly has become a city of winners.

Actually, Philadelphia fans were always winners, even when our teams weren't, because regardless of the standing of our teams, we were always totally supportive of them. For example, it could be the bottom of the ninth inning with the Phillies behind by six runs, with two outs and the count on the batter 0–2, and no one is leaving the stadium. Unlike in Los Angeles where, regardless of the score, even if a pitcher is throwing a no-hitter, the fans start pouring out around the fifth inning, so they can get a jump-start on the traffic. I once told Tommy LaSorda that the Dodgers should play only four innings. It would save wear and tear on his players and save them the embarrassment of hearing one stoned fan in the bleachers cheering them on.

On the other hand, in reference to the Philly fans, you could justifiably replace the word "great" with the word "ruthless" and/or "unforgiving." The City of Brotherly Love invented such phenomena as beer bottle throwing (leading to the mandatory introduction of the paper cup) and organized mass booing. Only in Philly would you see a player who had hit three home runs in a game get up to bat for his fourth time and if he strikes out, hear fifty thousand fans scream, "Trade the blind son of a bitch!" which would be followed by booing in unison as the player dejectedly walks back to the dugout.

Philadelphians love to boo. It's in their genes. It is a historical fact that when William Penn and his settlers got off the first ship on the new land, everyone started booing for absolutely no apparent reason. Okay, it isn't a historical fact, but it is funny. The following, however, is a fact. I've seen and heard it. Philadelphians will boo at funerals. I'm serious. While grieving graveside, you hear, "Boo! They're carrying the coffin all wrong! Boo! It's slanting to the left. Boo! Trade the short guy in the far left corner! Boo! The hole's not deep enough! Boo! Where's the booze?"

In spite of all of this, I loved the Philly fans then and I love them now. I also loved playing baseball, football, soccer, ice hockey, and running track and field. I loved roller-skating, ice-skating, bowling, and, my favorite, shooting pool, and, most of all, I loved the street sports: stickball, wall ball, stoop ball, wire ball, Atlantic City Baseball, box ball, et al.

Although I was such a sports fan and loved to play sports, I had a different perspective about it than any of my friends, and, actually, different from anyone I've ever met. I wanted to win when I played, and tried my best to win, but I realized it was only "a game" and in a matter of only a few, upcoming years even we, the players, would forget who won or lost, let alone the scores and stats. So sometimes, after we lost a game, as we walked off the field, I would say something like, "Wow, wasn't that a great game?" My friends and teammates would go into shock. "What the hell are you talking about, Brenner, we got our asses whipped?" I would reply, "Yeah, I know, but I was three for four and what about that great shoestring catch I made?" I wanted to win, but maybe even more important to me was how I played and, most importantly, the fun I had playing. When it came to this philosophy of sports, I was alone.

I also wanted my hometown professional teams to win, but I knew they were also really only "games," and that I was a fan of my local team only because of the sheer coincidence of my parents deciding to live in Philadelphia. If they were born and raised in Pittsburgh, I'd be rooting for the Pirates. If my dad became a bookie in Cleveland instead of Philly, I'd be cheering for the Indians. The idea of going bonkers over a sports team and getting all bent out of shape if they lost was and is totally idiotic to me. Taking it a step further, painting your face and/or body the colors of your local team is total asshole time to me. Even worse is breaking a blood vessel or going into a deep depression. Whenever I am at a sports event or watching one on TV and the fans are having shit fits, I always feel like standing up and yelling louder than they, "It's only a goddamn game!" but I never wanted to be tarred and feathered and hung out for the buzzards, so I just shake my head unnoticeably and scream the words internally.

One of the many times I was a guest on *The Mike Douglas Show,* when it was taped in my hometown, Mike asked me how the trip was from New York City. I complained about the horrible traffic in the city, because of the Flyers' Hockey Championship celebration parade. The audience, my fellow Philadelphians who have always been my best and most loyal fans, booed me. (I told you they love to boo.) As a true Philly son, I did not shrink or retreat from my position; instead, I looked right at the audience and said, "Why should I care about the Flyers? Do you think they're in their locker room right now saying, 'I hope Brenner does great on *Douglas* today'?" Philadelphians love a wise guy, so I got tremendous applause and whistles and, most importantly, forgiveness.

If you happen to be one of these sports nuts who gets all worked up in a lather over how you play or how your professional team or athletes play, you are suffering for absolutely no intelligent reason. Loosen up; enjoy the play instead of the end results. If you win or lose, if your professional team wins or loses, the only way it will affect your life is if you have money riding on the outcome. That aside, not a solitary moment of your life will be improved or ruined because you or your team won or lost. Your boss will still be an asshole, your job will still be shit, your marriage will still be whatever it is, your children will still be wonderful and pains in the ass, you'll still have to go to the dentist, your tendonitis will still hurt like a son of a bitch, your balls will still itch, and you'll still die. In other words—it's only a game! Have fun with it, have some laughs.

In order to get the right and less aggravating perspective on sports, let's now look at several of them through the comedic eye, maybe lessening their importance, which, in turn, should lessen your aggravation and lower your blood pressure.

The Olympics

People get so worked up about the Olympics. I have friends who don't go out for weeks, where there is real life to enjoy. When they are watching the Olympics they have screaming, raging fits because some athlete, who was accidentally born in the USA, and, therefore, represents the USA, doesn't run as quickly, jump as high, or throw a metal disk as far as some other guy who was also accidentally born in his homeland.

I am neither a big fan nor a TV viewer of either Olympics, Winter or Summer, especially since both became political balloons to be tossed about by the world's political baboons. The scandal of the 2002 Winter Olympics also turned me off. But I have to admit that I was thrilled to sit in the seat where Alexander the Great sat while watching the original Olympics in Greece. The athletes performed naked back then, but the schmucks didn't allow women to compete. By the way, I love historical references. It was the naked Olympics that led to the invention of the jockstrap and the expressions, "ass over heels," "nothing but elbows and assholes," and "running his balls off."

In spite of my finding the Olympic events tedious, I do follow some of the news stories, such as the disclosure that one of the male figure skaters tested positive for heterosexuality. While we're on the subject, I think it is stupid to disqualify an athlete because of steroids. Instead, we should hold a Steroids Olympics. Wouldn't that be great to see, athletes performing at their human maximum?

"Ladies and gentlemen, here is the high jump of . . . oh, my God, 106'4"! What a disappointment. Now for the four hundred meter ra . . . Vroom! . . . Okay, that was fun, and now, let's check in with . . ."

One of the strangest news stories to come out of the 2002 Winter Olympics was the announcement that curling was going to sweep the USA and become one of our most popular spectator and participant sports. A quote from the American Association of Curlers that I read in a newspaper account was, "Even though we only sweep for twenty seconds, it's intense." Intense? My mother and all the other women on my block used to sweep the pavements and front stoops for two or three hours, and I never heard one of them say, "Man, this is intense." And, on top of this, they call curling a sport? To me, it's more like janitors with an attitude.

If you are a die-hard fan of the Olympics, good for you. I hope you spend your lifetime enjoying them, but that is exactly my point—enjoy them. Don't get worked up into a frenzy over who wins how many medals for the USA as compared to other countries. Many of the countries participating in the original Olympics don't even exist anymore. In retrospect, think how stupid it was for a Mesopotamian getting bent out of shape because his runner got a bronze medal, while a Sumerian won the gold. Like every sport, the Olympics is supposed to be fun time, not heart attack time.

Football

My first love in sports was football. I became an Eagles fan when I was seven years old. I still am, although having lived in New York for twenty-five years, I added the Jets and the Giants to my list of favorite teams. My oldest son is a die-hard Jets fan, in spite of living in Philly. My eight-year-old son for some inexplicable reason has decorated his room with both Eagles and Jets paraphernalia.

I took him to his first football game when he was seven, the Jets versus the Raiders in Oakland. I thought we were not going to get out of the stadium alive. Sixty thousand fanatical fans were screaming, "Defense," in unison, physically rocking the bleachers, and one tiny voice was yelling, "Offense." In my fearful ears, both words were equally loud, and I was certain "offense" would be the last word my son would ever speak and the last word I'd ever hear. Luckily, or probably because my son is so adorable and displayed a big pair of balls, we were allowed to live.

This is my point. I don't understand why anyone would paint their face the color of their team or write their favorite player's name and/or number across their bare beer belly with a Magic Marker, or get a tattoo of their hero or team name, or put horns on their head or fright wigs on their head, or wave some kind of superstitious rag or stuffed animal. Then, instead of ducking when the TV camera points at them so no one they know will see them acting like a colorful asshole, they go crazy, waving and jumping up and down. I guess when they watch tapes of old NFL games, they must get hysterical seeing men in the stands wearing suits and hats and women in dresses and hats.

I guess schmuckdom, like beauty, is in the eye of the beholder, but I wonder if they also laugh:

- when they watch those athletes of yesteryear play football for the love of the game and not for the love of money;
- when they watch quarterbacks call the plays, not wait for someone sitting in a heated booth high above the field to tell them over their headsets what to do;
- when they see quarterbacks run hard, put their heads down, and crash into their tackler, instead of sliding to avoid being tackled;
- when they notice so many players playing offensive and defensive for the entire game;
- when teams call time-out only if someone gets injured or they want to confer with their coach, not because a beer commercial has to air;
- when they see players stay loyal to the same team through all or most of their careers;
- when most players can be understood when they speak; and
- when hardly any player gets in trouble with the law.

The evening my son and I returned from Oakland, I was sitting at my home office desk thinking about the differences I just mentioned, thinking that it was a shame my son couldn't take a time machine back to when football was a sport and so were most of the fans. My son ran into my office, interrupting my thoughts. He screamed excitedly, "Dad, I'm watching the tape you made of the Raiders/Jets game we saw today and I could hear myself screaming 'offense.'" I told him that it was great that he heard himself, holding back my laugh until he ran back to watch his first live football game, and I realized that it is still a great sport and maybe worth acting like an asshole to watch it.

Basketball

When I became six feet two inches tall as a teenager, the neighborhood choose-up teams, as well as my high school team, vied to get me to play basketball. It seemed so natural, because I was a good athlete in other sports and had become tall. But there was a twofold problem. I couldn't play on any organized school sports team, because I had to work every day after school to help support my family. The other problem I had with both the school team and the sandlot teams was simply that I hated basketball. I still do.

Yet millions of Americans go crazy over the sport, packing stadiums, screaming and applauding every move on the court, going apeshit when a basket is called, having severe anxiety attacks or heart attacks when their team loses, lamenting and losing sleep for days over a loss, and displaying general all-around asshole behavior. Watch basketball fans and you'll wonder why monkeys are in cages with us laughing at them, instead of the other way around.

The game never made any sense to me, especially the professional ones and, most especially, the professional teams of today. At least when I was a kid, most pro players were my height or a little taller. Wilt Chamberlain was the first exception. So-called shorter players had to actually shoot *up* to the basket. Nowadays, they dunk (or drop) it in from above. What is the skill in that? Raise the baskets a foot or two. My other suggestion is mechanize the baskets, so they are constantly moving side to side and up and down.

Die-hard basketball fans still insist that it is a difficult sport. If it were, it would not be so easy to score so many times. Think about it. The final score of most ice hockey games is something like 3–2, the average baseball final score is probably something like 4–3, and football maybe 21–14. So hockey players on both teams bust their balls to score a total of five times in the whole game, baseball players seven times, and football players five times. If the final score of a basketball game is 112–110, this means that the players on both teams scored one hundred and ten times! So how damn difficult is it?

I have a bigger problem with the score throughout the game. It is always like 26–24, then 43–40, 76–75, and as the clock ticks away the final minutes, 102–101. Boring! What they should do in pro basketball is give each team 100 points and let them play for two minutes.

Another gripe I have with basketball and most professional sports is the changing of the rules, which is almost always done to make the game move faster or to make more money. No one used to stop a football game to show a few minutes of commercials. The commercials ran only when the players stopped. Even in billiards, some idiot invented "ball in hand," so that after a table or pocket scratch, instead of placing the cue ball behind the line, the new shooter now can put the cue ball anywhere on the table his little heart desires, so he or she can make the easiest shot, "and we'll be right back after these words from Bud Lite."

Can you imagine if this rush to speed up sporting events so that more money can be made affected other sports, like boxing? Rule 247A—If a fighter fouls his opponent, the other fighter can place the offending fighter anywhere in the ring he so pleases, placing his jaw wherever he desires, and then punch him as hard as he so chooses with the intention of knocking his head off his neck. Rule 285B – The fight shall be stopped any time the company sponsoring the fight wishes, at which time the fighters will remain motionless until after the commercial break. Come on; give me a break, but not the commercial, moneymaking kind.

Not only does baseball follow the commercial break rule, making a sport that has become boring even more boring, it has some of the craziest new rules, the weirdest of all, in my opinion, being "The Intended Rule." This is where a player only has to get close to the man sliding into his base, showing that he "intended" to tag him. You used to have to not only tag the guy but tag him hard enough so an umpire with a Seeing Eye dog would see it. What would it be like if we applied this "intended" free pass to other aspects of life?

"I *intended* to pay you the money I owe you."

"I *intended* to hire you."

"I *intended* to give you a raise."

"I *intended* to fix your carburetor."

"I *intended* to get an erection."

"I *intended* to not screw your wife."

Golf

Golf is without a doubt one of the most popular professional and amateur sports in America, and, in my humble opinion, one of the most, if not the most, boring, although, I must admit, since the entrance of Tiger Woods, I have found it less grating, but that is because he is so damn cool. But even Cool Tiger can't convert me.

Even this sensational athlete cannot get me to even watch golf on TV, mainly because I can't stand whispering. Why do the golf announcers whisper? It isn't like they are two feet away from the golfer. They're in a TV truck a mile or two away, watching the match on TV monitors. They could shout and fire off cannons and it wouldn't disturb the golfer. Besides, they whisper so low you can't hear them. It sounds like "Comblesta gormayben hasfesser." And as you turn up the volume of your TV, they're screaming, "COMBLESTA GORMAYBEN HASFESSER!" Turn the volume up full blast and they're yelling, "I INTENDED NOT TO SCREW YOUR WIFE!"

I lived on a golf course in Aspen, Colorado, for almost five years. From my backyard Jacuzzi, a flute of champagne in my hand, I watched thousands of golfers. They all had three things in common:

1. They all dressed like schmucks. I have the feeling that when golfers leave the house to play golf, wives all over the country fall down and roll on the floor in wild hysterics at how stupid their husbands look in those stupid, short-sleeve, colorful shirts with an animal on the pocket, nonmatching, glow-in-the-dark chartreuse-colored pants, and shoes with scallop flaps covering the laces.

2. They were physically the most out-of-shape "athletes" in the world, with stomachs hanging over their belts like window washers descending on a scaffold. They looked like Sumo wrestlers who never learned how to wrestle. The only difference between them and bowlers was the size of their balls. Oh, by the way, did you hear that someone invented bowling shoes that, as you bowl, tone your legs? Tone a bowler's legs? Have you ever looked at bowlers? The inventor would make a lot more money if he invented bowling shoes you could eat with a beer.

3. Golfers became raving, livid lunatics whenever they screwed up a shot. I saw grown men throw themselves to the ground, kick and scream like my boys did when they were toddlers. Even back on my neighborhood street corner, local poolroom, or local church, I didn't hear as many "Jesus Christs, goddamn its, shits, and cocksuckers," and I can't tell you how many clubs were flung through the air and landed in my yard. Thank goodness none of them splashed into my Jacuzzi, or there would be a funny-dressed fat man walking around with a nine iron sticking out of his XXX-large-sized ass.

So why would anyone want to dress like a schmuck, hit a little ball, walk for twenty minutes only to hit it again, and keep walking and hitting until it finally falls into a little hole in the ground, all the while becoming so enraged that a heart attack could leap out from behind the next tree?

Now I'll tell you a story to show you how little I know about golf. This is embarrassing, but it is the truth, and it might be just the story you will need to think about the next time you are having a fit on a golf course and only a big laugh will save your life.

One early afternoon, I looked out my window in Aspen expecting to see, majestically standing across the golf course, the becalming sight of the lightly snowcapped Rocky Mountains. Instead, there were hundreds of people and TV cameras. It was some sort of major golf tournament.

I already told you that I had zero interest in and minus-zero knowledge of the sport, but my back porch was the best seat in town, so I took my coffee with me and stood against the railing, only yards from someone who I assumed was some big deal golfer.

Now, my house was situated next to one of those—what the hell is it called? You know where the golfer places the ball on this little piece of wood and hits it as hard as he can? I know it has a letter followed by the word "off." Okay, I don't feel like calling a golf friend, so let's call it where they "J-off."

My first observation was that golfers had to be the worst physically coordinated athletes in the world. This guy who was J-offing kept losing his balance, forcing him to keep moving his legs. I thought that any moment he was going to fall on his ass, but he finally stopped shaking and locked in his legs in what looked like an "I'm-going-to-take-a-shit-on-the-grass" position.

I also didn't know that the first swing was a fake-a-roonie. When this guy swung at the ball and missed, I couldn't believe it. It wasn't like someone was pitching the ball at him at over 90 mph. The ball was sitting stationary on top of that little stick.

Then he took a second shot at it, and this time, he hit it. Now comes the funniest part to me. Did you ever see golf fans? They're so weird. After this guy hit the ball and started walking away, all the fans followed him like little, obedient kindergarteners. Can you see this in other sports, like baseball? Say a batter puts one into the outfield and the announcer calls out to the fans, "It's a double. Come on, everyone, let's all go to second base."

What a ridiculous, boring "sport." If you play it and it gets you all uptight and angry, you can do one of two things: Find something else to do with your afternoons and weekends or put golf in its proper perspective and learn to laugh from hole to hole and all the way home.

Tennis

Talk about boring? To me, tennis is golf with a net and, of course, because I know so little about it, I was led into another very embarrassing situation that, unlike the limited number of people who saw me make an ass of myself at the golf game, this time it was millions of television viewers.

I never played tennis as a kid. As a matter of fact, in my macho neighborhood, a man couldn't even wear shorts, let alone run around with a racket hitting a ball over a net. Knife-throwing was considered sissy. There was tennis on TV. I just never bothered watching it. The glimpses I saw of it looked pretty boring. Now, to the future, when I'm a man, full-grown but still fully ignorant about tennis.

One day, when I was at the top of my game as a stand-up comedian and talk-show sub-host, I got a call from a press agent telling me that he got an invitation for me and three friends to go to the United States Openness or whatever the tennis event is called that is played in Forest Hills, New York. I told him to thank the network executive, tell him I'm not into tennis, but if he should ever have tickets to the Men's Nine Ball Finals or a championship fight in Vegas, I'd appreciate it.

Later that morning, I was having brunch with three of my friends (not from the old neighborhood) who were tennis nuts. I casually mentioned the tickets. They had shit fits.

"You turned down tickets to the Open? Are you crazy?"

"Brenner, those tickets are worth more than gold!"

"Do you have any idea who's playing? Jesus!"

"Okay. Okay. Stop. I'll call and try to get them for this afternoon."

"Great!"

"Love you, man!"

"I'll drive."

As soon as we pulled into the parking lot in Forest Hills, and I saw the fans piling in, I knew I was out of place. I was the only man not wearing a sweater over my shoulders with the sleeves flipped over each other once, in front of the chest. I had on a muscle T-shirt. I just said to myself what I always said in such a socially incorrect position—"Screw it!"—and continued toward the gate.

The guys flipped out when they saw our seats. We were right on the fifty-yard line, facing the TV network cameras. It didn't take long for me to figure out that this was going to be as boring as pigshit on a stick. I excused myself and walked around, figuring that I could raise my attention span and interest if I had a bet on the match.

Because my father was a bookie, I have an instinct for spotting someone making book at any sporting event. I walked over to a small man with a cigarette dangling out of the corner of his mouth and his eyes flitting about. Within thirty seconds I had a few hundred dollars wagered. I returned to my seat.

"Yo, you guys don't have to worry about me being bored. I just put some money down on that guy with the red stripe on his boxers."

"He's seeded," replied one of my friends, and continued looking at the program.

I thought, "I don't believe my luck. I lay all this money on a guy and he has some kind of problem from eating seeds."

"Is he going to be able to play with all the seeds in him?" I inquired.

The guys laughed. "Good one, Brenner. Throw it in the act tomorrow night."

I had no idea what my friend was talking about, but I instinctively knew that whatever it was, the explanation was going to bore the hell out of me, so I dropped it and tried to count the number of blue sweaters versus yellow.

Finally the match began. The guy I bet on kicked off. The other guy hit it back and so it went. Now, I had never seen tennis fans before. I am used to football, baseball, and boxing fans. Did you ever see tennis fans? The guy hits the ball and everyone goes "Ahhh," and then the other guy hits it back and they politely go "Ahhh" and maybe clap their hands like little girls watching their birthday friend unwrap a Barbie Doll.

I had money riding on this match, so when the other guy was running to hit back my guy's ball, I jumped to my feet, pointed at him, and yelled out, "Your mother sucks!"

I had no idea that at that exact moment the network was going to zoom in for a close-up of me. I actually didn't know about it, until people in airports, on planes, in the street, and in my audiences told me about it, over and over and over again, ad nauseum.

Actually, I really didn't give a flying shit on the moon, because I had won $500 on the match. I know a winner when I see one, even if he is dressed in funny shorts.

That was the one and only tennis championship I ever saw, but I used to party with some of the pro tennis players and they were a wild bunch, full of fun, even in their regular underwear.

I may not be the world's greatest advocate for people who spend every minute of their precious free time playing or watching sports, but I do relate to the passion that sports inspire. Whether your sport of choice involves carved fiberglass on your feet, a pole in each hand, a racket, a club, a cue, a bat, a rod, a gun, a sword, a table, an open field, sneakers, bare feet, bundles of clothing, a skimpy bathing suit, pads, gloves, ropes, ladders, or a broom, try to keep in mind that it is a sport, just a sport, only a sport, and it is supposed to be fun, so have fun, get some laughs the next time you play, instead of ulcers. The best way to get some of the laughs you can do easily. Carry a mirror to look into during the game, or take a video or audiotape of yourself and the people around you. Screen or listen to it and when you've seen or heard enough, remove the paint from your face and take the fright wig off your head and then relax in a hot bath and laugh, you asshole; the joke is on you.

Weather

It amazes me that there are people who actually worry about the weather. Oh, I can understand someone like a farmer, a sailor, a fisherman, or a homeless person worrying about it. Their livelihoods and lives depend on the weather, but why would the average Joe or Jane with a normal Joe or Jane job get all worked up over it? To me it's so stupid, and such a waste of time and energy, especially since there's nothing you can do about it.

In the lives of most people, it really doesn't matter if it's windy, cloudy, snowing, or raining cats and dogs. Unless, of course, it is literally raining cats and dogs. A German shepherd (the four-legged kind) or even a miniature poodle falling from fifteen thousand feet can do some heavy damage to your property and person. Other than that, what's the big deal about what is happening outside?

I have seen people with their eyes and ears glued to the TV, listening intently to the weather person's every word and watching their every scribble on the map. A person watching could be in Kalamazoo, Michigan, and, who knows why, he is worried shitless about a cold front sweeping across Maine or Budapest.

And for the millions of weather nuts in this country, we even have a twenty-four hours a day, seven days a week, 365 days a year Weather Channel, and thank God for it, too, I say. I don't know about you, but sometimes in the middle of the night I awaken in a cold sweat, suddenly worried sick that there might be a low-pressure system heading for Kutztown, Pennsylvania. I leap out of bed, turn on the tube, and click my remote as quickly as I can to the Weather Channel, screaming aloud to the weather person, "What about Kutztown!" Twenty-four hours of weather? I can't watch a TV weather report for twenty-four seconds. The only thing more boring to me than the weather is the weather forecasters. They try to make their report interesting by being melodramatic.

"There's a high front swooping down like a Japanese kamikaze from Canada and another high front slipping in like motor oil from Mexico." Illegally, we know that. And another high front . . . high front . . . high front . . . I always expect to look outside and see these giant H's moving across the sky. "Run for your lives! The invasion of the high fronts is coming!"

Or else, the weatherman becomes Merlin the Magician mesmerizing with visual aids that fly around on a screen behind him, which he creates with his superspecial magical touch. With only the tip of his forefinger, he draws on the screen a bunch of stupid arrows and circles that the rest of us got yelled at for doing in third grade. "Oh, my God, Martha, there's a yellow arrow whipping across the entire state. It looks like it's heading our way! Get the kids! We're heading for the hills! But don't wake your mother."

And I don't care how many times they explain it, although I have to admit that most of the time either I'm focused on another thought or I'm desperately searching for my remote. I have no idea what the hell they're talking about. Like what the hell is the barometer reading and who gives a flying shit on the moon about it, anyway?

Even though I travel extensively, and bad weather can really screw things up for me, I couldn't care less about the weather and rarely check it. There's nothing you can do about it. So if you want to know what it's like outside, do what I do. I stick my head out of the window. If it comes back wet, it's raining. If it doesn't come back, it's very windy.

I wish other people were as nonchalant about the elements as I, but even knowing they can't do anything about it, so many people are addicted to knowing the weather. A lot of the blame falls on the lap of the media. You can't pick up a newspaper without seeing some scary headline on page one about the weather.

COLD FRONT SENDS FLORIDA FARMERS SCRAMBLING TO PROTECT GROVES.

If you don't own or work in an orange grove, don't earn your living selling oranges, or don't eat oranges, why do you give a shit?

CHILL CANCELS NASA MARS PROBE.

Are you an astronaut? No? Then screw the chill.

HEAT SPELL ROASTS ARIZONA.

Do you, a friend, or a family member live in Arizona? Are you going to Arizona? Can you find Arizona on a map? No? Then screw the heat and Arizona.

Maybe I'm being a little harsh. No man is an island, so we should care for our neighbors, but even with our care and empathy, we can still tone down the worrying and lighten up. How? Look for the funny silver lining in every cloud. Here are some examples:

Let's start with the cold front I mentioned above. For years now, the winters have been devastating. Some years have started out with very mild weather and suddenly have become arctic zones or have been pummeled by unbelievable snowstorms. So what's so funny about that? Where's the joke? Let's see . . . okay, try this medicinal line:

"The South has been experiencing the coldest winter in its history. It was so cold last night in Arkansas, everyone's tooth was rattling."

Did you ever notice that people often do not evacuate their homes when warned a hurricane is coming? Everyone blames the weather bureau, claiming that it doesn't give enough warning time, and the weather bureau blames the police, claiming that they're not doing the job of evacuating people quickly and efficiently.

Neither one is to blame. I'll tell you who is—whoever gives the storms their names. That's who's to blame. Look at the names they give them: Hurricane Isadore. Who is going to be afraid of anything named Isadore, especially in Miami? Do you know how many Isadores go to Miami every year?

"Isadore's coming!"

"Oh, that's nice. Is he going to stay for dinner?"

Come on, if you want people to leave their homes, you've got to put the fear of God in their hearts. You've got to give hurricanes names like "Hurricane Mother Humper" or "Hurricane Rip Your Ass Off!"

"Rip Your Ass Off is heading our way! It's every man for himself!"

Lately, we've been experiencing a lot of lightning storms. One of the worst struck Philadelphia. The sky looked like it was decorated with cobwebs of lightning. Did you hear about the idiot who went outside, at the height of the storm, wearing retro jeans from the 1950s that had a metal zipper? Well, a bolt of lightning struck him right on the fly. I guess now he can rub his wife's head against it and stick her to a wall.

Even crazier was what happened to a young man in a small town in Italy. I forget the name of the town, but I think it ended in a vowel. Anyway, he was on top of this woman in a field right outside of town. They were really going at it full speed, when he got struck by lightning. At first, I felt so sorry for him and then I realized the person to really feel sorry for is the next guy who is having sex with this woman.

"Guido, you're nothing. Last week, while Anthony was doing me, my hair stood straight up and a ball of fire this big shot out of my ass."

There's a very serious weather issue plaguing many parts of the nation. Drought. In the winter of 2002, the governor of New Jersey declared a drought emergency, claiming that year's drought to be the worst in recorded history. Two thousand and two saw droughts in New Mexico, Arizona, and California, the tristate area. In New York, soil was parched, reservoirs were depleted, and streams were trickling. So what's so funny? Try this one—a true news story and then a joke:

The drought has gotten so bad in NYC that scientists are scurrying for new ways to increase the supply and cut the demand. In the meantime, the state said that if they don't get some relief from the drought by springtime, they are going to ask the people living in New York to drink toilet water.

Let me tell you something. There are two reasons why I will never drink toilet water. Number one . . . and number two.

Another real news story. This time out of southern Florida. The media reported that because of the drought, there had been a tremendous increase in the number of alligators running through the streets and across the lawns of towns and cities. (In a totally unrelated story, there was also a tremendous increase in missing old Jewish people.) Scientists claim that the alligators are running to get away from the drought.

I hate to challenge the scientific community, but I have an entirely different theory of why the alligators are on the move. I believe they are running away from us and here's why:

My theory is convoluted, so bear with me. Okay. As you know, Man has always sought the perfect sexual aphrodisiac. This is why we used to kill tigers and still kill rhinos. I don't know if you heard about the latest aphrodisiac discovery being sold across the country—alligator testicles. Very weird, but very true. The first thought that probably comes to your mind is how horny was the guy who figured this out. Was he walking through a swamp with some male buds, confessing, "I haven't gotten laid in two years. I tried . . . Wow, look at how that alligator is hung. That gives me an idea. Bob, hand me your knife."

Okay, enough joking around. Let's get serious. The reason I know so much about the "legitimacy" of this aphrodisiac is because a very good friend of mine uses it. As with all aphrodisiacs, they grind it into a powder. You have to sprinkle this powder on a food or into a liquid three times a day, seven days a week. If you miss just once, it is ineffective.

My friend has been using this alligator testicle aphrodisiac religiously for about two and a half months now, and as a result, he has this irresistible urge to fuck his shoes.

Let's get even more serious. Every year, this country, particularly the Midwest, is plagued by tornadoes. In some regions, they call them cyclones or twisters. You know what I'm talking about. Those funnel storms that always attack trailer parks. (This is why no Jew has ever been killed by a twister.) You'd think that people would wise up and stop living in trailers. They attract storms. The twisters are heading for a city, when one of them says, "Hey, everyone, there's a trailer park over there. Let's get it!" Vrooooooom!

Then the twister picks up like three cars and a cow. Meanwhile, all the chickens on the farm are always fine while four-thousand-pound bovines are heading into space. Whenever a cow sees a twister, she yells, "Hold on to a chicken!"

As soon as the storm subsides, the TV networks always send some cub reporter to cover the story. Why not? It's a simple and obvious story. Something was there, and it isn't there anymore.

So we see the young reporter, microphone in hand, standing with a resident of the trailer park that was annihilated, who is still stunned over what happened. To add insult to injury, this is probably his one and only fifteen seconds of fame, so the least the network could do is give him the dignity of having his name on television, but no, across his dust-covered chest they superimpose the words "Twister Victim."

So anyway, "Twister Victim" is standing on top of a huge pile of debris, splintered wood, half a toilet, a smashed refrigerator, all of which just a few short hours ago used to be his home. The man is still vapor -locked over what happened to him, staring into space like a zombie. That's when the reporter shoves the mike in front of his face, almost down his throat, and asks the question that they always ask, "How did you feel when you saw your house blow away?"

What do these reporters expect as an answer? "Oh, it was great! You should've seen my bed with my wife in it hanging on for dear life. It took off like a bat out of hell, probably in the next county by now. And my mother-in-law never let go of her enema bag the whole way up. Silly thing to take, wasn't it? Nobody gets constipated in heaven."

Yes, it was a silly thing for her to take, but no sillier than you being concerned and worried about the weather. So the next time the winter winds blow and the snow piles up, when the torrential rains fall and the heat smothers, whenever Mother Nature roars fury of one kind or another, look for the funny silver lining and remember tomorrow is a new day with new weather to worry about that you really don't have to worry about. Think of weather this way—getting soaking wet or being too hot or too cold is just Mother Nature's way of letting you know you're still alive.

Smoking

We all know smoking is bad for you, that it will take years off your life, and that it is a horrible habit. Yet millions of Americans smoke, with millions of new smokers joining the club every year. I would guess that smoking, and its deadly effects, is in the top twenty worries of Americans, either the negative things it is doing to them (if not by smoking, then by secondary smoke) or to people they love. I wish that instead of making you laugh about it, I could make you quit. Maybe I can do both by telling you about my long smoking habit and how I finally beat it.

Remember when they stopped placing a pipe in the box with Mr. Potato Head, because some lobbying group claimed that the pipe influenced children to smoke? I don't know about you, but I know my whole street corner gang started smoking because of Mr. Potato Head. It's bad enough the cute little toy is now in his fifties and comes with snap-on ears that have hair hanging out of them, but to blame him for making kids light up? Come on, reel it in. You've cast too far.

But I did start smoking when I was a kid, nine years old. It wasn't because of Mr. Potato Head; it was partly because all the cool guys in the neighborhood smoked. You know the cool guys who today are working in McDonald's with dreams of moving up to Burger King? A bigger influence was the cool guys in the movies who always had a lit cigarette hanging from their lip, cinema heroes like Humphrey Bogart and Yul Brenner, both of whom died of lung cancer.

My childhood habit was about one pack a week, only because I didn't have the money to buy more, although once in a while a few of us would chip in for what were called "loosies." These were cigarettes that were sold individually, not in packs. Because of what my mother called "David's gift of gab," I was usually the one who went into the store for the buy.

"Hi, Moe, I need four cigarettes for my father: an unfiltered Lucky Strike, one Camel, one Marlboro, and one Kool."

A suspicious Moe would ask me how come my father wanted four different brands. I always replied to him and the other neighborhood store owners, "He likes variety. That's why I have a sister, a brother, and a chimp." They would always laugh, and I would always get the smokes.

When we kids were low on change, which was most of the time, we would go on a "cig hunt." We'd walk around the neighborhood with one foot on the curb and one in the gutter in search of grown-ups' discarded butts. A real find would be a cigarette 95 percent not smoked, tossed away by someone who just lit up, maybe not realizing that the bus he or she was waiting for was about to turn the corner. To us kids, this was proof that there was a God, or, at least, an angel who smoked.

When we were stone broke and the rain was soaking all the butts in the street, we would become so desperate, we'd pick and light weird things that were long and brown and hung on trees. They were called "Johnny Smokers." If they were also soaked from rain or snow, we'd smoke drinking straws. I'm serious. Sometimes, a few of us would go into a luncheonette and start a loud ruckus or a fight, so the owner would chase us out, which was exactly what we wanted him to do, because one of us had stolen a pack of cigarettes from a distracted customer eating at the counter.

I went to work when I was eight and a half years old but had to give all the money I made to my parents. However, by the time I was ten, I was making enough to keep a dollar for myself. I used it for childhood necessities: movies, baseball cards, chewing gum, candy, balsa wood airplanes, or, most importantly, cigarettes. I could afford to buy a full pack a week, reinforcing the ones found in the streets. We were really in heaven the day Mutt got a job in a pharmacy and could steal a few packs a week.

By the time I turned twelve, I was smoking a pack a day. By fourteen, two packs. By sixteen, three and a half packs a day, one match. This number remained my habit into and throughout my adulthood.

I'd light up a cigarette as soon as my eyes opened in the morning and knocked off one right before I went to sleep, with or without sex. The only time I did not smoke was when I appeared on TV or stage, because I didn't want to influence any kids to emulate me and take up the habit. I knew it was bad, but so were a lot of things in life, including life itself sometimes. Besides, I truly loved smoking, everything about it: peeling open the pack, tapping a cigarette to get the tobacco to shift down tightly, putting it in just the right spot between my lips, lighting it, and, best of all, taking those deep drags and blowing it out with individual finesse and style. Smoking was so cool, as a little kid hanging on a street corner, and as a man.

Even though smoking was still so cool and still so enjoyable, and although I had no cough and felt physically great, I was no fool. I knew the cigarettes were taking a toll, doing hidden damage, and that I would have to pay the piper someday. The older I got, the more I thought about this and about quitting. I decided to give them up—often.

I tried everything to quit but nothing worked. The dumbest stop-smoking system was lighting up your first cigarette one hour later each day, smoking as many as you wanted for the remainder of your waking hours. On the first day, if you awaken at 8:00, you don't light up until 9:00. The next day 10:00 A.M., then 11:00 A.M., and so on. Instead of beating the habit in the promised twelve to fourteen days, I found myself one midnight stuffing a whole pack in my mouth and lighting up, like a human bonfire.

I don't think I would've ever quit if one of my best friends, George Schultz, creator and owner of the first comedy club in America, Pips in Sheepshead Bay, Brooklyn, and one of the funniest and nicest human beings ever to walk this earth, hadn't called to tell me he had the first touches of emphysema. The doctors said that he could beat it *if* he would quit smoking.

Here was an opportunity to pay him back for all the kindness, help, and laughter. I could save his life and throw in saving mine, too.

I gave George an offer he couldn't refuse. I would quit smoking with him. I smoked a pack a day more than he, so it should be harder for me. I would pay for whatever treatment we took to quit, and if he broke the habit, I'd treat him to an all-expenses-paid trip to Las Vegas, where I had a three-week gig coming up. George loved to fish and knew I kept a boat on Lake Mead, which was stocked with trout.

I found out about an acupuncturist in Manhattan who had an 85 percent success rate with smokers. I called and set up appointments for George and me. The day came, and I went in first. I was actually looking forward to getting acupuncture because, since I was a little kid, I was always curious about it, especially how the first guy came up with it.

"Aw, this pain in my shoulder is killing me. Hey, I got an idea. I'll stick these long needles in my chest and lip . . . Ow, I twisted my ankle. Quick, hand me some of those needles. I've got to put them in my eyebrows."

The acupuncture treatment was just what I expected it to be. I took off my shirt and stretched out on my back on a long, leather examining table. A man suddenly appeared holding handfuls of metal needles, hundreds of them. He walked over to me and, without a word, started to twist the needles inside everywhere, my arms, chest, legs, feet, the back of my hands, forehead, and in my earlobes. I looked like a giant voodoo doll. Then, as quietly as he came, he left. My first thought was, "Oh, my God, I hope he works here."

After about forty-five minutes, he came back in and removed the needles. I have to admit that for about the next hour, I had no urge to smoke. I was in so much damn pain, I couldn't have raised two fingers up to my lips, even without the weight of a cigarette between them. My biggest worry was taking a bath that night with all the holes in my chest.

George felt the way I did, and cursed me all the way to lunch. We shared egg rolls, cashew chicken, and a million laughs. The wildest thing was that after we finished eating, neither one of us had a desire to light up. It was a first for me and for George. As a matter of fact, neither of us had a cigarette for the rest of the day and that whole night.

We met at the doctor's office the next morning, cigarette free for twenty-four hours. It was remarkable. George and I went religiously every day that week, at different times, because of our personal schedules.

Neither of us smoked a single cigarette the entire week. We couldn't believe it. But then came Saturday morning. The doctor's office was closed for the weekend. From the moment my eyes opened, all I could think about were cigarettes.

"Would you like mustard on your hotdog?"

"Yeah, and can you light it for me? Matter of fact, give me a pack."

I found myself going through every pocket of every stitch of clothing I owned, hoping to find a cigarette, a butt, some loose tobacco. I had to resist rolling up a newspaper, a roll of toilet paper, or anything that could burn. I threw the cushions off my sofa and chairs and dug my fingers down real deep along the sides and backs, hoping a friend or I had dropped one down inside them. When I lifted the lid of the toilet in hopes there'd be a butt floating around that could be dried in my microwave, I knew I was going mad.

I charged out of my apartment, down the fire stairs, forget waiting for an elevator. I dropped to the pavement and ran the fastest I could up the block to the corner grocer where I bought six cartons of cigarettes. While still in the store, I ripped open the carton, bit off the top of a pack, shoved two cigarettes in my mouth, and yelled for a light. The first puff tasted like shit and made me dizzy, but I stuck with it, until it turned into that familiar, delicious treat.

It always struck me so funny that tobacco companies and scientists fought over the question of whether cigarettes were addictive, with cigarette manufacturing companies' claim that they are not. Yeah, sure, and elephants don't shit. Look, I love sex. I crave it. But, I don't search under cushions and in toilets for it. Cigarettes are addictive!

The Saturday I fell off the program, I smoked my usual three and a half packs and the same on Sunday. I was so happy, until Monday morning, when I had a 9:15 appointment with the acupuncturist. I didn't feel right telling him over the phone what I had done. He was a good guy and I wanted to tell him in person. I put out my tenth cigarette of the morning, just before entering his office. I figured he would know what happened when he saw smoke pouring out of the holes in my chest, but he just smiled and motioned me into his treatment office.

I confessed immediately and apologized. He reminded me that he had an 85 percent success rate. This made me feel like I was back in school and one of only five out of forty-two of my classmates who didn't know how many bushels of wheat the farmer and his two sons picked or the answer to some other problem you would never face if you lived ten thousand years. If they asked us how many nickel bags of grass could be sold, what time the cop on the beat went up an alley to take a piss, how much each guy in the older gang got from robbing the neighborhood supermarket chain store, we all would've gotten As. Who in a city slum knew anything about farmers, except the jokes about some salesman screwing their daughters?

The doctor asked me what my biggest problem was. I told him it was the unbearable craving for a cigarette. He said he would offer me a method that would eliminate the craving, allow me to smoke as many cigarettes a day as I wanted, and I would end up quitting. I didn't say anything, but I thought, "This guy plays with his needles." But I listened. I've listened to a lot of lunatics in my life.

The doctor asked me, "Can you follow one rule?"

"Of course, I can," I answered." "I obey one of the Ten Commandments."

"Okay, David, here's what you do. You smoke all the cigarettes you want, but (there's always a "but," right?), but, no pun intended (I hate stupid jokes, especially when I'm waiting to hear a top secret), when you light a cigarette, you are allowed to take only one puff from it, and then you have to put it out. You want to smoke more, light another, take one puff, and put it out. Still craving? Light another, one puff, out. Keep lighting and puffing, until the craving is gone. That's it."

He smiled proudly and put out his hand. I took his hand, smiled as sincerely as I could, and thanked him, meanwhile thinking that I had let a stark-raving lunatic stick needles in me for one week and paid for it.

I left the office and thought of calling George and telling him that his acupuncturist was probably one subway flashing away from being institutionalized for life, but I didn't because I'd have to confess that I fell off the wagon and George hadn't smoked one cigarette over that entire weekend. I decided that whenever I was with him, I would either not smoke or sneak them, like I did with my parents as a kid.

I wasn't going to try the doc's one-puff craziness, but then I thought I had tried a lot of other weird things in my life, so why not? I added one element to what the doctor said to do and that was, when I was home, I put the pack of cigarettes in the farthest room from where I was, so I'd have to also go to the trouble of getting up and walking to get a smoke.

That night, I attended a black-tie charity benefit. At one point, I found myself in a circle of about ten people—I knew only one. I lit a cigarette, took a puff, put it out, lit another one, took a puff, put it out, lit another one . . . by this time, even the person I knew for years walked away from me.

For the next week, whenever I went out, I had to carry ten or fifteen packs of cigarettes in my pockets. My whole body looked like it was covered with monstrous square boils. In addition, I was spending about $400 to $500 a week on cigarettes. I'd go to my friendly corner grocer, "Hi, Sam. Give me pastrami on rye and twenty cartons of Marlboros. Thanks. See you tomorrow." By day three, Sam asked me to please stay out of his store and to seek professional help.

Believe it or not, after day ten, I quit. George had, too. We celebrated with three of the most fun-filled weeks we had ever had together in Las Vegas. I had never seen George look healthier, and I had never felt healthier. Only when I quit did I realize how horribly smoking affected my body. It was as though I had been given a transplant of a twenty-year-old man's body.

So this is a story with a happy ending, right? Oh, you could never know how much I wish this were true. A few weeks after that trip to Las Vegas, George started smoking again and never quit, no matter what I promised or threatened.

The last time I saw him, this man whom I loved with all my heart, was a few short years after the Vegas trip. He was staying in his sister's apartment where he had gone to convalesce, after another several weeks in the hospital. He was wearing a crumpled robe and scuffed slippers. He no longer had that ruddy complexion of a fisherman. He was so pale and so weak. He kept a tank of oxygen always at his side with the mask constantly over his nose and mouth.

My comedian friend Steve Landesberg was with me that day. The three of us talked; we laughed; we knew that after over twenty years of friendship, this was the last time we'd all be together. George was very bad off. We continued talking and there was one of those pregnant pauses that often happen in the middle of conversations. Steve and I were staring at this frail man across from us, remembering how he used to look, how vital he used to be, how very alive. George lifted the mask a little, smiled ever so slightly, and said, "Glad you came, boys?" We all cracked up. It was the last laugh we ever shared.

George and I had a running, private joke from the time we first became friends. Whenever we parted, heading to our hotel bedrooms while traveling together through Europe, saying good night in a casino, going our separate ways after I came offstage, saying good-bye outside his comedy club, Pips, wherever, I would say, "George, give me a pose." The joke was, since George was fourteen years older than I, and would probably cash in his chips first, I would have a vivid last memory by which to always remember him.

George would then make one of his rubbery, silly faces and wave his index finger at me, as if to say, "Be seeing ya, kid." He always looked so damn funny and it was so damn stupid that it always made both of us laugh, every time.

Well, that night, Steve and I hugged and kissed George, telling him that we'd call him from the road on our separate tours around the country and then visit him when we got back home to New York. As I was leaving the apartment, I turned in the open doorway and looked at George. He made a silly face and waved his finger, but this time neither one of us laughed. I can see him doing that right now and will see it forever. I just wish it would've been one of the hundreds of funny ones.

Did I ever go back to smoking? No. Do I crave cigarettes? Yes. Sometimes, leaving a movie theater or after a meal, I find myself reaching into my shirt pocket for a pack. I often dream that I'm smoking. If someone came up to me right now and told me that I wasn't David Brenner, a human being, but actually, I was God sent to earth as a human, in order to better understand mankind, the first words I would speak would be, "Who's got a cigarette?" God is impervious to any physical harm. But as long as I am a mere mortal, will I ever smoke again? *Never!* Why am I so sure? I'll give you the answer in one word: George. I don't want anyone I love and who loves me to lose me sooner than they should and then spend the rest of their lives missing me as terribly as I miss George.

Think about what you just read, because a lot of it is nothing to laugh at.

Weight: Losing and Gaining

One of the most difficult, frustrating, and depressing challenges ever to face mankind, tougher than achieving world peace, landing men on Mars, or figuring out where in hell the guests on Jerry Springer come from, is weight management. Most Americans have a problem losing, not gaining, but both problems are equally near impossible.

I realize that most, if not all, of you, who either know me or have seen me on stage or TV believe that I was born thin and remained thin with little or no effort on my part throughout my entire life. I only wish this were true. I know about the problems of gaining and of losing weight, because I have done battle with both for most of my life.

It's true that I was born thin and remained so throughout my childhood and teen years. When I was fourteen, I was five foot six and weighed 126 pounds, a decent weight for my height. I also had a very nice, straight nose. During the three-month summer break from school, I shot up six inches and didn't gain one ounce. On top of this, during a choose-up football game, and then in a non-choose-up street fight, my nose was broken twice. The result was a camelback hump without water storage, in spite of enough space. So my body grew up, but not out, and my nose grew up, down, in, and out, and several other unappreciated directions.

I was freaked out by my new appearance, because the day before we went on our summer break, I was the most popular kid in my class, class president, leader of a street gang, and, most importantly, I was the boyfriend of the most beautiful girl in the school. The day we returned to school, I had turned into the tallest, thinnest, largest-nosed boy in the class. I was about as geeky looking as a boy could be, a sore sight for all eyes. I covered the mirror in my bedroom and contemplated a life in a cave somewhere in Outer Mongolia.

Fellow students who hadn't seen me during the summer were shocked. My girlfriend, who was away at camp, had the first recorded teenage cardiac arrest in our school's history. All of a sudden, I was the butt of jokes, including "no butt" jokes, as well as tall and big nose jokes, but mostly skinny jokes.

Not used to being the kind of kid to be the butt, but, rather, the one who kicked it, I compensated for my gawkiness by becoming the best dancer in the neighborhood and the funniest. I made up jokes about my shortcomings, or rather, my tall, skinny, and big nose comings, before someone else did. If they got in the first shot, I topped them. As a result of making people laugh at my own expense, I kept all of my school and neighborhood titles and even added a new one, Class Comedian. I held on to my girlfriend and even sparked the interest of a few other girls.

Looking at me and my life from the outside, nothing had changed. Some things even improved. But on the inside, I hated the way I looked. I also hated the jokes, not the ones I told, but the ones aimed at me by others. I fought back by topping everyone with a better joke about myself. I got the idea from seeing the movie *Cyrano de Bergerac,* starring Mel Ferrer. Whenever someone made fun of his humongous nose, Cyrano topped it. Here are some examples of how I turned the joke table.

If someone said, "You're so thin all you have to do to be X-rayed is stand in front of a lightbulb," I would add, "I also have to walk into a room twice before anyone sees me."

When asked, "With that big nose, can you smoke in the shower?" I'd answer, "Yes, and my dick hasn't gotten wet in two years."

When someone asked the cliché question, "Is that your nose or are you smoking a banana?" I would answer, "You see my nose? Of course you can. Even people walking in Camden, New Jersey, can see it. Well, when I was a kid, I thought my nose was going to be an arm."

Sometimes, the jokes got cruel, so I just got crueler.

"How much would you charge to let me use you as a pipe cleaner?" "Two dollars, and, as a bonus, I'll shove my leg up your ass and Roto-Rooter you for free."

"Do you have to use a flashlight to find your skinny dick?" "Do you have to use tweezers to jerk off?"

"Yo, kid, what did your mother do, make love to a broom?" ' Yeah, because my father was busy shoving a mop up yours."

The most asked and most annoying joke was from students and adults: "How's the weather up there?" I would reply, "It's raining," and then would spit on their head. Yes, it's extreme, but it makes you the winner, and I was always the winner. Once someone felt the sting of my words and realized that my tongue was sharper than my skinny elbows, I was left alone. I was even feared. There wasn't anyone I couldn't verbally humiliate.

I even became a local celebrity, of sorts. I won first prize in the neighborhood Best Halloween Costume contest. What I did was take advantage of my nose. I put on a black cape, slicked my hair straight back, turned to show my profile, and entered as a 1956 Pontiac.

I'll tell you something wonderfully ironic. On a few of my earliest appearances on television as a stand-up comedian, I told the costume contest story, and the audiences screamed. How would I, as a young boy, ever figure that someday that self-deprecating, self-defensive joke would help to make me famous? The power of humor!

My mastery of the spoken word and my sharp, rapid-fire wit softened the hurt I felt hidden inside of me over being so thin. Humor only stops the bleeding; it does not cure the problem. That is up to you. You can spend your whole life being funny about being too thin or too fat or you can do something about it and use your sense of humor on another problem.

So throughout my teen years, in my daily attempt to gain weight, I ate three solid meals a day. I drank a quart of milk with dinner every night and then, after dinner, I would go up to the street corner to hang out with my friends at Moe's Luncheonette where I would eat a large hoagie or double-meat, double-cheese, cheesesteak sandwich and wash it down with a double-thick milkshake that had a raw egg thrown in. When I came home from hanging on the corner, before I'd turn in for the night, I'd chow down two or three chocolate Tastykakes and a big glass or two of milk.

Two years later, at age sixteen, I had grown two inches, topping me off at six foot two. Thanks to my twenty-four-month eating regimen, I hadn't gained one damn pound! I still weighed a whopping 126 pounds and thought that I was destined to remain geeky looking throughout my teens and maybe all my life, but I wouldn't give up. I kept putting the jokes out and putting the food in, plus I played sports and did manual work to stay as tuned as possible. By age eighteen, I had built up to a mighty 145 pounds, which I eventually pushed up another 10 pounds and my natural weight then fluctuated between 157 and 160. Although six foot two, I was no longer skinny; I was thin and muscular and was happy with how I looked and felt.

So when was the flip-flop? When did I suddenly have a too-much-weight problem? After all, I could always eat whatever I wanted, as much as I wanted, whenever I wanted. The eat-all-you-want knell sounded when I turned thirty. My metabolism slowed down and so did I. It was as though someone was holding back the minute hand of my internal clock. All of a sudden, a few too many French fries (with gravy on them, mind you), a slice of chocolate cake à la mode, a bacon cheeseburger, the whole hoagie or cheesesteak, and instead of the food taking a hike into outer space where it would disappear, it would now stick around; that is, around my stomach and my ass. The top weight I hit was 185 pounds, which sounds fine for someone my height, but the extra 25 pounds found love in all the wrong places.

It was as though while I was asleep, a group of invisible, masochistic elves were busy building misshapen, skin-toned sand castles all over my body. My washboard abdomen became a small, vibrating washing machine and my six-pack became the sack the six-pack came in. My v-shaped chest-to-waist turned into disgusting parentheses ( ), misnamed "love handles," as if some gorgeous woman would actually hold on to them for her dear life during sex.

Although in clothes I looked fine, because my face remained thin, I knew how I really looked and, as I was an active bachelor, so did others. Self-improvement of any kind should be just that—for the self. It is always a matter of having pride in your physical self, the same as having pride in the quality of the work you perform, regardless of the job. It is true that whatever you think of yourself is what you will project and, thereby, what others will think of you. I had to get in shape for myself.

My first plan of attack was the obvious one: decrease the amount of food and avoid the known fattening food, which is exactly what I did. It worked just fine; that is, until life played the next joke on me. I turned forty and turned down Body Change Two Boulevard.

Whatever I had been doing during the thirties decade was no longer working. I had to take other measures, a little more drastic. I cut my meals down to one a day. If, on occasion, I had to eat two or three meals, at business meetings and such, I simply spread the one meal into three. I would eat my dinner roll and coffee for breakfast, my soup and salad for lunch, and only my entrée and dessert at dinner.

I don't have to tell any of you who are around the middle of your lives how Father Time keeps messing with the middle of your body, and at an increasingly alarming rate. In addition to my self-imposed diet, I began exercising with free weights three times a week, walking three to five miles every other day. I am still doing exactly that. I have to, or I will gain weight. But even this regimen is not enough to keep off the unwanted pounds and restore the shape of yesteryear.

After trying several of the commercial diets, none of which really worked that great and all of which were either boring or a pain in the ass or both, I invented some diets of my own. One was the "Tailor Diet." I took my entire wardrobe of pants and suits to a tailor and told him to tighten all the waists to thirty-one inches and I'd be back in one month to pick up everything. This worked, until waist size thirty-one became physically impossible to achieve, even with two hundred daily crunches and some hot as hell steam baths tossed in. I returned to the tailor and had him let out an inch. I ended up going to the tailor so often, I had very little clothing left to wear and it was costing me a fortune. Plus, a few tailors were worried that my obvious psychosis could endanger their lives, so they refused to allow me in their shops.

Another one of my homemade diets was "Mr. Water." Twenty minutes before the food arrived at the table, I drank eight glasses of water. I looked like a schmuck in the restaurants, but I didn't care, because, by the time the food came, I was full of water that drowned most of my appetite. This diet worked great, but I couldn't be further than ten feet from a toilet at any given time. In retrospect, I think my leaving a date every few minutes to pee was sometimes responsible for my not getting laid. I know it was very annoying to diners at tables between me and the urinal. A list of restaurants that refused to serve me at this time in my life will be furnished upon request.

Then I came up with the "Halves Diet." I ordered, more or less, whatever I wanted, but as soon as the dish was placed in front of me, I divided everything on it into half portions, pushing the "leftovers" off to one side or, better yet, onto another plate, preferably one on a neighboring table, which pissed off people sitting there for some reason. People in restaurants get so uptight over little things.

A friend suggested a diet she created. She called it "The-I-Don't-Want-My-New-Lover-to-See-This-Body-Diet." Whenever she met someone who she believed had the potential to become her next new lover, she practically starved herself and lifted weights equal to the Empire State Building. I thought the motivation was great, but—and I hope this doesn't come off as an arrogant male brag—I usually moved too fast to have enough time to shape up. I just reread the last sentence, and it does come off in that negative way, but it is the truth, so I'm not deleting it.

One day, I had a brainstorm, an epiphany, well, a thought, anyway. I decided that if all I ate was protein, I couldn't possibly gain weight and would even lose the few pounds that bothered me. Nowadays lots of people follow this strategy on the Atkins diet. It kind of works, but come on, how do you think it looks and tastes, having tuna tartare as an appetizer, bacon as a second course, a burger and swordfish as an entrée, and pigs outside their blankets for dessert? Not to mention the fact that this diet gives you bad breath, so you'll end up looking great, but no one will want to get within six feet of you.

I've witnessed other peoples' homemade diets. One of the popular ones I have seen I entitled "The Just Diet." No matter what a person orders, they believe it won't be fattening, as long as when they order it, they use the word "just":

"I'll have *just* a double bacon cheeseburger and *just* some French fries with *just* some gravy on them and *just* a chocolate sundae for dessert and a cup of coffee with *just* a little heavy cream. Do you have Sweet'n Low?"

I was never a great believer in commercial diets. I always thought that all they did was give people false hope and make a lot of money for their creators, who could then go out and eat up a storm. If these diets really worked, there wouldn't be so many overweight and obese people in this country. We have more diet books and more fat-free food than any country in the world and we have the fattest people.

We are becoming overcrowded without increasing the population. According to the latest study, 65 percent of Americans are overweight, and 26 percent of us are obese. I have my doubts about the accuracy of this study. As I travel, I see a lot of overweight Americans, but I don't think it's anywhere near 65 percent. I think they arrived at such a high figure because of the way they test whether someone is overweight. You have to take all these weird measurements, like add the measurement of your chest to the circumference of your wrist, multiply the circumference of your forearm and add it to the total, which you then multiply by your wrist and divide the total by the distance from your Adam's apple to the middle of the back of your neck and then . . . What the hell is all this? If you want to know if you're overweight, it's so simple. All you have to do, the next time you are seated in a theater, or on a subway or a park bench, is look at the person seated next to you. If that person is still you—*bam!*—you've got to trim off some poundage.

To get people to know they're overweight and to control their food intake, scientists have also developed a pill where your brain tells your stomach it is full and to stop eating. They should invent a pill where the brain tells the ass what it looks like in Spandex.

Recently, I read about a study that claims that if you smell a banana twenty minutes before you eat, it will curb your appetite. The same is true of dog shit, by the way.

I'm sure some of the commercial diets, if followed religiously, along with an exercise regimen, may work, but in my opinion, many of them are just plain stupid. One of the most ridiculous is a pill called Orlistat. I checked it out on the Internet. (You can find anything on the Internet. Do you know that there is a website for people who stutter? I'm serious. It's www.stutter.comcomcomcomcomcom.)

Anyway, back to Orlistat. A friend of mine was using it. It supposedly helps you drop major pounds, which fall off of you like a rock slide. Well, it is true that there is a slide, but it is not fat or rocks. One of the side effects is "loose, oily bowels." Once I read that, I couldn't follow a fat person down the street without looking on the pavement for a trail. I know. I'm a little disturbed.

A big problem is the excuses, or false reasons, people invent for why they are overweight. Understand, if you are heavy, and you are happy, truly happy, looking the way you do and not the least bit concerned about how you are damaging your health and cutting down the length of your life, then stay the way you are, eat all you want, whenever you want, and to hell with what people think. Let their words roll off your back like water off a duck's back, or like a cannon ball off an elephant's ass, whichever may be more apropos in your case.

However, if you are unhappy and/or worried about being fat, then do something about it. The first thing you can do is to stop bullshitting yourself. I had an uncle who claimed that the only reason he looked like a hippo in trousers was because he retained water. I remember when I was a little boy at a family gathering, after hearing this claim for the millionth time, I whispered to my father, "Yeah, the Atlantic Ocean." It is true that some people retain more water than others, but there are pills and treatment to combat it. You don't have to look like a beached whale that moved inland.

The most popular excuse, maybe even a myth, is "my weight is all genetic." It is true that genes have something to do with everything. I have a friend who is humungous, maybe 350 pounds. He blames his genes for why he is not able to get into his jeans. Meanwhile I have watched him stuff food in his mouth like it's incriminating evidence he must hide from the police. As he was finishing off his second helping of food, he started in again about the family genetic that gave everyone with his last name, even those who had married into the family, ironically, a disposition toward gaining enormous amounts of weight. I was tired of hearing this bullshit and posed the following argument:

"If it is true that for some people genetics can be blamed for being fat or obese, then how come when they freed all the concentration camps in Europe near the end of World War II, they didn't find one fat woman lying there saying, 'I don't know what it is with me. I eat a piece of bread and drink one glass of water a day and look at me; I'm a blimp?' So take that ten-pound wedge of cow's ass out of your mouth and the bullshit out of your head and lose the goddamn weight, before you can legally be registered as a condominium." (I'm happy to announce that today he is down to about two hundred pounds and no longer has to grease his hips to get into a cab.)

There was a popular study that supposedly supported the genetic theory. Scientists altered the eating gene in one group of mice, which they claimed was the "thermostat" that regulated food intake. When the scientists turned up the thermostat, the mice stuffed themselves with food, until they were four or five times the size of their fellow mice, whose genes were not altered. The scientists then claimed that the fat mice were not aware that they were so much bigger than their thin brothers and sisters and also didn't realize how they looked, so they kept eating. Their supposition was that this was applicable to human beings. Well, we humans have something that mice don't have—mirrors!

Scientists can conduct a million experiments and studies, but I believe that the bottom line is, "You are what you stuff down your throat." Therefore, you are in control or can get in control and do something about it. It's not easy. As a matter of fact, it is unbelievably difficult, but a lot of things in life are, especially the most important— among which are health, a long life, and happiness. Being fat interferes with all three, and this is a scientific fact!

But let's say I'm wrong about genetics and it is proven beyond a doubt that they are responsible for some people becoming fat or obese. Well, there are lots of negative genetic dispositions, such as alcoholism, drug addiction, learning disabilities, etc., but people work to overcome them and they do! And so can you!

Each of us can make up an excuse for weighing too much or gaining weight. I spend a lot of time on the road, traveling around the country from club to club, hotel to hotel, always on the go and not always able to eat properly or exercise enough. Recently, I was 10 pounds over my normal weight of 162 pounds and feeling like shit, a lot of shit, physically, mentally, and psychologically.

What did I do about it? First, I stopped using the excuse that it was a natural result of working extensively on the road. Then I initiated my latest diet, "Combo." It is a modified combination of many of my old diets. I drink a glass or two of water (or vodka—an improvement) twenty minutes before my meal. I don't order fattening food, no bread, and no dessert. By drawing a 50 percent battle line, I don't eat all of anything. I keep only healthy snacks in my hotel rooms and my home. Whenever it's at all possible, even for only fifteen or twenty minutes, I exercise, including power walks. Most importantly, I don't get upset about what I can't change, such as my body's natural shifting sands of time and, above all, I keep my sense of humor about it and laugh, especially at myself, hoping that I will physically laugh my ass off, or, at least, the parts of it that I wish would leave. The result? I now weigh 242 pounds. Of course, I'm kidding. That's my job. The truth? My weight is on target, and I'm going to keep it there!

I believe that until you lose the weight, or you have decided to live and die fat, the intake you should increase daily is a big serving of humor and laughter. Now I am going to give you some fat jokes to help you do this. That's right, jokes about being fat. But instead of being offended, laugh. Maybe you can use them to counterattack anyone who looks at you or speaks to you in an offensive way. When people hear you make fun of yourself and they laugh, they are less anti-you and, maybe, might even become more tolerant of you and others who weigh a lot. I know from my personal experiences, when I was the victim of looks and comments, how much they hurt. I also know how much humor took away the pain, replacing pain with laughter.

Maybe you could even create your own funny fat jokes about yourself. But even if humor works and makes your life less unbearable, don't stop there. Rethink and maybe decide to get rid of the cause of your pain. Do something to lose the weight. Don't let your butt be the butt of others' jokes. Lose the extra weight so you can live longer, so you can laugh longer, genuine huge belly laughs but not from a genuinely huge belly. Okay, here we go:

You know you're fat and have to diet if . . .

You sit back in a recliner chair that didn't have a reclining feature until you sat in it.

You sit on a whoopee cushion and the escaping air kills six people.

When you sweat, heat lightning shoots around in your blouse.

A kid accidentally hits you with a Frisbee and it sticks. And you don't notice.

When you sneeze, your overcoat splits up the back seam.

When you cough, your hat rips.

When you fart, the coat on the person behind you splits and his hat rips.

You get in your car and it crushes the cat that was sleeping underneath it.

You laugh and a man's fly unzips.

It's been years since you've seen your dick.

When you lie down on a beach, people who forgot to put on sunblock gather close to you.

You're lying on a beach and well-meaning people try to push you back into the ocean chanting, "Save the whales!" And a real whale yells, "Mother" (or "Father").

When you stop waving to friends, the bottom of your arm keeps flapping for another ten minutes.

When you walk, you hear the swishing sound that corduroy makes and you're naked.

You're jogging or quickly walking down the street and you hear applause behind you and there is no one there. Your ass is telling you something.

If you don't feel well . . . if you're embarrassed about how you look . . . if you don't like yourself . . . if you're worried about your health . . . if you are afraid to die . . . if you love your family and friends . . . right, this one isn't a joke—neither is allowing yourself to get or remain fat. Lose the weight. Do it sensibly and slowly. As much time as it took you to put it on, allow for taking it off, but do it. The other thing I am telling you is while and until you lose the weight, keep your sense of humor and, above all else, laugh, laugh, and laugh!

PS—A Mystery Solved

As I was driving through the desert one day, I had an epiphany. It provided me with the answer to one of the world's longest and most baffling mysteries. Very, very fat people cannot see their feet. So if they step in dog shit, they're not 100 percent sure they did. What they have to do is back up, kick off their shoe up into the air, and look at it. And this is why you always see only one shoe on the highway.

Check one of the following:

☐ A—That joke made me laugh until my stomach hurt.

☐ B—I didn't get it.

☐ C—It made me hungry.

☐ D—It wasn't funny, you thin asshole!

☐ E—I'm going to throw out all the single shoes in my closet and lose the weight!

Fear of Flying

Everyone has fears. Regardless of what you're afraid of, or how ridiculous it may seem to others, it is very real to you. People can explain rationally why you shouldn't be afraid, but that usually doesn't lessen the horror or make the fear disappear. Laughter can't do it either, but it can help shrink your personal monster enough so that instead of looking way up at this frightening giant, you will be able to stand toe-to-toe with him, look him straight in the eyes, and deal with him staring back into yours. Who knows, you might even scare the shit out of him, and it'll be his turn to find the laughs.

All people who deal with fears are in the same boat, or, as in my case, on the same airplane. I have a chronic fear of flying. I have had it from my first flight, and having flown on thousands of flights since then has not relieved my fear an iota. For example, at this very moment, I am sitting on a 747 jumbo jet flying 38,000 feet above the Atlantic Ocean on a fourteen-hour flight from Atlanta, Georgia, to Cape Town, South Africa. It has been an extremely smooth flight so far, so I would describe my present condition, in medical jargon, as scared shitless.

I could tell I was not alone in my fear by looking at the faces of people in the boarding area when the flight was called and they got out of their uncomfortable, but safe, plastic seats and prepared to board. I could tell which ones were no longer thinking about sunny walks on the beach and yummy meals in the vacation moonlight. My guess is that even those who are great at faking their feelings and hiding their thoughts were thinking the same thing I was: "This giant piece of steel is going to drop out of the sky faster than the dot-com stock market and we're all going to die!" In fact, every time I take those thirteen steps down the ramp toward the open door of the plane, I am always hoping someone will run in and yell, "Stop! There's a call from the governor!" It has never happened, and even though I still have hopes, I adjust my rubber underwear and board the plane.

When you suffer from a fear, there are so many things that are catastrophic for you that others don't notice or couldn't care less about. For example, the other day I read a tiny newspaper article that catapulted me into a top-level panic attack. The airlines are beginning to offer live TV on planes. To most people, the normal ones, this might have been welcome news. Me? I immediately thought that with my luck, I'll be watching CNN in my seat, and they'll be talking about a bomb on a plane. Then they'll cut to a live, close-up shot of my face in the window of that plane, watching CNN!

In defense of myself and others like me, I must state that there are lots of sound and rational reasons to be afraid of flying. For those of us who weren't paying attention to the physics teacher in high school, the sheer improbability that a mega-ton metal tube could hurtle through the air at 600 miles per hour, 35,000 feet above earth, and that any passenger could actually survive, even with a seatbelt, requires two key assumptions: faith in the design of the airplane and confidence in the pilot, crew, and airline personnel who now control your destiny. Yet the whole flying experience is filled with evidence that can shake your faith and confidence. The key to managing your fear is to understand, or try to suppose that some of that evidence is just plain funny.

Let's start with the pilot of this plane I'm on right now. We'd been up in the air for about two hours, when the pilot came out of the cockpit for his visitation period. You know, that's where the pilot walks around saying hello to everyone. I hate that! To me, that's like being in the back of a car and, all of a sudden, the driver climbs over the seat. Who the hell is driving?

I once had a pilot scare the shit out of me on a *nonstop flight* from New York to L.A. He came out of the cockpit to greet passengers, recognized me, walked over, and said, "David Brenner, where're you going?"

It's my humble opinion that airline announcements need vast improvement. One that scares the hell out of me is when the pilot announces that we are 34,000 feet up in the air. I don't want to hear that! I want to hear we're twenty-five or thirty-five feet above the ground. When I fly, I like to look in people's bedroom windows, and I like to think that if anything goes wrong, I can simply jump out. Sure, this may sound stupid to you, but to me, although there may be some doubts about the physiological probability of survival, it is psychologically sound, an intelligent coping strategy. Besides, you should never underestimate the healing powers of denial. You would never want your surgeon to tell you that he is going to cut out forty-four feet of your intestines, right? It wouldn't matter if you had five hundred feet of that tube inside you; the thought of forty-four feet of anything being pulled out of you is goddamn scary! So, in my perfect world, it is two inches of intestines and thirty-five feet of air.

Other expressions inducing panic in me, and I assume in millions of passengers, are, "We are making our *final* approach," and "This is the *termination* of Flight 107." The airlines should never use the words "final" and "termination," unless they are talking about the end of turbulence. Then there is the safety instruction "In case of a decrease in the cabin pressure, an oxygen mask will drop from the ceiling. Just put it on and *breathe normally.*" This is not possible to do when you are plunging 34,000 feet out of the sky. I've been on a few flights when the plane dropped suddenly and the oxygen masks dropped, and every time, I sucked in half the air in the cabin, the mask itself, and, one time, the toupee of the guy seated in front of me. Plus, I'm always afraid that, with my luck, the little door above my head will open, and out will drop a pair of dirty socks on a cord. "Whose goddamn laundry is this?"

Another one of my fear-inducing favorites is, "In case of a water landing . . ." First of all, how the hell is a big-ass mountain of metal going to "land" in water? Did you ever see a three-hundred-pound man jump into a pool? He doesn't land, he *explodes!* That's as stupid as a "crash landing." It's not a crash landing; it's a crash, period! And why is it that after a crash, with millions of pieces scattered over two square miles, the "black box" is in perfect shape, not even dented? Why aren't planes big black boxes with wings?

Another thing that reinforces my fear is the stupidity that's evident in the design of airplanes. Recently, a few airline companies announced that over the next two years they are going to conduct intensive cooperative studies to determine whether we need more legroom on airplanes. Two years of studies! Why don't they just look inside of a plane? Everyone is crunched up like Quasimodo. The only one who is comfortable in an airline seat is a penguin and that's because his legs come straight out of his ass.

The most frightening part of the whole airline experience for me is going to the bathroom. First of all, who designed them—a sadistic dwarf? They're so small, you can hardly get inside, and to stand up, you have to be a contortionist. Then, when you throw the latch to lock the door, scary things start to happen: Fans try to blow your head off; blue water starts swishing around in the toilet. And did you ever make the mistake of pressing down on the sink plunger to empty the water? (Excuse me, sink? More like a metal dollhouse teacup.) Talk about scary. When you push the plunger, it makes a sound like some kind of deranged, prehistoric monster.

I like the signs in the airplane bathroom that read, "As a Courtesy to the Next Passenger, Please Clean the Sink." Excuse me, but I just paid $2,300 for an airplane ticket, and I've got to clean the sink? The other sign in the bathroom I always wondered about is the one above a slit in the wall: "For Used Razor Blades." Who in their right mind would try to shave on an airplane? You'd come out of the bathroom looking like you ran into Freddy Kruger in there.

By the way, not to get too personal, but I never sit on the toilet in an airplane. I'm always afraid I'm going to get sucked out over Oklahoma. The last thing I want to do is to die on a toilet in an airplane. "Now, a news bulletin. The body of David Brenner, comedian, was found in the middle of an Oklahoma barley field today. He was sitting on a toilet. More laughs at eleven."

Of course, there have been times I have had to sit down, especially when I made the mistake of eating airplane food. Inevitably on these rare occasions, just as I get started, the pilot makes an announcement: "Fasten your seat belts." There are no seat belts in there. You start pulling the toilet paper around you. Worse than this is when the pilot says, "Return to your seat!" I can just hear the water cooler conversation and see the reams of e-mails: "We were on a flight with David Brenner, the comedian, and he did the funniest thing. He came running out of the bathroom with his pants around his ankles, and . . ."

Still, no matter how well designed your plane is and how competent your crew, there's no getting around the fact that flying is just plain dangerous, and that sometimes shit happens. The most frightening flight I have ever had was a night flight from Los Angeles to the Cayman Islands.

Shortly after takeoff, I was in the bathroom when I heard an explosion, followed by the plane being tossed around as if it were being attacked by a giant with a battering ram, or worse, a terrorist. As a result of the explosion, I lost the hearing in my left ear immediately and heard ringing in my right ear. I was also pretty banged up, after being thrown around in a small space.

I managed to open the door and step out. Everyone was strapped tightly in their seats; some were hurt, but not too badly. I could hear people screaming and crying. As I worked my way back to my seat, I saw people praying.

The plane was literally dropping out of the sky, headed straight down. We dropped ten thousand feet in minutes, maybe seconds. We plunged so fast, everyone looked like Don King. All I kept thinking was, "Shit, what a stupid way to go!" Even in what looked like the last moments of my being, I also learned something. You get a whole different perspective on life when the plane you're on drops ten thousand feet and you see, not your life, but your dick pass in front of your eyes.

Miraculously, or so it seemed to those of us who thought this was the end, the plane stopped falling and leveled off. The pilot came on and apologized for not talking to us sooner, but he was busy. Really?

Then he first told us that all was well and we were landing in Austin, Texas. He explained that the windshield had imploded, but, luckily, neither he nor his cocaptain or the flight attendant who had gone in to serve them food was hurt. He had to drop the plane because of the loss of oxygen. That seemed like an excellent decision to me, because it meant we were going to live. He told us that arrangements were being made to put us up in a motel for the night and a new windshield would be flown in from another city, along with a specialist to install it. No one complained about the inconvenience. Only an idiot would. We were alive!

When we landed safely in Austin, Texas, and were waiting for buses to take us to the motel, a woman approached me and asked me to help make her ten-year-old daughter feel better. The child was traumatized by what happened. She was trembling and couldn't stop crying. I couldn't believe that she was actually turning to a comedian for help. I love Richard Lewis, but he is one of the last people on this earth that I would call upon to help calm my nerves.

It was complete lunacy in my opinion, but the little girl looked so scared and helpless that I agreed to try. I sat next to her and spoke softly, like spy to spy.

"I heard this is entirely your fault. Do you have any idea how much that new windshield is going to cost you?"

She gave a little smile. It was a start.

"You can forget your allowance for at least forty years."

This time, she emitted a solid giggle. I was on the right track.

"And, if you think that experience on the plane was frightening, wait until you get a load of Austin, Texas."

This time the little girl's laugh was right from the deep belly. She was fine. I felt great and so appreciative that a toss of the genetic coin had given me the wonderful and powerful gift of humor.

So when you feel that your fear, regardless of what it may be, is beginning to overwhelm you, try to find one funny thing about it, then two, then three, and as many as you can. Then, the next time you are at your computer or have a paper and pen in hand, write about the fear, but don't think frightened, think funny. Read what you wrote to a friend or even a stranger and see if they look scared or if they laugh.

You can even e-mail me what you wrote. Hell, what you write might even be in my next book. Damn, I just created a new fear for myself, the fear that people are going to want me to pay them for what they write. There must be something funny about that. Hmmmm, let me think.

Dentists

Show me a person who isn't afraid of a dentist, and I'll show you a person without teeth. Well, let's find some laughs, so the next time you go to a dentist, you'll be able to handle it. I need this as much or more than you, because I'm terrified of the dentist. I'd rather have a far-sighted armadillo operate on my testicles.

I wasn't afraid of dentists as a child. That's because we couldn't afford to go to one. Well, that isn't entirely true. It was more a matter of choice. You know what being poor is like, or maybe you're lucky enough not to know. It is said that money gives you choices. Well, so does poverty. We had to make such choices as, "Should we get a couch or a front door?"

Another choice in my house was whether to go to a real dentist or wait for the free clinics to come to our school with college students who were still deciding whether to go into dentistry or modern dance. The clinics would put on a puppet show to relax the children who would soon be in the grip of this heavy-handed novice sadist. In their show, they presented puppets named Mr. Tooth, Mr. Brush, and Mr. Cavity. They never showed you Mr. Pain and Mr. Blood.

The other choice was to decide between going to a real dentist and getting a pair of new shoes. My parents couldn't afford both. My older brother opted for the new shoes, so he could be "cool." I opted for the new shoes, too, so I could be just like my cool older brother. My sister was smart. She went to the dentist, so she ended up with beautiful, arrow straight, white teeth. Her feet paid the price. Whenever we went anywhere, my brother and I carried her, and she smiled for us all night.

As a result of the cool-shoe decision, I ended up with fillings in all my teeth. I could've given tours of the silver mine I had in my mouth. When I started earning money exceeding the costs of essentials, I decided to get my teeth fixed and went to a real dentist in Manhattan.

Now, I'm going to tell you a story that was physically, excruciatingly painful, costly, and traumatic, but I am going to make comments and embellish it, so that it will become hysterically funny. You are probably not a professional comedian. You may not even have a keen sense of humor. Regardless, you can learn to look for the funny part in any event. Even one joke will ease some of the gloom. Now, keeping in mind the real horror I was experiencing, read and learn how I made it all better with humor and laughter. Honestly, you can do the same.

The dentist took X rays and told me that he could fix my whole mouth with caps, or, as he called them, crowns. When I got the bill for the first one he did, I understood why they call them crowns—because you are getting the royal shaft. If something that small costs that much, my nose must be worth millions. I always admired anyone who, when they sneezed or blew their nose, could use only one Kleenex. I range between a dish towel and a bedsheet.

Anyway, the dentist gave me a shot of Novocaine, which I hate. For hours afterward, you can't feel your lip. You think you're saying, "I'll have a slice with pepperoni," and he's hearing, "Lyle hep lice who wit poppa Corroni." When you drink, you dribble down your shirt, and you walk out of a restaurant without noticing the piece of chicken hanging out of your mouth.

The dentist performed a root canal and put a cap on my tooth. When I looked in the mirror, I almost broke down in joyful tears. For the first time in my life, I had a real tooth in my mouth like a real human being. Like someone with enough money to live on a street where every other house is missing.

I was flying to L.A. that afternoon. I was so proud of my real tooth that I smiled at everyone in the airport, even the people sleeping at the gate. On the plane, I kept running back to the bathroom to look in the mirror at my tooth. I was so happy. Then the Novocaine wore off. All of a sudden, I had a hernia in my jaw. The pain was blinding. I swore to myself that when I got back to New York I was going to cap the dentist's dick.

We finally landed in L.A. I had a friend meeting me at the airport. I told him that he had to get me to his dentist right away. He made the call and drove as fast as he could to his dentist, who took me as soon as we arrived.

The dentist put me in the chair and X-rayed my jaw. My luck, the part of the tooth that remained under the cap was abscessed. He gave me a shot of Novocaine, hung a piece of chicken from my lip, and started drilling.

After a moment or two, I realized he was drilling into my cap. I pushed his hand away and said, "What are you going to do about the hole you just put in my first, only, and brand-new cap?"

He said, "I'm going to fill it."

For the next six weeks I was working on the road with a cap in my mouth that had a silver filling in it. That's like getting a glass eye with a frame around it, or, worse, a wooden leg with varicose veins.

Of course, I got it fixed and, eventually, my whole mouth fixed. It was worth it, but the pain was horrible every time I went to the dentist. I think someone should invent a device, and I'll put money into it, that fits between the dentist's legs. When he's about to hurt you, you can put just the slightest pressure on his testicles and wave your finger at him. "You hurt me; I'll hurt you." This would be a great advancement in painless dentistry.

So did you laugh at my dental disaster? Then next time laugh at yours.

Pets

I know I'd better preface this or I'm going to get umpteen million pieces of hate mail and e-mails. I'll be called all kinds of nasty names, like "shithead," "double asshole," and the one that makes it to the top of the list every time, regardless of the motivating reason—"Jew bastard."

Okay, in the name of not being called names, I prequalify the following by swearing to you that since the day I was born, I have never mistreated or hurt an animal that had more than two legs, never, so help me. I believe that animals are fantastic. I have taken about sixty photographic safaris in Africa just to see them in their natural habitat.

I am opposed to zoos and any other form of confinement. On school trips to the Philadelphia Zoo, I was always trying to figure out how to free the animals. I was also trying to figure out how to get Sheila to go behind the monkey house with me, so I was not a total altruist.

I am also against using animals for the sake of amusement, labor, and clothing, or to make money. Sometimes animals have also expressed their opposition toward the same.

Recently, a "working" elephant in Nepal, India, walked off the job before quitting time and went berserk, reminiscent of human behavior, except instead of going home to get a gun, he pushed his weight around. He crushed a dozen people and trampled twenty-five huts and three police stations, before turning the foot on himself.

You might recall another berserk elephant incident in Hawaii a few years ago. A circus elephant had enough of show business and being on the road. He became depressed over having to go out every night and balance on a ball like a schmuck. First he crushed his trainer or agent, I forget which, and then ran amok in Honolulu, overturning cars, demolishing anything in his way.

In both cases, on the Nepal job, and in the circus, all the other elephants said that each of the perpetrating elephants was quiet, always kept to himself, was a former Scout, and sang in their church choirs. I think it is such human qualities that endear us to animals.

It is incidents such as the ones above that reinforce my belief that elephants and other nondomesticated animals belong in their natural environments. Fuzzy little newborn chicks never expect to end up sitting in a basket with chocolate Easter candy and being manhandled by human toddlers. Baby turtles have no idea that some of them will be selected to have numbers painted on their shells and be forced to "race" to be the first to cross the line. Exotic birds were meant to fly freely, high above the jungles of the world, not to be perched on the shoulder of some stoned guy in Key West who wears an obnoxious flowered shirt and hustles tourists to take a photo with his fine feathered partner. The purpose of the porpoise is not to swim across a tank in southern Florida or California, with a person holding on to his fin, or to leap in the air in unison to get the rewards of a fish and the clapping of human hands. Tropical fish were meant to grace the warm waters of the world, not spend their lifetimes swimming in an endless circle inside a glass bowl that sits on a dining room table in Buffalo, New York. Horses were not put on earth to run their asses off so we humans can win money. I'm not going to even start with the animals that end up wrapped around our necks, waists, or feet, or whose heads are stuffed and nailed above our fireplaces, or whose feet are stuffed to be used as doorstops, or that are subjected to scientific experiments. I think I've made my point.

But I have to admit that it seems to me that there are some animals that were meant to live with Man. A good way of separating those who were born to be free and those who were put on earth to be our pets is simple. If the animal has to be locked up in a cage or in a house, in order not to run away from us, then it is obvious that that animal wants to be free. We humans should understand this. It's why we invented the automobile and divorce.

Most dogs and cats pass this qualifying test. There is enough proof from early cave paintings around the world that they have shared our spaces and lives since we first began walking upright, and no one's ever found a drawing of a cave that had a door on it, so one has to assume that these two species voluntarily stayed with our cave-drawing ancestors, which is more than I would've done.

I have no objection to this animal/human arrangement. I take umbrage not with the pets, but with the pet owners and their treatment of their animals. I'm not talking about cruelty, just the opposite—pets being placed on a pedestal by their owners, high up, exalted above all human beings.

Rarely do pets go to bed hungry, but 25 percent of the children in this country do, every night. Rarely are pets abused, and if they are, the owners are punished quickly and to the maximum of the law. Often not so with our children. Pets are cuddled, hugged, kissed, protected, fawned over, and loved. Not all of our children are. Few domesticated pets sleep in the streets. Hundreds of thousands of adult humans do. There are more children in orphanages than pets in shelters. No wonder the SPCA, the Society for the Prevention of Cruelty to Animals, was formed years before the establishment of the SPCC, the Society for the Prevention of Cruelty to Children.

I remember sitting in a packed movie theater watching the opening scene of the movie *Patton*. The camera panned a battlefield slowly, showing hundreds of dead and mutilated bodies of young soldiers. Then it panned a dog tied up to a tank and everyone in the theater gasped. That's the moment I came up with an idea of how to end the Vietnam conflict, which can be used in all the other senseless wars our government leaders get us into. What we do is kidnap a couple hundred household pets. Then, every day, we send to all the print media and TV news outlets photos of a noose around a dog's neck, a gun to a cat's head, or a meat cleaver resting on a parrot's neck. We include a note that reads, "If one more American soldier dies in this unnecessary conflict, we are going to kill Rex, Tabby, and Polly."

You know the owners of these pets and other domesticated-animal lovers will have shit fits and spring into action, go into an uproar, march on Washington, make demands. "Stop the war now, you political warmongering assholes!" Strange, isn't it, that no one would do that for Rex, Tabby, and Polly if they were two teenage soldiers and a young army nurse?

There should be a balance between the treatment and tender understanding we give to pets and that which we give to humans. The lack of this humanity to humanity, and to the other animal life with which we share this world, is one of my biggest gripes.

You might think that this is a subject about which even I don't see or can't find the funny side. Wrong, my dear reader. I think humans and their pets are hysterical, and I can't imagine I'm the only one who thinks that pets are wonderful and their masters are ridiculous. For those who agree, let me give you my take on the subject, in an effort to make life in the world of stupid pet masters less annoying and, hopefully, funnier. Here's how you appear to me and lots of others. Think of it as a little pet food for thought.

Let's begin by looking at a recent survey by Waltham that I read. It was titled: "Percent of People Who Say They . . ."

Talk to their pets: 100 percent. Now, I understand saying such things as stay, sit, fetch, or kill. It drives me crazy to hear people hold complete conversations with an animal. Although adorable and comparatively bright, house pets have a brain ranging in size from a golf ball down to a BB and an IQ even lower than that of an airport screener. I used to ask people if their pet ever answered back, but gave up after a lot of them said, "No, but we can read each other's minds." The pet owner couldn't do the same thing with human beings, because I never had my face slapped.

Think pets understand what they say: 97 percent. Even more frightening than this is that the 3 percent who don't believe their pets understand them still talk to them. Then again, this is also true of most human husbands and wives. When I first moved to New York, I lived in a one-room apartment in a building on East 69th Street. There was an older woman who had a little dog, and whenever she was leaving the building, she would say to her dog, "Cuddles, say good morning to Joe, the doorman." About the one-hundredth time I heard it, I cupped my hands and in a dog's voice, said-barked, "Good morning, Joe." You know she told everyone in the building about the talking Cuddles and went to her grave believing he actually greeted Joe.

Display photos of their pets: 84 percent. I can't tell you how often a complete stranger on an airplane or in a restaurant has whipped out a snapshot of their cat or dog to show me. I finally figured out a way to put a stop to it. I, in turn, whip out a photo of "my" hunting rifle, aligning the end of the barrel with their pet's cute, itty-bitty, furry head.

Think of their pets as their children: 78 percent. How could anyone with half a brain think they gave birth to an iguana? I could understand having sex with an iguana, but giving birth to one?

Are more tolerant of their pets' shortcomings than of their spouses' or children's: 75 percent. If you don't believe this, take a shit on your living room rug and see what happens.

Allow their pets to sleep on their beds: 76 percent. This calls for more than a comment. This calls for one of life's true experiences.

Years ago, when I was a fun-loving bachelor in Manhattan, full of spunk and heavy doses of testosterone, I met a gorgeous young woman walking along Fifth Avenue, my favorite location for meeting gorgeous young women, but that is for the book I'll never write. Words were exchanged, smiles, laughs, a little tap touch here and there, and a dinner date set for that night.

The dinner was delicious and so was the woman, full of life, quick to laugh, bright, articulate, and built from the original mold. After dinner, we enjoyed a hand-holding-and-stopping-to-kiss walk on the streets of the Upper West Side. I lived on the Upper East Side, so we went to her place.

It was one of those chemical reactions in which each person physically wants the other person with the same degree of desire and intensity, so, in a matter of minutes, we were naked on her water bed. Things were heating up to the point where I started fearing being boiled to death (I love when I am living a movie scene, because life is not a movie), but the entire time everything was progressing perfectly, I had this uneasy feeling that we were being watched. I tried to shake it, but couldn't. We rolled over. She was on top. In the space between her right arm and her large right breast, I saw a pair of eyes staring at me at quite a height off the floor. My first thought was an eight-foot-tall husband, but the shape of the eyes was not human. I thought I was being calm, but my voice even scared me.

"What the hell is that?!"

"You don't like what I'm doing, David?"

"I love it, but I love life more. Do you collect glass animal eyes that move?"

She laughed. "Oh, that's my pet ocelot, GiGi."

"What's an ocelot?"

"A cat, like a small tiger. Now turn over."

"Are you crazy?"

I pulled myself free, ripped off my leather mask, and switched on the bedroom light. Jesus Christ, there it was, just like she said. A tiger stretched out on the mantelpiece. The cat yawned and her fangs were long, sharp, and I just knew longing for Jew dick.

I don't ever remember being able to do what you see in cartoons, where the drawn character rises several feet into the air while in a prone position and then takes off like a rocket, but I swear I did it that night. Somehow, while strafing inches off the floor, I scooped up my clothes and got dressed and rocketed out of the apartment, down the stairs, and out onto Columbus Avenue. As soon as my feet came down to earth, I took off for the nearest cab and to the safety of my jungle-animal-free apartment.

That was the night I learned the difference between pussy and *pussy*.

I'll tell you another wild story about an unusual pet. In the beginning of my career, I was living in a tiny, one-room apartment on the Upper East Side of Manhattan. One day, when I opened my door to leave the apartment, I saw a rat sitting right outside. I immediately slammed the door shut and called the doorman to report it. He said he would send up Louie, the handyman. I told him to tell Louie to knock on my door when he had gotten rid of the rat.

A few minutes later, I heard the recognizable and familiar, near-deafening noise of a baseball bat slamming against my door and on the hall rug, accompanied by the loud cursing of Louie. "Take that and that, you rat bastard!" Louie was rumored to moonlight as a loan shark enforcer for some mob boss, so he was proficient with a base-ball bat. I guess that whenever he wielded his bat, he probably always said, "Take that, you rat bastard." A professional rut.

Louie knocked gently on my door. "Yo, you can come out now, David. I got the cocksucker." I opened the door and there was Louie smiling ear to ear, holding up a small, brown paper bag. He shook it, as if to prove he had made the kill. I guess he had to do this in his other job, too, but with a much bigger bag, of course.

We rode down to the lobby together. The doorman, Joe, and the superintendent, Mike, were there. The four of us discussed the hunt and the kill. I mentioned that I had never seen a brown and white rat before. Louie said he hadn't either and that the rat looked at him in a cute sort of way before he bashed in its head.

Just then, the elevator opened and out stepped a very shy and dainty man who had just moved into the building a few weeks earlier. He approached us, a very concerned look on his face.

"Excuse me. I'm Mr. Rabe in 7B. Did anyone report seeing my pet gerbil, Baby Barney? He ran out when I opened the door to get the morning paper."

I had no idea what a gerbil was. I was born and raised in the ghetto streets of Philly and spent my entire adult life in big cities. Dogs, cats, sparrows, pigeons, cockroaches, goldfish, silverfish, light-ning bugs, house flies, mosquitoes, mice, and rats were my animal kingdom. Well, I thought I knew rats.

Louie looked at the man and asked him if this animal of his was brown and white with a cute face. The man got optimistically tearful and said, "Yes, have you found Baby Barney? Where is he?"

Louie, the New Yorker, attacked as only a New Yorker can. He held up the bag. "Baby Barney's here. Why the hell did you buy some-thing that looks like a rat, you asshole?!"

Doorman Joe from the Lower East Side piped in, "You know pets ain't allowed. It's in your lease."

Superintendent Mike from Bedford Stuyvesant threw the final punch. "I could get you thrown out of this building, if I wanted, you schmuck!"

Baby Barney's daddy was thunderstruck and almost fainted when Louie offered him the paper bag. "You wanna give Baby Barney his final resting place down the incinerator or you want me to do it?" The man backed up and retreated into the elevator, pushed his floor button, and was gone. I felt to blame for Baby Barney's horrific demise.

"Maybe, we could buy the guy some flowers or something."

The three guys looked at me like I was crazy.

Mike said, "What for? You wanna date him or something?"

They laughed. I smiled. Louie walked away with the bat over his shoulder, real professional-like, and the paper bag swinging in his hand. I walked out, went down the block to the flower shop on the corner, and sent a huge assortment of flowers to Mr. Rabe and Baby Barney. I signed it, "A Friend of the Gerbils of the World."

Mr. Rabe moved out a couple months later. We had bumped into each other on the elevator a few times, but he had learned enough about New Yorkers not to speak to me or anyone else. I was never sure if he knew I was the accomplice to Baby Barney's murder and also the man who sent the flowers. I hoped he didn't. I also hope that the statute of limitations on gerbil murders has expired, just in case Mr. Rabe reads this book.

I'll tell you one animal I know little about but feel genuinely sorry for—the horse. The only horses I saw growing up were either pulling fruit-and-vegetable wagons or had poles shoved into their backs which came out through their stomachs and were imbedded in a wooden floor that went around and around in a circle as organ music played and children squealed as they rose up and down on the backs of these brightly colored and bejeweled wooden animals.

I never had a desire to ride a real horse, but when I was a young man, a young woman talked me into going horseback riding up a mountain in Lake Tahoe, Nevada. I had zero desire to climb up on the back of a horse, but the nth-degree desire I had to climb up on the back of this woman sent me leaping onto the saddle.

After a briefing by our guide, we each mounted a horse. As soon as my legs straddled the animal, I hated it. When we started moving in a single-line procession of one horse following another, I hated it even more. About thirty minutes into it, just as we were reaching the height of the mountain trail, I reached the height of my hate of horse-back riding. Oh, I forgot to tell you that I suffer from acrophobia, the fear of heights. Just looking down from the corner of my eye caused me to break out in a cold sweat. My only choice was to stare at the ass of the horse in front of mine. Now, I am an ass man, but more of the female human kind.

I called for the guide to stop. He did, giving the hand signal taught to us in class which, of course, I had completely forgotten immediately. It might have been because it closely resembled a Nazi salute. Something else to hate about this experience. The straight line of horses came to a complete halt, and the guide called out to me.

"What's the problem, Mr. Brenner?"

Everyone's eyes were on me, including the horses'. Maybe it was my imagination, but my horse's eyes were glowing red.

"Well, I'm just a little bit concerned," I called out. "This is a helluva drop, a few thousand feet, I'd guess, and, well, the horse's feet are right on the tippy edge, and I —"

"Hooves," he interrupted semi-angrily. "Horses don't have feet; they have hooves."

"Whatever they are that hang down to the ground from each corner of their bodies are very, very close to the edge of the cliff."

This time, he addressed everyone, not just me, a big smile on his face. "Let me reassure all of you that these horses are surefooted."

"Don't you mean sure-hoofed?" I yelled out, unable to resist.

Some fellow riders chuckled; most glared along with the guide, who continued.

"They have been doing this for years." Now he looked directly at me. "And your horse, sir, has gone up this mountain six to ten times a day for nearly twenty years. Now, if there are no other questions, we'll —"

"Twenty years? Six to ten times a day?" I screamed, my voice breaking up from fear.

I don't remember if the instructor answered me, ignored me, threw a rock at me, or what, because I was deep in thought. I was imagining my horse getting up every morning in what was probably a cold stall, being given a few handfuls of hay to eat, and then going outside where some 240-pound housewife from Albuquerque would climb up on his back and up he would go, up the same damn mountain, six times a day, every day for nearly twenty years. I felt his pain. I read his mind. He awakened this morning and said, "I'm mad as hell, and I won't take it anymore!" This was the day he was going to end it all, leap off the mountain with me on his back. No way!

"He's not taking me with him," I yelled, and jumped off the suicidal horse's back and started walking down the mountain. I've never climbed onto another horse's back since, but that night I did climb on a woman's back, on the edge of a bed that was only three feet off the floor.

Okay, I've told you why I felt sorry for this particular horse, but I haven't told you why I feel sorry for every other horse.

First, a horse is an ugly animal. I know a lot of people think a horse is beautiful. Well, if that's true, then how come when you're a little kid in school and there's an ugly girl in your class, you say, "Look at that one. She's got a horse face"?

Secondly, horses are stupid. They have a brain the size of your testicle (or your boyfriend's or husband's). They're so easy to con. Like back in the days of the knights. Whenever they were going into battle, the knight would con his horse.

"Here, I'm putting this piece of leather on your head. It'll keep you from getting hurt."

"Oh, okeydokey, Master, get on my back wearing all that heavy, ball-busting armor and off we'll go to where they'll stab us with swords and throw spears at us."

And that's another reason I feel sorry for horses. We used them in just about every war. How's that for animal rights? And from the beginning of time, what has a horse been to man? Mainly a beast of burden, pulling heavy things, a life of shlepping. And if the horse wasn't pulling, it was running with a person sitting on its back whipping its ass to make him run as fast as he could to beat fellow horses also running their asses off.

And if in all this hell of his life, a horse should fall down and break its leg, we shoot it! If a dog or cat breaks a leg, we take them to the vet, who wraps some tape around the leg, and then, three or four weeks later, the little bastards are terrorizing pigeons or mice again. Horses we shoot, and they know it. Did you ever see a horse fall? It gets up right away.

"What the hell are you doing with that gun? I sprained my ankle. Look, I'm dancing. Sing something."

The poor horse: He's stupid, ugly, a beast of burden, fighting in wars and getting shot in the head. The way I figure it is that God knew He made a mistake as soon as he finished the prototype horse, the first horse. God must have said to Himself, "Oh, my G . . ." Wait, he couldn't say that. Okay. "Oh, my Me." So God, to make up for all the mistakes He made with the horse, in His infinite wisdom, God gave the horse a quality that no other animal possesses. The horse is the only animal in the world that can run and shit at the same time. Did you ever see a horse go over a fence? Midair—plop, plop, plop. Every other animal has to stop to go. Even the turtle.

Let's leave the horse behind, as opposed to the horse's behind, and move on to my biggest animal gripe—the relationship between man and dog. But first I want to tell all of you dog lovers that I, too, love dogs. I've had "little doggies" since I was a "little boyyie." I love 'em, love 'em, love 'em! But—hold on to your leashes, dog owners— to me, a dog is a dog is a dog is a dog. That said . . .

Only in America would we set aside a "Take Your Dog to Work Day." I feel sorry for any dog whose master works in a Korean restaurant.

"Anyone see my Andrew?"

"About ten minutes ago, I heard him barking in the kitchen. Excuse me. Yo, Kwan, could I have more of that delicious meat. What do you call it?"

"In ol' country called 'An Drew Lum Sung.'"

The other day, I was with my dog in the pet section of my neighborhood supermarket looking for a rubber ball, the kind that whistles when you bite it. It takes so little to make a dog happy, doesn't it? Why can't children be more like dogs?

The first thing I saw on the shelf was a shampoo for dogs that "is guaranteed to make your dog more attractive to a dog of the opposite sex." I thought, "What a coincidence," because just that morning, while I was walking my dog, I was thinking, "How can I get more dogs in the neighborhood to hump her?"

The wildest product I saw was an expensive, small bottle of small pills, called Clomical. You know what dog ailment they treat? Keep in mind that we are talking about America, so something as obvious as worms is out. They are for dogs that suffer from Separation Anxiety. You know, that's when you leave for work in the morning, your brokenhearted dog runs to the window and barks, cries, and pleads for you to return immediately. The only problem with the pill is there are side effects—vomiting and diarrhea. So you return home in the evening to a happy dog and a house full of vomit and shit.

You can buy a hearing aid for a dog. What? A hearing aid! They also sell nose warmers for dogs. How do you get the dog to wear it? Unless it's in the shape of another dog's ass.

I once saw a powder that you sprinkle on your dog's food if your dog is shy. Shy! What dog is shy? How can an animal be shy that thinks nothing of sitting naked in public and licking its ass?

"No, please don't pet my Bootsy. He's very shy. When he finishes licking his ass, I'll introduce you."

Here's another "only in America" dog story. There is a best-selling book that is all about how to enhance the spiritual connection between you and your dog, thereby making your dog happier and more in love with you and vice versa. Of course, like most dog lovers, the author reminds us that dogs love us no matter what. I don't know if this is really an attribute, when you recall that Hitler's dogs loved him without reservation. Then again, they might not have known what a crazy bastard he was, because maybe he never had them join their cousins in hunting down Jews, and they didn't have a chance to hear the truth about him after the war, because in his bunker Hitler tested his suicide cyanide pills on them first.

Dogs also have a dark side like humans, or they couldn't be trained to be watch dogs and police dogs, and to fight in wars. Even nonviolently trained household pets have been known to attack people. A study done at the University of Pittsburgh concluded that over 450,000 Americans were bitten by household pets. Did you hear about the dog that ran after a man, caught him, and bit off his testicles? True. When I read about that, I finally understood that stupid book they made us read in school as kids. "See Spot chase Dick. See Dick run. Run, Dick, run! Run your balls off . . . oops, never mind, too late. Yikes."

Okay, back to the book. Hopefully, you didn't forget the book about how to connect spiritually with your dog that I was telling you about. Obviously, I almost did. The author suggests that you should meditate with your dog. He claims that in addition to connecting you and your dog spiritually, it reduces stress for both of you. What kind of stress does a dog have? "Should I scratch my left ear or my right ear?"

Then, the author advises you to "see the world through your dog's eyes." He writes that you should walk around your house or apartment on all fours and see it from your dog's point of view. I guess if you have a Mexican Chihuahua, you'll have to crawl on your belly. I suggest you also go outside and walk around your neighborhood on all fours, too, and maybe stick your nose up a neighbor's ass and hump the mailman's leg.

Another suggestion made by the author is to think like your dog. You know, curl up in an easy chair in the living room and really make believe you are your dog and think like him.

"Hmmm. Well, I guess I'll go out in the backyard and take a shit. Oops, ten after four, time to lick my balls."

Now I'll tell you my favorite dog/master story. I was living in Los Angeles. I had a neighbor who lived next door to me in a big, gray house. That's what I called him, "Mr. Grayhouse." I didn't know him. I didn't want to know him. I have enough friends. I don't need another. This is a real New York attitude. In New York you go out of your way not to meet a neighbor. You become friends with someone because you spend time together and find out all you have in common. Suppose you move into a place and make friends with a neighbor, and he turns out to be a real asshole. For the rest of the time you live there, you have to keep ducking him.

"Get the kids down on the floor of the car, honey; the asshole is on his lawn. Duck, everyone! A.A., A.A.—Asshole Alert, Asshole Alert!"

But I couldn't completely avoid the asshole in proximity, because I sometimes saw him in the mornings walking his dog when I was walking mine. I didn't say hello to him, but I did wave. I was such a dumb schmuck. I even practiced in the mirror how to look sincere. It didn't work.

One day I was having breakfast with a very good friend of mine of many years. He actually knew my neighbor and said, "Did you hear what happened to Mr. Grayhouse last night?"

"No, what happened to him?"

"Nothing happened to him. His dog died."

I said, "Oh, that's a shame. It was a cute little dog."

We finished breakfast and I drove home. Just as I was pulling into my driveway, I saw Mr. Grayhouse at the curb getting his mail. Of course, his mailbox was shaped like a dog, and he was pulling the letters and magazines out of its ass.

Now, if this had happened back in New York, someone's dog died, you would be sorry, but you would go home. There's nothing you can do about it. Dead is dead. But I was living in L.A. and might be living there for a while and "when in Rome . . ." Besides, I was practicing how to be insincerely friendly, so I got out of my car, walked up to Mr. Grayhouse, and said—and I meant it—"I'm sorry about your dog."

He let out a sigh, a very long sigh, and said, quietly, "It should have been me."

'Should have been me'? Let me tell you, I love my dog, but if Death walked into my house, I'd say, "Wait a minute. Take the bitch."

Then he asked me, "You're coming to the funeral today, aren't you?" I thought, "It should've been you," but I resisted saying it. Then I realized that he knows who I am and is just being funny. I also meant to be funny when I said, "This is my first dog internment. Should I wear a suit? Are we sitting Shiva? Should I cover all the mirrors with sheets? Should I bring you a fruit cake? Tell me."

Next thing I know, he's saying, "That dog was a member of my family, and I am going to give it the same kind of funeral as I would for anyone else in my family."

I said, and again, I was still just trying to be funny, to cheer the guy up, but he got so bent out of shape, "I have a great idea. For old times' sake, on the way to the cemetery, why don't you let your dog's head hang out the window of the hearse?" (A little-known scientific fact: If your dog has his head sticking out of your car window, and you speed up to exactly 82.4 mph, your dog's tongue will fly out of its ass in 2.6 seconds.)

Grayhouse got so pissed off at my hearse joke. Actually, he was lucky I didn't say what I was really thinking. He kept going on and on about the funeral, finally telling me that he was having the dog cremated for $1,850! I wanted to say, "Listen, give me $200, and I'll throw him in my Hibachi. Good for you; good for me."

In that one moment, Mr. Grayhouse turned into a New Yorker and never spoke to his neighbor again. The son of a bitch never even waved.

Advice: Here are some tips on how to keep your sense of humor when you are becoming annoyed by a pet and/or a pet owner.

For pet owners: Remember, there are a lot of people who are not crazy about pets and will act strangely when encountering you and your pet. Look for the funny side.

For non–pet owners: Remember, there are a lot of people who are crazy about pets and will act strangely when encountering you. Look for the funny side.

For pets: I'm sure you have found out plenty about schmucky human beings to laugh about, so you don't need any of my advice.

Now that I have reached the point where I have said all I have to say on this subject, why does my gut tell me that I'm still in a lot of hot water with pet owners and animal lovers? Okay, let me try to extricate myself and get back in your best graces. I already told you that I love dogs and have had dogs all my life, and believe in a just world for animals in the wild and freedom for those in captivity, but this might not be enough. If you are really steamed at me, just leave me a message on my website (www.DavidBrenner.com) and, for the person who writes me the best pissed-off one, I'll send you my fuckin' dog.

Studies and Statistics

Studies

Did you ever read the results of a study and get upset, especially when you are in the percentage of those who are getting the short end of the stick? You find out that your car is the most dangerous, your marriage has little chance of working out, your kids are likely to have a drinking problem, you are at high risk of dying from a new disease, your next-door neighbor fits the profile of a serial killer, your dick will probably fall off and kill your dog, and all other kinds of horrible moments and events hiding around the next corner ready to pounce on you and ruin moments or years of your life. Welcome to the frightening world of studies.

To me, the most annoying studies are the ones that use taxpayers' money, our money for some kind of foolish shit. One of the stupidest studies I've seen recently is the federal government's grant of $590,000 of *our* money to do a study on how to make catfish dumber so they are easier to catch. Now, is that stupid, or what? I could have saved the government all that money. All they had to do was cross the DNA of the catfish with the asshole who came up with the idea.

A lot of money is being spent on a study to find out why old people fall. They fall because they're fuckin' old!

I read a study in which they divided an old age home into those residents who prayed regularly and those who never prayed. As they watched over the years, the ones who never prayed died sooner. So the conclusion of the study is that prayer helps you live longer. I thought, "Wait a minute. Suppose the prayers prayed that those who didn't pray would die?"

This one might be me, because I've always seen most things differently than anyone else. Anyway, in a health study, I read that acupuncture relieves the pain from body piercing. Is it me?

There was an extensive study conducted on health. Excerpts from it were published in a popular men's magazine that, although a fine publication, will remain anonymous, because unsubstantiated lawsuits have plagued me my whole adult life.

Anyway, a couple of conclusions from this study stayed with me. One was, if you are with someone who passes out, do not feed him. Now, I don't know about you, but that's the first thing that would come to my mind.

"Oh, my God, Tony just fainted. He loves scungilli. Go get some. We'll stuff it down his throat."

In all fairness, there was another conclusion I am very glad I read, because I would have never thought of it, otherwise. If you have a friend who suffers from severe diarrhea, do not invite him to swim in your heated pool. Why not?

In another health study, it was reported that riding a bike could make men impotent. I can challenge that study with only one word: China!

Here is a study that really upset me. It was featured on a newscast that I was watching. It was reported that it is absolutely, scientifically confirmed that cellular phones give rats cancer. As soon as I heard this, I turned to my rat and yelled, "Put that down! Send an e-mail!"

I heard another study result on TV: "More people are killed while talking on their car phones than while talking on their phones at home." I don't know about you, but I never sat at home on my phone, looked out the window, and yelled, "There's a house heading right for us! Run for your lives!!"

Talking about car accidents, did you read the survey in *USA Today* conducted by State Farm Insurance about dangerous roads in America? At the top of the list was Roosevelt Boulevard in my hometown of Philadelphia. It's a road that runs for about ten or twelve miles in the northeast section of the city. It took the prize for the most accidents, but the most dangerous intersection in America is in a town in Florida named Pembroke Pines. At the intersection of Flamingo Road and Pines Boulevard, in a twelve-month period, there were 357 accidents! Now, wouldn't you think after . . . say, forty-two, someone would've said, "Let's put up a goddamn light!?" This is a town of four hundred people. Only three are still alive.

Another discovery in the road safety study was that the worst highway traffic during rush hour in the country was in Los Angeles. The average time a driver there spends sitting in his car without moving ahead one millimeter is 136 hours a year. That's six straight twenty-four-hour days. Imagine if these were concurrent.

"Where's Daddy, Mommy?"

"He's in his car. He'll be in a week from Tuesday."

Even wilder than that is a study being conducted in Arizona, resulting from a number of people getting high by licking toads. They are investigating a liquid secreted by toads that when humans ingest it, they get high. I think they should forget studying this and study how the first guy discovered it. Were a bunch of men on a camping trip, and one of them stood up at the campfire and said, "Wow, look at all those toads. Want to run over and lick a few and see what happens?"

A cocktail of so-called anti-antigenic drugs administered to a dog by a student at Tufts University School of Veterinary Medicine in Boston resulted in totally eliminating all traces of cancer from the dog. Researchers are now studying its application with human beings, which, so far, has been encouraging, except some men have snapped their spinal cords trying to lick their balls.

At Cambridge University in England, researchers are studying using dogs to screen for prostate cancer. A dog's sense of smell is so keen, but the dogs have to examine very quickly, because they can't breathe for very long with a rubber glove over their noses.

My question is, again, how someone discovered this. Was there a medical researcher in his lab one day, when the door to his lab opened and a Labrador came through the door into the lab? So, the researcher closed the lab door behind the Labrador . . . Okay, I know I'm being silly. No more puns. What did the researcher do?

"Hmmmmm, I got an idea. Rover, when I drop my pants and bend over, I want you to stick your nose up my ass and see if you smell prostate cancer. No, Rover, Goddamn it! Your nose, you horny bastard!"

I read a study about men who keep their hands in their pants pockets, jiggling their change or whatever. I remember older guys hanging out on the street corners in my old neighborhood who used to do that. I always thought they were real cool. Au contraire, my reader. According to this study, men who do this are very shy and awkward around women and have a difficult time meeting the opposite sex. I think this is totally wrong. You keep jiggling your hands in your pockets, you won't need a woman.

Here's an interesting study I came across that concludes that the warmer a man is in the sexual part of his body, the less active sperm he produces. Sex therapists, upon reading the results of this study, are now suggesting that if you want to have a baby, you should make love in a room where the temperature is forty degrees or less. As a man, you have to hope you can turn on your wife with the little BB balls and peanut you have down there.

"Come on, you know I'm bigger than this! It's snowing in here for crying out loud. Help me look for it."

This is one of the most interesting studies I've ever read. They wanted to know where the most honest and least honest human beings live. So what they did for five continuous years was travel to 117 cities around the world, in which they "lost" 1,100 wallets, inside of each of which was $50 in local currency and a card with the name and phone number of the person who supposedly lost it. God, what kind of job is this?

"Hi, Bob. Long time no see. What have you been doing since high school?"

"Well, for the past five years, I go into a city and lose my wallet. Then I sit in the hotel room and wait for someone to call me."

"What are you doing now, Bob, working as an airport security guard?"

The results of the international study were interesting:

Around the world, 44 percent of the wallets were never returned.

In Norway and Denmark, 100 percent were returned. This is where the most honest people in the world live.

This one surprised me. In the USA, 70 percent of the wallets were returned. Not in my old neighborhood. We used to find wallets in pants. Sad but true.

If you're going to lose your wallet in America, lose it in Seattle, Washington. It was the only city returning all the wallets. They are our most honest people.

Do not lose your wallet in Atlanta, Georgia.

And, in Brooklyn, New York, three of the men who lost the wallets are still missing.

There are a lot of studies that never should have been done. They are a waste of time, money, and intelligence. The following is one of them. I thought it was a bogus study, at first, but by surfing the Internet, I confirmed it was a true study.

For over three years, scientists traveled to every country in the world. One of the big conclusions of the study is that the men in India have the smallest penises of any nationality. Now, why do we have to know this, and, more perplexing, how did they conduct the study?

(Read aloud with an Indian accent) "Okay, let me see your dick. That is not a dick! Go buy a dick and come back."

The final study I want to discuss is the most valid of any study ever conducted. It is scientifically conclusive and the knowledge gleaned from it is beneficial to all mankind.

Study Conclusion: You'll live better and possibly longer if you learn to laugh.

Statistics

Closely interrelated to studies are statistics. Actually, studies can't be conducted without statistics and without studies there is little reason for the gathering of statistics. In this world of mini-second communications, rapid-fire news, and computerized analyses, studies and statistics abound. They are frequently frightening and, therefore, a lot of people worry when they read them. This is understandable, but completely unnecessary.

Think of statistics as putty. They can be molded into any shape, according to the person molding them. This is why politicians have been able to bullshit us for over two hundred years. Twist and turn, mold and shape, con and connive, bullshit and bullshit.

But understanding human nature as I do, I know this is not enough to convince you or to get you to ignore statistics. However, there is no reason why you can't do a little molding, twisting, and juggling of your own and become the bullshitter, instead of the bullshitee.

Here's an upsetting statistic, especially to me. My live performance act is based entirely on current events. Therefore, I read about eighty magazines a month; I continually watch TV news throughout the day and night; I watch news-oriented TV programs, such as *Meet the Press* and *60 Minutes;* I surf the Internet for a couple hours in the morning and before I go to bed, but my main source of information and therefore the majority of my jokes come from all the newspapers I read. Lately, I've been thinking that I am being stupid putting all my factual eggs in my newspaper basket, because I read that 42 percent of the American people don't believe anything they read in the newspaper. But I read that in a newspaper.

Here's a statistic that is even more upsetting to everyone: 44.3 million Americans suffer from a serious mental disorder. Think about it. That comes out to about one person in almost every seven. Since reading this, every time I am on stage, I look out at the one thousand people sitting in my audience, and I think, "Oh, my God, there are 166 lunatics sitting near me." Actually, it's 166.66666666. The .66666666 of a person is the scariest.

Here's a stat I just discovered on the Internet last week. It is also scary. According to pollsters in Chappaqua, New York, 40 percent keep secrets from spouses.

It can't be true. It's got to be around 98 percent. A husband and wife can't be totally truthful with each other. Who's going to stay with you, once they find out what you are really like? I believe that keeping secrets is one of the most vital platforms on which to build a firm, long-lasting relationship. Of course, I've been married and divorced three times (an impressive statistic, right?), so maybe you shouldn't be coming to me for relationship advice.

Now don't think that I was always a statistic cynic. I must confess that in my youth, I became a fanatic worrier. It was all due to my coming across a statistical analysis of the causes of death, from falling off a ladder to dying in a car accident. Regardless of the fact that I've never been on a stepladder and had no intention of ever using one and did not own a car at the time, I was terribly upset. I did some research at the library in city, state, and national documents and insurance company studies.

The odds of my getting through the rest of that year without losing a limb, hearing, sight, my mind, or life itself, from falling out of a train or out of love, slipping in a tub or on ice, crashing into a tree or a murderer, collapsing from heat exhaustion or just collapsing for no reason, and hundreds of other injurious, maiming, or death-causing horrors was a negative 450,020 to 1.

I made a list of all activities that must be prevented: no riding trains, dry showers only, avoid loud noises, no sun, and hundreds of others that if followed would have forced me to stay in bed in a dark, air-conditioned room curled in a prenatal position. But I had done all the research, had checked and double-checked my calculations. There was no doubt that the most common activities and actions of human beings were razors at the throat of survival. On almost a daily basis, I was becoming more worried, more psychotic, and less popular. Come on, what woman wants to go out on a date with a man who is wearing sunglasses, carrying an umbrella, peering at rooftops with binoculars, and wearing rubber gloves?

Then the unexpected happened, which jarred me back to reality. A man I knew broke his neck sneezing too hard, and a neighbor of mine was cleaning her toilet when the shower curtain fell, knocking her medicine cabinet off the wall, which crashed down on her head, knocking her out, and she drowned in the toilet water. I spent the following two months trying to find the statistics and probabilities of these two types of deaths and found nothing. I then realized I would have to throw these causes of death, as well as all freak accidents, into the mix, all of which would increase the odds of my eminent demise manyfold. To do this statistical analysis, I would be spending my last few hundred minutes on earth inside musty libraries and offices.

I came to a quick and sensible conclusion that I live by to this day—I'm going to live as long as I live and not a moment less or more, so the hell with statistics and their resulting odds. If you agree with my conclusion, I'll bet that your chances of living a more fulfilling and happier life are 100,000,000 to 1 in your favor, give or take 16,623,000 or 27,802,345. Want to bet? Okay. What odds will you give me?

Baldness

To most men, if not all men, who are bald or are going bald, either of these is an unfathomable tragedy, second only to having their dicks fall off—maybe. If you're a man going bald or have already gone bald or a woman who has been with a man going or gone, you know exactly what I am talking about. It is such a devastating phenomenon that most men who are going bald also simultaneously go into denial.

"Wow, Bob, you're losing your hair. You're going bald."

"No, I'm not. It's just thinning out a little."

"Well, if your apartment is thinning out like this, you're going to have only a chair and a throw rug within a year."

Yes, I know, I'm very lucky to have a full head of hair with no evidence of my going bald. My father died at the age of ninety-two with a full head of hair. My three sons have my hair and their sons will have it, too, or else! No Brenner male has ever gone bald. In my family, you can marry out of your faith or race, but God help you if you marry a bald man and bring the bald gene into the family pool. One cousin of mine violated the family code and married someone from the Dome Head Clan. Luckily they never had any children. Their dog went bald, which is something no one has ever understood and that has been discussed only in muted tones well out of their earshot.

In spite of having lots of hair, even hairs to spare, I know a lot about baldness and the trauma of it, and I empathize. My four best friends in this world are guys I grew up with in the neighborhood. I met them when I was seven and a half years old. We are inseparable, blood brothers. Each of these childhood friends is bald, so they have hated me for years. I have had this unconscious, nervous habit my whole life of running my fingers through my hair. Every time I do it, they get all over my back (which, by the way, doesn't have a hair on it, thank God).

"Why the hell do you always have to do that, Brenner?"

Of course, I counter immediately and without mercy. "Well, you can pat your heads."

The best aspect of having friends, bald or hairy, who go back that far in your life is, if you need to know the absolutely truthful answer to a question, regardless of how hurtful the answer might be, the best persons to ask are the guys from the street corner. We are brutally honest with one another. We pull no punches, gild no lilies, speak no bullshit—the truth, the whole truth, and nothing but the truth, so help you, or I'll kill your dog.

I am very pissed at one of my lifetime friends and it has to do with hair, not mine, and only God and a doctor in north New Jersey know whose. Actually, I'm pissed at all four. One of them did something and didn't tell me, and the others knew that he did it and also didn't tell me. I hadn't seen the friend in question for about ten months, but we talked on the phone regularly. Also, in defense of my actions, I not only talked to the other three friends, I saw them. There were plenty of opportunities for one of the four to be forthright, but no one said one word to me.

The friend I hadn't seen, the culprit, was completely bald, except for the sides and back—the monk look. What I didn't know was that since I had seen him, he had gotten those things they sew into your head. God, how does anyone have the patience and the pain threshold to keep his head under the machine for an hour? And can you imagine you go to a party, think you're real cool, and there's a thread hanging? "Here, Tony, let me get that for you." One pull and the guy's head unravels.

Anyway, I was in concert in New Jersey, across the river from my hometown, Philadelphia. Whenever I am close by, we street-corner best friends get together for a few cheesesteak sandwiches and hoagies and a million belly laughs. The guy who had plugged his head called and said that he would pick me up after my show and take me to meet the rest of the guys at Pat's Cheesesteaks, a South Philly hangout we have been patronizing since we were kids.

Now, you have to keep in mind that the last time I saw my friend his head looked like it was waiting to get three holes drilled in it. He was always nervous in bowling alleys. After the show, I was in my dressing room, my back to the door, when I heard, "Yo, David!" I turned around and my mouth dropped open. There's my bald pal smiling and pointing to his head, which is now covered with a wisp of hair or a brownish cobweb.

"Well, what do you think, David? Does it look natural?"

"Yeah, if your hair is falling out in rows. You look like you have a little farm on your head. What you should do is call the government; they'll pay you not to plant anymore up there."

Natural? Come on, was he serious? It's about as natural as a wooden nose.

But being the best friends we are, we joined the other baldies and had a thousand belly laughs and lots of unwavering friendship. The cheesesteak sandwiches were great, too. I saw a hair in mine but didn't say anything and kept eating. They would get so damn jealous and upset. Hopefully, it was one of mine.

Prior to this incident with the transplants, I had a "hair incident" with one of my other childhood friends. He was the first one in a male crowd of forty-five to go bald. He had just turned nineteen. It was a tragedy. Not only because he was first and so young, but because he had the hugest head you have ever seen on a two-legged animal. He was also very skinny. When we were kids and played hide-and-go-seek, he would hide behind a stop sign.

Anyway, here's what this guy does with his casaba melon top. First, whenever he gets a haircut, his barber is only allowed to cut the hair in the back and on the right side of his head. He hasn't had the hairs on the left side cut in well over a decade. I went on a vacation with him to St. Maarten. It was so frightening, waking up in the morning and in the bed next to yours is a bald man with fourteen inches of hair hanging off the side, like I'm shacking up with Rapunzel.

Then, when he got up, he did something I had never seen him do in person. He parted his hair on the left side of his head directly above his ear and carefully combed each strand of hair across the top of his head. He's always been a Perry Comb-Over, but this was the first time I had ever seen the detailed process. He really believes that when he walks down the street, no one can tell that he's bald. Sure, if he is living in a land of only midgets, maybe. And when the wind blows, he has this long mop whipping people in the face. I swear, someday in a bad storm, he's going to whip someone to death. He could get a job as a torturer, maybe working on those al-Qaeda detainees in Guantanamo Bay. "No, praise be to Allah, please, no more hair whip. I'll talk."

These are just two examples of some of the extremes a man will go to who is in a hair-losing situation. Such a man will go to just about any lengths to have a length of hair and will buy practically anything that claims to either restore his own natural hair or make it look like it is restored. If there is the remotest chance that it will result in a small patch of fuzz or a couple sort-of–looks-like-hairs-in-the-right-light-and-angles, a man will make the long leap of faith.

"Just rub this virgin-guppy-oil-soaked sponge on your bald and thinning hair parts at midnight every night while standing on one leg and within a few weeks you will see a major difference." Most likely, the "major difference" will be the disturbing glow of oil on your dome and leg cramps.

Then there is the actual magical comb that according to the advertisements fires some sort of laser beam into your scalp, which somehow makes your hair grow thicker without somehow putting a hole in your head. Personally, I'd rather shine a flashlight up my ass for absolutely no reason whatsoever.

I'm sure you have seen the following full-page ad that has run in *USA Today* and most national magazines. The ad's headline, in my opinion, should win every advertising industry accolade. It is way more effective and more eye and ear catching than The Pepsi Generation or Where's the Beef, or even the award-winning classic by Coca-Cola, It's the Real Thing, or the Marines' Were Looking for a Few Good Men.

The ad's banner headline is "A Full Head of Hair in 30 Seconds!" So if you're bald and uptight about it, and who besides a professional basketball player or a newborn baby isn't, in less time than it takes you to say, "Peter Piper picked a peck of who gives a shit what," you'll have a massive mop of hair on your head and, as a result, enough brass in your balls to approach that gorgeous woman you always see bending over the fruit counter where you shop and end up in her bed in a matter of a few short minutes. Glory be to God and the person who invented this miracle product.

Exactly what is this miracle product? It's a spray, but the ad tells you right off the bat that it is not paint like the last time. Remember that fad? You'd see all these men walking down the street with the bald areas of their heads painted black.

"Look at the guy. The back of his head is painted black. What's he think he is, a billboard?"

No spray paint this time. This hair-growing miracle is called Hair Building Fibers, which the manufacturers and distributors claim are made out of the same thing as your hair. Now, I always thought hair was made out of hair, but it's not. It's made out of the shit that flies out of their spray can.

Then these fibers bind or cling to whatever hair you've got left or your whole bald head. How? They are magnetized with static electricity (that's a new one, right?). In the ad, they show a before and after (only thirty seconds after, of course). It looks like dirt is hanging in this guy's hair or is matted onto his head. Actually, he looks like someone who forgot to put on his hat and got caught in a shit storm.

Then they go on to make other wild claims, like being able to drive in an open convertible at great speeds, play any contact sport, and dive or swim in a pool or an ocean. This is followed by the claim that all you have to do to remove this miracle whatever from your head is put a little water on it.

Before this ad, I used to think that the wildest product was the pill that they came out with a couple years ago that was supposed to grow hair. Great, suppose it gets caught in your throat? And have you ever seen a toupee that looks real? Besides the fishnet in the front, they never sit flat in the back. It always looks like the guy is hiding a wallet in there. And how about the ones that sit on top of the head like a hair helmet?

(Did you ever notice that you never see a bald-headed homeless man? They always have these bushes of matted, dirty hair. They don't wash it or put anything on it. Now, I'm not suggesting that once a week you spend the night with your head in the gutter. It's just an observation.)

There are many bald or balding men who don't fall for these miracle ads. Instead, they invent their own way of disguising or hiding their handicap. One of the strangest ones I ever saw was in an airport when I was trying to change my flight. I kept staring at the man behind the counter who was working on my problem. From the moment I said "Hi," I thought that he was one of the weirdest human beings I had ever seen and I couldn't figure out why. Then, after a few moments of staring at him, I realized that his hair was coming toward me! When he turned around . . . wait, I've got to stop laughing . . . okay . . . when he turned around, I saw that he parted his hair at the base of the back of his neck and combed it up, over, and out. A Perry Comb-Up.

But the prize for the most bizarre "top secret" was in a restaurant in New York City. At the table next to me, with his back to me, was a man who had a tiny tuft of hair on the top of his head. Now, you know that a man parts his hair on the left or right or in the middle. Not this guy. He drew a part across his head, from one ear to the other ear. You understand? He is sitting in a public place with a wide part going across the top of his head, east to west, instead of north to south. I was so tempted. I wanted to lean over and quietly say, "Excuse me, but did anyone ever whisper in your ear? Someone twisted your head around, man. You're all screwed up. Your eyes are supposed to be over here."

So how do we becalm our bald citizens and stop them from making assholes of themselves from the ears up? One of my beliefs in life is that when we are born, we are given a genetic blueprint from God Himself, and we are going to live out that blueprint, looking the way God wanted us to look every single day of our lives, unless we do things to violate our bodies, like use drugs, smoke cigarettes, eat too little or too much. So if you are a bald man, you should be very proud, because you have been selected by God Himself to be in His bald army!

I know I shouldn't be talking about this with the mop of hair sitting on my head. I'm very lucky. This doesn't mean that I don't empathize with or care about those less fortunate than I—the baldies. Oops, I mean men who suffer from hair loss. Is that better? Are we still friends?

To all of you hair-loss victims, I am telling you that, first of all, denial is stupid. You're losing or have lost your hair. It's a fact. Stop denying it. I don't go around denying that I have a big nose. I don't say, "What're you talking about? I don't have a big nose. I have a small face." I have a big nose. So what? It doesn't bother me. Of course, when it's windy, I spin around a lot.

I made you laugh with that nose joke, right? It was at my own expense. That was the idea. Now, go look in a mirror. Stare at your bald or balding head, have a good laugh, then salute and say, "Thank you, God. I'm reporting for duty." And if this is not enough, keep in mind that when the archeologists of the far future dig us up, all of us, even hairy head me, will be bald. Maybe even God is bald. Now that's a theological thought to ponder, isn't it?

Bald or covered with hair, all that really matters is what is inside that head of yours, not what is on the outside of it, and how you use what's inside to make life as good as it can be, including the ability to make fun of and laugh at what isn't exactly as you would have or want it to be.

Plus, it has been said that bald men are more virile and better in bed. This should make you feel better, even though there is no doubt in my mind that this statement is full of shit. Come on, laugh, Mr. Bald Eagle, and keep laughing. Why not? You have nothing to lose, especially on top of your head. Gotcha again, baldy.

Aging

Growing old is a biggie with me. I rank it right up there with being poor and dying, in that order, of course. I've been uptight about aging since I was nine years old. I'm serious. I can remember telling my friends that I didn't want to become ten, because no one in the neighborhood who had double digits in their age was happy.

Maybe this wasn't true where you grew up, but it sure as hell was where I'm from. It just seemed that when you had only one digit there were very few things that were major problems, or real causes of grief. So what if you can't afford to buy a baseball glove, baseball, or a bat? No big deal. Just slip a few small paper bags into each other, cut holes for your fingers and thumb, shove a rag in the bag for padding, and you've got a glove. Wrap a rock with black plumber's tape and you've got a ball. For a bat, I always lived in or near a Sicilian neighborhood, so there were plenty of them lying around. Sometimes you had to lift a body to get to them, which was no big deal. I'm only joking, of course. You could give someone a quarter to move the body for you.

So, from ten years of age on, birthdays went from annoying to traumatic for me. For some reason, fifty was the worst. I remember going to bed at age forty-nine and waking up the next morning at age ninety-nine. At least, that's how I felt. It was so hard to tell anyone how old I was when asked. The number got stuck in my throat like a ball of sandpaper. And once you turn fifty and every year after that, you say your age differently. Instead of saying, "I'm fifty-five years old," you angrily blurt out, "I'm fifty-fuckin'-five years old! Next year, I'll be fifty-fuckin'-six years old!"

This age hang-up of mine was even more ridiculous, because I inherited great genes from my mother. She came from a family of Dorian Grays, no one showed their age. I had an uncle who fell in love with a twenty-two-year-old when he was forty-five. He told her that he was twenty-five and he looked it. They married and had four daughters. He never told her his true age. When he turned sixty-five, he couldn't retire and collect social security or she would find out his age, so he worked until he was eighty-five. When he died at age ninety-five, with all his original teeth, a full head of white hair, and needing only reading glasses (well, not anymore), she thought she was burying a man of seventy-five. She died ten years later, never knowing the secret. I guess if there is a heaven, he's catching hell.

My mother passed away at age eighty-six without a wrinkle and with the hands of a young woman. The genetic pool from my father is pretty damn good, too. My dad died at age ninety-two with all his hair, 20/20 vision, and still able to walk up several flights of stairs spryly and unaided, and, as far as I know, based only on unsubstantiated rumors, he was still a lady-killer.

With all these wonderful genetics going for me, what is my hang-up all about? Well, you can't get all the plums without getting some of the pits. Maybe I am too critical or look too closely, but I see and feel every physical change in my person. Parts of my body that were always silent now creak a bit. Sections of the body that were flat and tight are slowly heading for the pavement, because as you get older, you lose the war with gravity. If you were to live to be two hundred, as you took your morning walk, your ass would be scraping the sidewalk behind you like a duster and your stomach in the front like a snowplow, one that can't lift for speed bumps either. Ears that once could hear the breathing of a sleeping cat in the next room now miss "Would you like a lid on this?" Eyes that could spot a fly walking across the top of a window curtain now miss a yellow cab turning the corner. And a penis that once could . . . That's enough about body parts.

So, how do I cope? How do I meet Mr. Age head-on and battle him blow for blow? You guessed it: with Mr. Humor and Mr. Laughter. They're not just a young person's partners in the aging game; they're for anyone who wants to play, and, man, do I play, hard and without mercy. It's survival in its purest form.

Let's start with finding the humor in the physicality of getting older, and remember I hate every change in my person, regardless of how minute or unnoticeable to anyone without a magnifying glass.

One morning, I was looking at myself in the mirror, which I rarely do for obvious reasons. No reflection, no aging. This philosophy was reinforced when I noticed crow's feet next to my eyes.

"Jesus Christ, what the hell are these lines?"

A very young friend said, "They're laugh lines, David."

"I just don't want to look hysterical," I replied, and shaved and brushed my teeth with my eyes shut, which I have done ever since.

A childhood friend of mine has an aging problem with his eyes, too, but didn't try to find even a giggle in it, let alone a laugh. Instead of crow's feet, he has bags under his eyes. His brothers, sister, and parents have bags. In the old neighborhood, they were known as the Bag Family. So, of course, he eventually joined the clan. Instead of joking about it, like, "These aren't bags; they're suitcases," or "Can I carry these on or do I have to check them?" he bought one of those gravity tables where you strap yourself in with gravity boots and hang upside down, supposedly fighting gravity. The premise is sound.

Religiously, every day, my friend hung upside down for two solid hours. He did this for three straight months. Now he has bags *over* his eyes.

One night after taking a soothing hot bath, as I was sitting on the edge of my bed, my legs dangling over the side, I noticed a flap of some kind where my lean and mean lower abdomen used to be. I stood up. It wasn't as bad as when I was seated, but it was still hanging in there. Somehow, when my eyes and stomach were turned, Mr. Age had sneaked up on me and put a fanny skin pack around my lower abs.

Even when I tripled the number of my daily sit-ups and crunches, even when I sucked it in and held my breath, the fanny pack hung there defiantly. I realized that instead of continuing to panic and killing myself on the floor for hours, I had two other choices. I could get a tummy tuck or I could paint it black and put a zipper on it.

When you are getting older, you've got to learn to roll with the punches, or, at least, crawl. It's horrible to be stretched out on a beach, enjoying the warm sun and the melodic sounds of the ocean waves caressing the sand, feeling as you did as a teenager, when some real teenager looks at you and asks, "Why are you wearing leather on such a hot day?" It hurts when you've got to face the chilling truth that you are ever so slowly metamorphosing into a large wallet, but you must go on.

Such aging signs as the aforementioned, you can control, but others you can't. One that drives me crazy, and there is nothing you can do about it except laugh and bear it, is one my father called "The Midnight Runs of Paul Revere." Doctors would probably diagnose it as an aging bladder.

I get up in the middle of some nights as often as three or four times to go to the bathroom. I have stopped drinking liquids at noon, but I still have to run. When I was a kid, I used to be able to hold it in for a month or two. What happened? What happened is that I turned fifty and this is my birthday present from God. In the middle of the night on your fiftieth birthday, you hear a booming voice in your sleep. "Happy birthday, my son. Go pee pee!" "Yes, God," and off you go, groggily, stumbling in the dark, hoping you don't break a toe, hoping that you find the toilet, that you remember to lift up the cover and the seat before you start and put them back down when you are finished, not in the middle, and that God will forgive you for being too lazy and tired to wash your hands or at least a few fingers. Worse than the Midnight Run, and a sure sign that you're very, very old, is when you pee a few times in the middle of the night without bothering to get out of the bed.

The truth is that all kinds of terrible shit happens to you as you get older, from head to toe, inside and out, 360 degrees. This is why, as a kid, I never understood when you would ask an old-timer in the neighborhood, like a little old lady . . . Why do we always say "a little old lady?" How come you never hear anyone say, "I met this giant old lady today. She must've been eight or nine feet tall"? Anyway, why is it whenever you would ask an old person, "When is the best time in life," they'd always give you the same answer:

"The best time . . . the best . . . the . . . What was the question? . . . Never you mind, I got it . . . The best time in life . . . The best time in life is . . . right now."

I used to think, "Who the hell are you kidding? Now? Are you crazy, you dried-up white prune? Now?"

"Right now" is a bullshit answer. The real answer is twenty-one. It never gets better than twenty-one. At twenty-one, you can do it all: go sleepless, smoke a carton of cigarettes and a few joints, do some blow, drink a quart of Scotch, screw your brains out for hours and hours, get in your car in the morning, hit a few trees on the way to work, and *life is great!* After you turn fifty, you just feel like all those things happened to you.

As I grow older, I have more empathy for older people. For instance, I'll tell you something that really burns my ass, something that is so unfair. I've been thinking about addressing Congress about it. I'm serious.

Here's my gripe. Most American manufacturers take into consideration most physical differences among their customers. This is why we have left-handed monkey wrenches and handicap accesses. One of our industries that, in my opinion, completely ignores our senior citizens is the automotive manufacturer.

The makers of automobiles know exactly how many senior citizens purchase their new cars every year, because they have to put their birthdate on the car loan application. So I think that the automobile makers should produce a certain percentage of cars every year, keeping their senior citizen customers in mind, and make these cars where the windshield is *below* the steering wheel! There is no reason why our elderly have to stretch to see out the window. Did you ever go to Miami and watch cars going by? All you see is this little tuft of white hair, like a rabbit is driving.

The other day, I saw an article in the paper showing statistics that prove that very few senior citizens are victims of road rage. The study attributed this to the experienced driving and calm demeanor of senior citizens. I have to disagree. Do you know how hard it is to shoot at just the top of a head in the window of a car?

Growing older, and finally, just being plain old, happen to everyone, everyone, that is, who is lucky enough to make the trip that far. Father Time doesn't pass up the rich and famous. He might pass them by for a bit, chuckling at them as they shoot their faces full of Botox, until their only expression is "I'm a little scared," or suck enough fat out of their asses to insulate a two-story house, but he knows he's going to catch up to them someday.

This doesn't mean that if you are old, you should give up on life, pack it in, and wait for the final bell, but—and this is an important but—make sure that whatever you do fits your age. You can *think* younger than you are, but don't try to *act* younger. Nothing is more ridiculous than seeing an older guy with a ponytail and nose rings, unless he's a real pirate.

I read that Sean Connery has agreed to do another James Bond movie. He's a wonderful actor, one of my favorites, but, come on; he's in his seventies. I can't wait to see that Aston Martin speeding along in the passing lane at 12 mph, the seat belt hanging out of the driver's door, and with the right blinker on for forty miles, and a bumper sticker that reads ASK ME ABOUT MY GRANDCHILDREN. I can just see Sean shuffling up to a bar—"I'll have a prune juice, shaken, not stirred"— or looking the bad guy in his eyes, or trying to look in his eyes, and in that deep, crackling voice blurt out, "Hi, the name is Bond . . . eh . . . something Bond."

Yes, aging is a bitch, but not as cruel as it may seem or may actually be, if you do what you can and should do with every aspect and phase of life and, that is, find the humor in it. A lot of jokes have been written about getting older. I've written a few myself, not made up from my imagination, but based on actual news items or real personal observations. As you read the real news and observations, I want you to remember that without sprinkling some humor on them, the stories or observations might have been sad, or maybe even terrible, and, therefore, so might have been the aging process. Maybe you'll see reflections of yourself, as you are today or will be tomorrow, and, hopefully, will keep in mind what I jokingly said about it.

A man 103 years old got married. On his wedding night, he said he was going to slip into something more comfortable. It turned out to be a coma.

How about this man ninety-seven years old whose wife left him, because he was cheating with a next-door neighbor? Ninety-seven! I guess he got caught when he came home with two sets of teeth in his mouth. By the way, that is one of the signs that you are getting old—when your wife says, "Nibble on my ear," and you reply, "Sure, throw it in the glass with my teeth."

I saw a commercial for the world's smallest hearing aid—it's absolutely undetectable. I don't get it. Look at most old guys. They have a bush of hair hanging out of their ear. They're going to care about a little piece of plastic in it? "Excuse me, Bob, what's that piece of plastic in your ear bush? No, sticking in the hedgerow right next to the weeping willow tree, by the wheat field, across from the jungle."

This is true. I swear. I saw a man, he must have been around ninety-four years old, and he was buying condoms. I thought, "God bless him. He not only *bought* Trojans, he probably *fought* with them."

One of the greatest medical breakthroughs for elderly men has to be Viagra, and, thanks to prominent senior citizens and athletes, the public has become aware and open-minded to its use.

I have a friend who uses Viagra, and it actually saved his marriage. Honest. I was over his house one day, and I had to use the bathroom. On a shelf right above the sink was a little blue box. It was his Viagra pills. I know I should not have done this, but I was so damn curious. I picked up the box and read it. On the bottom was written "WARNING: After taking a Viagra pill, DO NOT operate heavy machinery." Now, I can't speak for other men, but when I get aroused, I like to get on a bulldozer and look for women. There was also another red flag:

"WARNING: If while having sex, you experience pain, dizziness, and nausea, stop having sex immediately." What kind of animal would continue? "No, no, keep moving, just don't spin. Ouch! No, I'm okay. As soon as I throw up, I'll feel better."

Another possible side effect of Viagra would keep me from using it. There's a chance you can lose your hair. That would be horrible. But you know what would be worse? If the opposite happened. You take a Viagra pill and your pants fill with hair and you can't get your head up.

By the way, did you know that they are giving Viagra to sheep? Just what I always wanted, a sweater with a stiff collar.

Let's face it, growing old is a bitch but way better than the alternative. One of my most vivid memories in life was walking with my mother on the boardwalk in Atlantic City, New Jersey. She was in her early eighties at the time, and, like a lot of women her age, she walked slowly and bent over, as though she were sneaking up on someone. I used to kid her about it. "Who are you after, Mom?" She would giggle and keep a steady course on the person she was pursuing.

Anyway, on this particular early spring afternoon, the sun shone brightly and it was unseasonably warm. My mother was legally blind, caused by a degenerative disease of the retinas, so I would always describe what I saw. She had been an artist and an avid reader, as well as a world traveler, so she appreciated hearing my descriptions as she envisioned them in her mind's eye.

As we walked hand in hand, as we had all of my life, I told her that because of the unseasonably mild temperature there were a few people actually in the ocean. She didn't say anything for a moment, then, turning her face in the direction of the unseen sea, she pointed and said quietly, "David Darling, when I was a little girl, fourteen, sixteen, I used to swim way out in that ocean, until all you could see from the beach was my head bobbing in the far-off waves." She paused for a moment, let out a deep sigh, and added, "When you get old, there is so much you must forget to remember."

We continued our slow walk in the sunshine. I felt so sad, for I understood what she meant. Recalling the activities and joys of one's youth, of what was in your life and will never be again, can torment one's so-called golden years.

A few years later, while summer-vacationing in Aspen, Colorado, where I had lived for a period of four years, I was walking along the dirt path that runs alongside the Roaring Fork River. An old woman was approaching me. She reminded me of my mother, the sweet look, the permanent smile, the advanced age, but unlike my mother in her later years, this woman was spry, quick of foot, and, from the way she turned to look at everything, she had her vision and could enjoy the wonders of nature that my mother had so enjoyed when she had her sight.

When the woman got closer she said good morning, and I said good morning in return. She stopped and smiled at me. I stopped and smiled at her.

"And it is a glorious morning, too," she said. I nodded. She continued, "And such a tragic shame that most people wouldn't even notice."

I said, "You're right on both counts. It is a glorious morning, and it is a shame."

She giggled, similar to my mother, and said, "But not a shame for you and me."

I smiled. She bounded away. I turned and watched her walk up the path, seemingly so young, so full of life, so appreciative, and so right. As I continued my walk, I thought back to that time on the boardwalk with my mother and what she had said about growing old, and I realized that my mother was right, but she was also wrong. Yes, growing old is horrible, but life, at every stage, regardless of its trials and tribulations, or its setbacks and horrors, life remains a sweet mystery forever. It is still a fantastic journey into the exciting unknown. It is still a glorious celebration.

Yes, Mom, you were right. When you get old, there is a lot you must forget to remember, but what you can never forget to remember is how to laugh, because laughter can keep you internally young forever and who wouldn't want that? Who? . . . Sorry, you'll have to speak a little louder.

The Future

One of the most universal and idiotic worries concerns the future. Almost everyone worries about what will happen to them and to their loved ones, yet most of life is out of our control. Everyone wants to live longer, yet the very next millisecond of one's life may never even happen. It's only luck that I was alive long enough to finish the last sentence, and this one, too.

I believe that most human events are mere accidents and that the only guarantee we have is that we might not have the future in which to do anything; and yet, defying all rational thinking and common sense, people worry about the time that might never lie ahead. Seeking to get a glimpse into this non–promised land of the future, we turn to what, at best, can be called the supernatural or inexplicable, or, at its most realistic and honest, the super-ridiculous and inexcusable, or, for short, a big crock of crap.

Some people search for the faraway future, light-years ahead, to the last ridges of time. Others look no further than the span of their own lifetimes. Some are even less ambitious and want to know only what is going to happen that day. Regardless of how far-reaching your vision, there are ways to focus on what lies ahead. These methods have various names but one claim to fame—each possesses a magical power to peek into the future, and, in some cases, transport you there or bring someone back to tell you all about it.

For those desiring to peer merely into the next twenty-four hours or less, they need not look any further than in their morning newspaper, turning the page to what is entitled with great reverence by the believers, Today's Horoscope, or, as a realist might entitle it, Today's Bullshit.

To delve into this very popular delve into the future, we must trace its roots of origin. The mother of horoscopes is astrology. Its premise is that our lives are determined or at least influenced by the stars. I'm no expert in the intricacies of astrology, but I know that the basis for it is that the arrangement of the stars at the exact moment you were born gives you what believers call your "sign," which among other things determines your traits as a human being and your future. You slide out of Mom at a great alignment, lucky you; plop into the birthing room blanket when a bad alignment is happening in the heavens, and you are the same as the act that created you—screwed. Believers believe all has been written in the stars. It sounds good, and it certainly has a wonderful element of mystery, intrigue, and romance of sorts.

A skeptic would look at astrology a bit differently. First, he would probably question how this "science" is applicable regardless of whether one's birth was a natural birth, as were all births during the time when astrology itself was born, or by Caesarean, possibly accompanied by mind- and body-altering drugs that throw off your natural arrival. Therefore, your true astrological birth date and time can be off by minutes, days, weeks, or even months. Your birth sign isn't in line with the stars is but a result of circumstance, such as a medical necessity or an impatient doctor or mother.

Then one might wonder how two babies born at the exact time, thereby receiving the same exact sign, do not have the exact same personal makeup, lives, or futures. For example, a white child born in a posh hospital suite in the wealthy community of Shaker Heights, Ohio, versus a black child born on a dirt road in Bangladesh, as its mother is trying to escape from murdering revolutionists. It is doubtful that their lives from second one to the last second will in any way resemble each other. If their horoscopes were really views into their futures, one would read, "Buy IBM and build your second summer home in East Hampton," and the other would read, "Run your sorry black ass off and hide behind a bush."

I once had an executive assistant who showed up in the morning and wouldn't type a word, open an envelope, or even have her morning cup of coffee until she read her horoscope. It was so annoying, but

I said nothing, until one day, when she finished reading it, she cheered and read it aloud: "This is your lucky day." This was followed by some technical stuff I don't remember exactly, but it went something like "Mars is aligned with Jupiter and you are in the cusp of Saturn." Whatever. She continued, "During the next twenty-four hours, you should ask friends to join you for dinner and a night of good wine and entertaining conversation from which you will learn much that you will use in a career change coming your way soon. Today is also the perfect time to plan a trip to an exotic island." She was absolutely giddy with excitement. "Isn't this wonderful," she asked? I replied, "Yes, splendiferous. You must share it. Call state prisons, find someone on death row with your exact sign, and tell him the great news. You'll make his day."

A lot of people in the world have the same astrological signs. There are many with the exact sign as Osama bin Laden and Saddam Hussein. Maybe it's President Bush or you. Check it out. It might explain why you have to constantly resist the urge to blow up a building or build twenty palaces.

I guess by now you can tell I am not a believer in astrology and its offspring, the horoscope. As a matter of fact, I hate when people ask me my sign. I always answer "I was born under a stop sign at Fourth and Dickerson, now leave me alone." Usually, I get a response like, "You must be a Taurus." "Yeah, and you must be an asshole."

Let me tell you what I do believe: If a Sagittarius and a Gemini walk in front of a moving bus, they're both dead. Okay, so as not to alienate all you believers, let me leave it open that the Gemini might be half dead, half alive.

Let's trace the history of how all these personality traits, such as being secretive or stingy or introverted, were determined, the process employed to develop this into the science as we know it. All you skeptics out there, keep an open mind. Maybe you don't, but millions of other people worry themselves sick because of their astrological traits and how they have manifested themselves uncontrollably, sometimes damaging or even destroying their lives. This is very serious business for many, so let's not treat it lightly.

Way back, and I am not sure how way, but I understand it was far enough in the past that it was during the time when there were thirteen months in the calendar, but it can't be true, because, if it were, it would throw every sign determined by a twelve-month calendar out the window. This is too simple a way to negate the validity of astrological signs, so let us move on, as if this is false information. Let us deal only with intelligent, deductive reasoning. Isn't this just typical of an Aquarius with penis rising in the cusp of his fourth moon?

So how did those astrological pioneers find out that people born under one sign were aggressive, while people born under another sign were passive, that certain signs meant you were stubborn while your brother born in a different month, on a different day, at a different hour and minute, was easygoing, et al? How did this intricate science come to be?

The way I heard it, and you can check out the validity of this information, especially those of you born on September 9, 1980, at 10:51 A.M. I only have so much free time and don't want to spend it on the Internet or in a library, and because I'm an Aquarius and you know what sticklers we are about not wasting time and our love of peanut butter–chocolate ice cream and the color red.

Anyway, I understand that the originators of astrological signs traveled to many small towns and spent endless hours in the local graveyards, collecting the birth dates and names from gravestones, until they had all 366, counting leap year. Then they interviewed townspeople to find out what their dead neighbors, friends, and relatives were like. So if someone said his dead uncle was a stubborn son of a bitch, this might explain why you've been told that you are one, too. These men and women of science had to do a lot of traveling, spend a lot of time in cemeteries, and interview lots of people, in order to develop a detailed analysis for every birthday. The dedication of these unknown and unrecognized heroes of science has paid off, for their work has resulted in millions of intelligent and rational human beings believing in and practicing the knowledge gathered and gleaned by these unsung scientific heroes of a bygone time, at a time by the way, when most people believed flies were born from meat and the earth was flat.

Let's move on to another science that causes worries for a lot of people—the science of ESP, Extra Sensory Perception, as it is known by the believers in it, and Extra Schmucky Putz by the nonbelievers. ESP is the ability to read minds, feel others' feelings, thereby being able to know what is happening somewhere else or to someone else or about to happen—a true look into the future.

The way ESP works is someone gets a "feeling" that something dangerous is about to happen, like a hanger will fall from a closet and poke out the eye of a pet belonging to a family in Albuquerque. Sometimes the ESP "visions" are specific, like the example I just gave, but at other times they are sketchy; regardless, they are always accurate. People have gotten off of planes that went on to crash, have run to their children's school, because they could "feel" that something terrible was about to happen, or have put all their money on the spin of a roulette wheel because an internal voice "told them" that the little ivory roulette ball was going to fall into slot twenty-three.

Oftentimes, a person's ESP or premonitions are correct. Most of the time, they are meaningless, primarily because people only remember the ones that come true. Yes, Aunt Sally did trip over the ottoman and broke her hip as you "predicted," but cousin Jeremy never called and neighbor Betty's breasts were not surgically removed. Selective memory is a vital ingredient in ESP and other "marginal sciences." It also is very beneficial in marriage. Yes, you did forget my birthday just as I "felt," but you weren't having an affair with that bitch Claudine and you didn't mow my mother down in your car on her way to church.

I am not experienced nor am I knowledgeable enough about ESP to vote for it or against it, although my cynical and skeptical nature has led me to believe it's a ten-pound bag of steaming horseshit. My opinion has not changed over the years of listening to firsthand ESP revelations. For example:

At a house gathering of about thirty people that I attended, a young woman joined in the conversation of the supernatural, ESP in particular, telling us a story of what happened to her and how ESP saved her life.

She was shopping with two of her girlfriends at their local supermarket. The other two women put their groceries in the trunk. Because she was getting out first, she decided to climb in the back of the car with her groceries. Right before her friend started to drive out of the parking lot, she had this "feeling" that something terrible was going to happen and that she should sit up front with her two friends. She was worried, actually terrified of what was in her future. She proceeded to tell her driver friend to stop the car. She placed her bag of groceries on the seat and got in the front with the other two women.

About ten blocks later, a man ran a red light and smashed into their car, at the exact spot where she would have been seated had she not had this ESP experience and acted upon it. Her bag of groceries was smashed to smithereens. She described in graphic detail how the watermelon "exploded" as she would have, had she not had the ESP about her immediate future and had not followed its instructions. Everyone was mesmerized by her story and chattered like birds about the power, miracle, and foolproof validation of ESP. I interrupted the ESP praises, addressing the young woman who had told her amazing story.

"Did you ever consider the *fact* that had you not had this ESP message or had it and ignored it, you would have remained in the back of the car, instead of taking the time to move into the front seat, which put your car at the intersection at the exact time the other car ran the light, instead of passing it minutes before. So believing in this ESP bullshit almost killed you."

I didn't need ESP to tell me that I had worn out my welcome, so I left. I am sure some of the people in the crowd said that they "knew" I would leave.

A lot of people believe in the first cousin of ESP, dreams. How many times has someone told you they had dreamed something and it happened exactly as they dreamed it? Again, this is selective memory. How many times has anyone seen a blue gorilla eating a convertible as naked people ran up the walls of buildings with flames shooting out of their asses? (I decided to use this dream I had last night as an example.)

Looking into crystal balls to see into the future has been around for a few thousand years. I have to admit that I own a crystal ball, but I don't try to read it. It just looks so great in my billiard room at home. I've seen some people sneak glances into it, I guess to see what might lie ahead. Usually, it was merely a reflection of someone trying to sink the nine ball. Yet, intelligent, rational people pay money to sit across from someone who stares into a crystal ball and tells them what lies ahead. I'll tell you when I'd believe they can really see the future. If as I am heading up their walkway, they are heading for a phone to call the police, because they know I'm not going to pay them.

A lot of people believe in the "science" of palm reading. I always wondered about one aspect of it. If these people can really see into the future, how come they always live in such dumps? You'd think that they'd look at their own palm. "Oh, my God, let's get the hell out of here. Maybe open a massage parlor or a Starbuck's."

One night, my date and I and three other couples went to one of New York City's finest Indian restaurants. After we finished our delicious meals, an Indian palm reader approached our table and offered to look into our futures. None of the men wanted to do it, but the four women were giddy to try it, so we sat back and watched the show.

The Indian palm reader took the first woman's hand, and after moments of peering intensely at it, tracing lines with his finger, he spoke quietly in a thick Indian accent.

Palm One: "You are a very trusting person but have learned not to be too trusting. You are open and yet closed. You are full of love and want to share it but only with the right man. You like . . ."

Palm Two: "You love children and would like to have many, but you worry if all of them would be happy, and you worry about the world they will grow up in. You like to be with people, but a part of you wants to be with just yourself. Sometimes, you . . ."

Palm Three: "You have been basically very happy in your life, but you have also known sorrow and disappointment. You miss someone who was very dear to you, but you have learned that life must go on. When you were . . ."

Palm Four: "You like to go out and have a good time with crowds but can also curl up in bed with a good book all by yourself. You do more to help other people than other people do to help you, but you wouldn't change the way you are. There are many times . . ."

When he finished reading the last palm, he bowed, and tucked all the money we gave him into a satin fanny pack and moved off to the next table. Our women were dumbfounded over the accuracy of what he had said about each of them, exclaiming that he had revealed things about themselves that they had never revealed to anyone. After a few minutes of this palm-reading adulation, I had had it.

"Excuse me, ladies, but that guy is so full of shit, he lives in a giant toilet."

Of course, the women immediately ganged up on me, defending their newfound guru. The other men were too afraid to defend me. Did I tell you that they were married and I was single? Alone, I finally recaptured the floor.

"Okay, please. One second. I'll make you all a deal. We'll come back here tomorrow night, my treat. Each of you women will dress differently; change your hairstyles and makeup and us guys will look as different as we can. We'll switch women just for dinner and sit in a different seating arrangement than this."

They agreed; anything to prove me wrong. We showed up the next night as planned. At the end of the meal, the same palm reader approached the table. We signed on for readings of the women's palms. He took and studied the hand of the first woman, who had been Palm Two the previous night.

Palm One, former Palm Two: "You are a very trusting person but have learned not to be too trusting. You are open and yet closed. You are full of love and want to share it but only with the right man. You like . . ."

Palm Two, former Palm Three: "You love children and would like to have many, but you worry about if all of them would be happy, and you worry about the world they will grow up in. You like to be with people, but a part of you wants to be with just yourself. Sometimes, you . . ."

Palm Three, former Palm Four: She tried to back out, but I wouldn't let her, so she sat there listening to the verbatim recitation told to her friend the night before.

Palm Four, former Palm One: She got up from the table and headed for the ladies' room, not to piss but definitely pissed off. What was most unfortunate was that she was my date, and somehow, call it what you may, I knew without even glancing at my palms that the rest of my night was going to be lousy and sexless.

As good as I am at pricking a balloon filled with vapors of bull-shit, Groucho Marx pulled off one that will remain the envy of every comedian and realist who lives or ever will live.

Séances were the rage in trendy Hollywood in the 1930s. A group of famous show business people would sit around a large, round table holding hands, their eyes closed, breathing evenly, and keeping their minds blank. The latter has never been a problem for people living in Los Angeles to this day. Directing and guiding the celebrities was a Gypsy woman (or a woman from Central Casting) who would peer slowly across the ceiling of the darkened room that was sweetened by the swirling smoke of burning incense. She would call upon "The Great Spirit," an entity who could travel between the worlds of the living and the dead.

When The Great Spirit was contacted, whirling around the room as a whitened apparition, in order of seating, people could ask any question of the spirit or any deceased relative, who would then speak through the spirit.

"Oh, Great Spirit, how is my dear, dead husband?"

After a moment during which the only sounds were the swishing of the flying spirit and the piped in, muted ethereal music, The Great Spirit would answer. Remember this was before digital wraparound sound and satellites.

"Marty is doing just fine. He is happy, and he still loves you. He . . .

Wait he has a question . . . Marty wants to know if you still have his favorite pipe, the one with the moose carved on it that you gave him on the first Christmas you spent together."

"Oh, my God, no one knew about that pipe! No one! *(Crying)* Yes, darling, I sleep with it under my pillow every night."

"Marty wants you to know he still loves you and he wants to tell you that it is between you and Bette Davis for the new film *Dangerous*."

"Marty, should I have my agent call the studio; should I . . ."

The Gypsy woman would groan and grunt and her eyes would reach back into her head. Then she'd whisper that Marty had "returned," and she'd go to the next person. The questions for The Great Spirit ran the gamut, from where a stolen tiara might be to where a dead relative had hidden his stocks and bonds to if a recently recorded song would be a hit or how long one would live. The answers were all forthcoming and always amazing to the questioner and the others. The Great Spirit always said something that "no one else in the world knew." This convinced everyone that he was real, everyone except an acerbic, cynical, brilliant Jewish comedian named Groucho Marx. (Acerbic, cynical, brilliant, and Jewish? How's that for the epitome of redundancy?)

The Hollywood crowd had tried for months to talk Groucho into attending a séance, but they were never successful. They didn't give up and the badgering became more and more annoying. To end it, Groucho finally agreed to attend but only on the condition that he didn't have to ask a question or say anything. It was agreed and, as difficult as it must have been, he kept his end of the bargain.

That night, The Great Spirit was in rare form, giving pinpoint details about the past and the future, as well as his usual no-one-else-in-the-world-could-know answers and comments. Groucho was next in line and, as agreed, was to be skipped over, but someone pleaded with him to ask a question. Groucho declined, but the others joined in, some proposing the argument that this was the only way he was going to be convinced that this was legitimate. Finally, Groucho agreed to ask a question, to the delight of everyone, especially the

Gypsy, who called upon The Great Spirit, who had flown into a dark corner. He reappeared and was circling above the table. The Gypsy called upon Groucho.

"Mr. Marx, please ask The Great Spirit any question."

"Any question?"

"Yes, Mr. Marx, any question. The Great Spirit knows the answer to all that can be asked, of the past and the future, of this earth and the beyond."

Groucho's eyes followed the flight of The Great Spirit as it continued to swoosh in a tight circle above the table. Finally, Groucho spoke.

"Oh, Great Spirit, knower of all answers, past and future, here on earth and the beyond, what is the capital of South Dakota?"

The Great Spirit kept swooshing and swooshing and swooshing, not saying a word. The Gypsy closed her eyes. And you know that somewhere in a back room close by, but out of earshot, a conversation such as the following was raging:

"Jesus H. Christ, Charlie, you found out the name of Groucho's childhood dog and you got a pile of sheet music he used on tour with his brothers in the 1930s, why the hell didn't you pick up a goddamn atlas? Come on, one of you guys must know the damn capital!"

"Is it Harrisburg?"

"No, asshole, that's Pennsylvania! We're looking for South Dakota!"

"Where the hell is South Dakota, down south?"

"Great, it's back to cheating in card games for all of us!"

Needless to say, séances soon fell out of favor with the Hollywood crowd, and I like to think that a lot of the credit for that happening can be attributed to Groucho.

But reaching the dead is not dead. It is very much alive and well, but living on TV. The flying sheet of The Great Spirit and the darkened, incense-laden room have been replaced by bright lights, TV cameras, large studio audiences, and millions of Americans glued to their sets in their homes to watch a few different guys who can reach the dead, those persons who have "gone to the other side," as death is now called in the twenty-first century.

The goal is the same, only the "tricks" are more sophisticated and electronic. The only aspect of talking about or with the dead that remains the same, and is the most important aspect, is finding people gullible enough to suck it all in and swallow it, by hook, line, and bullshit sinker.

Even though I don't know all the tricks, there is one that I do know about, and I laugh every time I see another sucker fall for it. It is as old as the spoken word. The Spirit Guy picks someone out of the audience and the conversation goes something like this:

Spirit Guy: (Holding his hand over his eyes, his head facing heaven and the studio's klieg lights) "I see the capital letter A and it's either a B or maybe a P. Do any of those letters have anything to do with anyone you know?" (Take a moment and think of what your answers would be.)

Sucker: "My father worked for the A & P supermarkets." (It could've just as well been his father's dog—Pete—or his son's latest report card—all As and Bs—or one of hundreds of other things with dozens of people he knows.)

Spirit: I am getting the feeling of illness or maybe even death.

Sucker: My father was recently diagnosed with the Syph.

Ducking and weaving with generic, open-ended questions, the sucker fills in with finite details that no one else in the world would know (sound familiar?), until the twenty-first-century, TV-rated Spirit has told this sucker that his mother is going to be fine, that the woman who broke his heart is going to disappear from his life, that his gold watch will be found in the summer, that he will have to wait for that trip to Puerto Rico, that his father knows he really loves him, but he should tell him (unless he is watching this bullshit show and just heard you say it), that the future will be fine and not to worry. The audience in the studio goes apeshit, the people at home wonder how they can be on the show, and the Spirit laughs his balls off all the way to the bank.

Now I'll tell you a personal experience that I had with a mind reader, a well-known psychic, a medium who reaches the dead, and, overall, a great act. He was not the Amazing Kreskin, who is truly amazing and also a great act.

I was booked to do a college Homecoming Weekend concert in the Midwest. My opening act was a mind reader. There were about 3,500 people in the audience. The mind reader did the usual stuff that all mind readers/psychics/magicians do, but he did them extremely well. You know what I'm talking about—he asked someone to hold his driver's license against his forehead and then recited the numbers. He asked someone to take her driver's license out of her wallet and not only knew the numbers but announced the state in which it was issued and gave the numbers of her home address. He had someone write the numbers of a dollar bill he had in his pocket on a piece of paper and tear it up. Then he wrote the numbers on a blackboard and made the torn paper reappear whole. The numbers matched perfectly.

He ended his act with a spectacular finish. He had asked the Dean of Men to hide the check he was going to get for his performance anywhere in the large theater. If he didn't find the check through the process of mental telepathy, the check would be returned to the university and his show would be for free. The audience cheered, and I, witnessing this from the wings, said "Schmuck." Give back fifty bucks, maybe a hundred, not the entire amount, which had to be about $5,000.

With his fingers pressed against his temples, he found the check taped under the seat of one of the 3,500 chairs in the theater. Everyone applauded wildly, including me.

When he came offstage, I rushed over to him and told him what a great performance he put on. Usually, I don't like to know how a magician does his bits, but I couldn't help asking. "How'd you do that last trick with the check?"

He hissed angrily at me, "I don't do tricks; I read minds!" and he stormed away. I looked at him and thought, "Read this, you asshole!" The whole hour I was onstage I kept thinking of what a schmuck he was.

After I came offstage, the students from the Entertainment Committee who had booked us told us that they had a little setup of food and drinks in their dormitory lounge where we could pass the time before we had to leave for the airport.

There were about twenty of us sitting and standing around in the small lounge that was no more than fifty feet square. Now, here's the kicker. When it came time to leave, the mind reader couldn't find his coat. I couldn't resist. I said, "Next time, tape it under a chair."

I admit that I am one of the world's biggest cynics. I don't believe in anything I can't see or cut with a knife. At the top of my Can't Believe It List is anyone claiming to see into the future. At the top of my Believe It List is that the way to live your life is to believe that now is real and anything beyond it is merely a vague possibility. So live what is real the best way you can live it and hope it lasts a lot longer, even a little longer. One way to live life at its best is to live it laughing. My father took this a step further.

Two of my father's favorite sayings were, an original, "If every day of your life, you make one person have a big belly laugh, you can say you lived a worthwhile life," and the cliché, "Always leave 'em laughing." My father lived by them. Whenever I was with him, and I tried to be with him as much as possible, we always left wherever we were—a relative's house, a store, an elevator, a poolroom, a neighborhood bar, wherever—we always left to the sound of laughter generated by this brilliantly funny man, my father, my best friend.

When my father was ninety-two years old, he was near the end of his fifth cruise around the world, when he became ill and had to be hospitalized in the ship's hospital. Ironically, this was aboard the same ship and in the same bed where my mother had passed away two years prior. The doctor told me of my father's last moments.

The doctor and four nurses were making their nightly rounds. They stopped at the foot of my father's bed. The doctor asked, "Are you comfortable Mr. Brenner? Is there anything we can do for you? Is everything okay?" On the wall behind the doctor and nurses was a shelf on which there was a row of bedpans. Now, here's my father, who for ninety-two years has done it all—running in the tough streets of Philly, serving in the navy, touring in vaudeville shows as a song-and-dance man and comedian, becoming a numbers writer for the mob; a man who has traveled to just about every country in the world, who has seen it all and then saw it again, leading the fullest of lives. Now, here he is ending up in a small bed, in a small, antiseptic hospital room. This life's doer and world traveler's last world is a floor, a ceiling, and four blank walls, except for the one in front of him that had on it a shelf with four bedpans. In answer to the doctor's questions, my father pointed to the bedpans and said, "Great view."

The doctor told me that he and the nurses couldn't stop laughing, and when they finally did, they looked at my father. His eyes were closed and he had a smile on his face. He had left 'em laughing for the last time.

I'd like to go out that way, only I'd like to be 250 years old and in the arms of a gorgeous, 25-year-old woman I had just satisfied. At the same time that I came, I went. *Yeah! Viva Vida!*

You know I couldn't end this with the story of my father's last act in life. I have to make you laugh. I am my father's son. But it is up to you to continue laughing for as long as your future may be, and I can promise you that if you do, you will have a much happier and less worrisome future, and you don't need the stars, signs, spirits, palms, ESP, mind reading, or any other bugaboo thing to validate that this is the truth. But if you have more than three letters in your last name, do not go outdoors between the hours of 10:12 A.M. and 4:22 P.M. on any shady Thursday and never wear dark blue above your waist. You've been warned.

Epilogue

I truly hope that this book has given you a lot of laughs, but more importantly, I hope it has taught you how to find your own laughs, which will make your life easier and happier.

From the moment the doctor slaps your ass to bring you to life, life itself keeps slapping your ass. Life is anything but easy, but if you keep your sense of humor, if you search for and find the laughter inside the dark clouds, then whenever you do, you are slapping life back—right on its ass.

Please try to do it. Please never give up. Please make life better for you. If anything I wrote helped you to do this, then you will be validating the importance of laughter and humor and the importance of my life.

One problem—by finishing this book, I have afflicted myself with a new worry: book sales. So please, if you enjoyed this book and/or found it useful, tell others who you know could use some laughs, or, better yet, buy them a copy or two. Thanks, I needed that.

Quick Fix Jokes

The purpose of this chapter is to provide you a quick fix laugh if you're inexplicably feeling a little down and could use some fast, temporary relief or in case a new worry or problem is not one listed in this book. For example:

A forty-year-old South Vietnamese shows up on your doorstep and calls you "Daddy."

Your wife calls to tell you she can't get the dead deer off the hood of your car.

Your new boss was your old boss at your last job; the one you handed a bag of dogshit when you quit.

The check-in clerk at the airport informs you that your airline ticket reads Philadelphia, Mississippi, not Pennsylvania, but it doesn't matter because that flight is sold out anyway.

You look like a clone of America's latest most-wanted serial killer.

The burning sensation has returned.

These Are the Jokes, Folks

Scientists confirmed that in spite of popular belief, sharks don't eat people; they only bite them and spit them out, which the scientists can't explain. I can explain it. When a shark bites you, you shit in your pants.

Did you ever look at birds with envy and think, "Man, I wish I could fly"? Did you ever think that birds look down at us and think, "Man, I wish I could cross my legs"?

How come pilots are the only professionals that let you know what they do by wearing little gold pins of wings on their lapels? You never see a proctologist wearing a little gold asshole.

The difference between a drunk and someone stoned on drugs is a drunk will drive through a stop sign. Someone who's stoned will sit and wait for it to turn green.

The Kentucky Derby winner Facachi Pegasus was sold for $31 million to stud. I was surprised, because I heard he was hung like a person.

I love the Country/Western Award Show, because I love to sit in front of a TV and listen for three hours to why life sucks.

The al-Qaeda and Taliban "detainees" in Guantanamo Bay have given us no information and have been cursing, spitting on, and slapping our marines. We could solve this problem and get even with Fidel Castro at the same time. Let them escape.

Nature magazine wrote that scientists have discovered a prehistoric insect that could clasp things with its testicles. Italian guys would love to be able to do this. They could scratch themselves while still playing the accordion.

A woman was rushed to a hospital when her pet boa constrictor swallowed her hand. I'll never complain again when my dog humps my leg.

The oldest man in Italy was celebrating his 112th birthday at an outdoor luncheon when the wind blew his cap off his head. He chased it and suffered a heart attack and died. What's really shitty is the present his hometown friends had wrapped to give him was a new cap.

Justices suspended former president Bill Clinton's license to practice law on the grounds that he was untrustworthy. I always thought these were prerequisites for becoming a lawyer.

The latest aphrodisiac in China is tiger penis soup. I can just about get through a matzo ball.

Someone has invented a toilet that runs off electricity. Just what I always wanted—to sit on something naked, with my most precious body part close to water, that runs on electricity. Perfect!

One of the best-selling books in Japan is an instructional book on how to commit suicide. To give you an idea of how popular it is, the author had a book signing and no one came.

Alabama has passed a law that it is a crime to have sex with a corpse. What's frightening is that they had to pass a law.

I never understand when I read in a newspaper or magazine that some man is a practicing homosexual. How much practice does it take?

Australian scientists have announced that they have developed a tranquilizer for turtles. How slow are the Australians?

Italians are fantastic cooks. In the preparation of certain foods, they often use parts of their bodies, such as for pizza, they toss the dough up in the air and catch it on their fist, or they stomp on grapes to make wine. They often use parts of their bodies. This is why I have never eaten an Italian doughnut.

Did you ever get a return envelope in the mail that reads that there is no postage due if mailed in the USA? I don't know about anyone else, but sometimes I like to take my mail to Guam to mail it.

Do chickens laugh when you show them a skinny, naked, rubber person?

If a cow laughs heartily, does milk come out of her nose?

A study has confirmed that Japanese blink more than any other people while watching the news. What the hell are we supposed to do with this information?

Scientists claim that eating tuna fish eyeballs helps fight dementia. Forget about it. The last thing I want to remember is that I ate tuna fish eyeballs.

People who don't hold grudges live longer, unless they run into someone who is harboring a grudge against them.

There's a book *The 101 Lies Men Tell Women*. The first is that there are only 101 lies.

The Dear Abby newspaper column is very popular in China. Can you see it? "I have a friend, Wing Pang Pock, not his real name . . ."

There's a commercial for an at-home IQ test for only $29.95. If you order it, we know your IQ.

The number one complaint of New York cab drivers is passengers defecating in the backseat of the cab. I have the solution—slow down!

To cut down on road rage, L.A. police warned drivers not to taunt any driver who is pointing a gun at them. I'm glad I read that, because my natural tendency would be to say, "What are you driving there, asshole, a Pinto reject?"

France has designed a golf course in the shape of a woman. Of course, there are bushes under the arms.

The number one activity of nudists is deep-sea swimming. Are they crazy? The last things I want any hospital report of mine to have written on it are the words "tortoise" and "dangling."

Did you hear about the convention of three thousand ventriloquists in Las Vegas? There were four speeches and no one knows who made them.

A study claims that people are a lot less trustful than they were twenty-five years ago. I don't believe it.

Scientists have proven, without knowing why, that women with big rear ends live longer. Of course, husbands who tell them that, don't!

TV cable operators had their annual meeting in New Orleans. It was on a weekday sometime between 9:00 A.M. and 5:00 P.M.

A company in Florida is offering cruises for nudists. I was just saying to myself the other day, where can I go to see naked senior citizens bent over playing shuffleboard?

I like when on the news, they show a courtroom scene and superimpose "Artist's Rendering," as if we were really thinking that people were running around the courtroom with charcoal all over their faces.

An eighty-year-old woman robbed a bank in Florida. Police said when they chased her they reached speeds in excess of 20 mph.

Why do they always show us profiles of criminals? How many criminals commit crimes sideways?

I don't think that older people are more spontaneous. I think they just forgot their plans.

Berlin threw a party to commemorate the anniversary of the tearing down of the Wall. Everyone was celebrating. Well, almost everybody; the Berlin Handball Team is still pissed.

The Japanese have produced a movie about a radiation leak at a uranium processing plant. It is about a worker who was exposed and is titled *The Amazing Colossal Man*. He stands about six feet tall.

France paid tribute to the first successful parachute jump by a Frenchman, Andre Jacques Garnerin, in 1797. Actually, the parachute was invented long before that, but there weren't any successful jumps until the invention of the rip cord in 1797.

The FDA has warned men who use hair dye that it often contains concentrations of lead that should not be ingested by children. I know this upset a lot of guys who enjoy having their kids lick their heads.

On a medical TV documentary, a doctor showed a technique where he injected an anti-impotence drug into a grapefruit, which was supposed to be a man's penis. Are bananas out of season?

A study in a British medical journal reports that men who have sex twice a week live longer than men who have sex once a month, which is great news, unless you're serving life in prison.

While swimming in Winterhaven, Florida, a college student was bitten in the groin by a turtle. Boy, there's a story he can tell his adopted grandchildren.

This year marks the seventieth anniversary of the first nudist camp in the USA. People who defend nudism say the naked body is a beautiful thing. I wonder how they'd feel if the original members were standing in front of them right now.

A recent survey claims that there are more cabs involved in accidents in New York City than ever before. Just the other day, there was a six-turban pileup.

Fifty-two percent of married men reported that they prefer doing yard work to having sex. The other 48 percent reported that they can't have sex until they do yard work.

Hollywood has gotten its first Hooters restaurants and in typical L.A. fashion, they are already doing construction to make them bigger.

According to sex experts, men who wear loud-colored clothing are less anatomically endowed, which probably explains why there are no clown porno films.

An article in a New York paper claimed that the squirrels in Central Park are starving "because their nuts keep slipping out of their hands." What man wouldn't understand?

Two men in Utah were arrested for drilling holes in a woman's head to relieve her depression. She should have been a little suspicious when they introduced themselves as Dr. Black and Dr. Decker.

7-Eleven is now providing twenty-four-hour check cashing. I was just saying the other day, "Where can I get my check cashed that has a very high incidence of robberies?"

Harley-Davidson has applied for a patent of the roaring sound their motorcycles make. You know what it'll mean if they get it. They'll be able to sue everyone walking out of a Taco Bell.

A five-year-old Colombian girl was arrested in an airport; her two suitcases were filled with heroin. Meanwhile, in an unrelated story, Keith Richards was seen checking into a hotel with two suitcases filled with Barbie Dolls.

New York City is a finalist in a bid to host the 2012 Olympics. If they win, it'll be the first time that so many people from different countries in the city are not driving cabs.

To counter Southwest Airlines' policy of charging obese flyers for two seats, Amtrak announced that they will charge obese people half price. I guess they figure the extra weight will keep their trains on the track.

The inventor of the infomercial died. In his will, he asked for his ashes to be scattered by a salad shooter.

The creator of miniature golf passed away in an ironic way. He dropped his heart pill, which rolled down the hall, banged against two walls, and got wedged under moving panels.

Houston, Texas, was voted the fattest city of 2002. The people were so angry, they formed a one-million-pound march on Washington.

At some performances, a show called *The Vagina Monologues* charges up to $1,500 a seat. I would pay that much to hear one of them talk. Even whistle.

My father would never let me kill a fly. He'd say, "Leave it alone. They only live three days." We had houseflies in our kitchen eighty-four years old, senile with beards. They flew crooked. "Do you have any prune juice?"

Why do we camouflage our long-range missiles, so the enemy thinks we're shooting trees at them? They should be painted sky blue with little puffy white clouds. "Look how windy it is, Abdullah Abdullah."

Whenever a moose wanders into a town and sticks his head through a store window, the papers always describe him as "a disoriented moose." How do they know he didn't wake up in the woods that morning and say to his moose wife, "I'm going to wander into town and check out the specials at Wal-Mart"?

The chain store 7-Eleven announced they're going to make all their stores brighter. What about their clerks?

I think that what cities ought to do with people who walk around talking to themselves is pair them up or give them cell phones.

Police raided a Brooklyn bingo parlor that was a front for prostitution. I think the name gave it away—Badda Bingo.

In Los Angeles you can have your dog legally marry another dog. I guess if it doesn't work out and they get divorced, the bitch gets the house.

I think we're approaching the problem of air pollution all wrong. We're trying to decrease it. What we should do is increase it, that is, make the air pollution particles so big, they can't fit into your nose. At least, you could see it coming. "Duck, Betty, pollution!"

Who started the expression "Duck"? In the beginning, a lot of people didn't know it and must've gotten whacked on the head. "What the hell's wrong with you? Why'd you yell 'duck'? Why didn't you yell 'hippo' or 'elephant'? Then I would've ducked."

I hate when a doctor puts on that rubber glove, because you know in a few seconds, you're going to know exactly how a puppet feels.

I always wanted to go to Korea. I always wanted to meet #4 Shirt Inspector.

They've made a full-sized car out of thousands of children's

Legos. It's beautiful. The only problem is that in order to drive it, you have to snap yourself down on that little peg.

Why do they ask on commercials, "If you have unwanted hairs on your nose or coming out of your ears . . . ," as if there's someone in this world who would want it, excluding Italy and Poland, of course.

A vegetarian is someone who won't eat anything that can have children—well, almost.

Why do old men put their initials on their handkerchiefs? "Will the old man with the initials G.W.B. please come to the Lost and Found? We found your snot rag."

I saw a sign on a wall of a Manhattan restaurant that read, "For Bathroom Use Staircase," and in New York, you know they will.

It's a $100 fine if you get caught honking your horn in Manhattan. Meanwhile, you can expose yourself and it won't cost you a dime. So if you're going to honk your horn, you might as well whip out your dick and have a little fun for the same money.

An oldie but a goodie and surefire: I was sitting on a subway, and I was sitting on a newspaper. A man said, "Are you reading that paper?" I didn't know what to say, that I'm nearsighted? So I said nothing. The next time it happened to me, I was ready. I said, "Yes," stood up, turned the page, and sat down.